THE GEOGRAPHIES OF SOCIAL MOVEMENTS

NEW ECOLOGIES FOR THE TWENTY-FIRST CENTURY
Series Editors
Arturo Escobar, University of North Carolina, Chapel Hill
Dianne Rocheleau, Clark University

This series addresses two trends: critical conversations in academic fields about nature, sustainability, globalization, and culture, including constructive engagements between the natural, social, and human sciences; and intellectual and political conversations among social movements and other nonacademic knowledge producers about alternative practices and socionatural worlds. Its objective is to establish a synergy between these theoretical and political developments in both academic and nonacademic arenas. This synergy is a sine qua non for new thinking about the real promise of emergent ecologies. The series includes works that envision more lasting and just ways of being-in-place and being-in-networks with a diversity of humans and other living and nonliving beings.

New Ecologies for the Twenty-First Century aims to promote a dialogue between those who are transforming the understanding of the relationship between nature and culture. The series revisits existing fields such as environmental history, historical ecology, environmental anthropology, ecological economics, and cultural and political ecology. It addresses emerging tendencies, such as the use of complexity theory to rethink a range of questions on the nature-culture axis. It also deals with epistemological and ontological concerns, building bridges between the various forms of knowing and ways of being embedded in the multiplicity of practices of social actors worldwide. This series hopes to foster convergences among differently located actors and to provide a forum for authors and readers to widen the fields of theoretical inquiry, professional practice, and social struggles that characterize the current environmental arena.

ULRICH OSLENDER

The Geographies of Social Movements

AFRO-COLOMBIAN MOBILIZATION
AND THE AQUATIC SPACE

DUKE UNIVERSITY PRESS   DURHAM AND LONDON   2016

Printed in the United States of America on acid-free paper ∞
Typeset in Quadraat by Westchester Publishing Services

Library of Congress Cataloging-in-Publication Data
Oslender, Ulrich, author.
The geographies of social movements : Afro-Colombian mobilization
and the aquatic space / Ulrich Oslender.
pages cm—(New ecologies for the twenty-first century)
Includes bibliographical references and index.
ISBN 978-0-8223-6104-6 (hardcover : alk. paper)
ISBN 978-0-8223-6122-0 (pbk. : alk. paper)
ISBN 978-0-8223-7440-4 (e-book)
1. Social movements—Colombia—Pacific Coast. 2. Blacks—
Political activity—Colombia—Pacific Coast. 3. Blacks—Land
tenure—Colombia—Pacific Coast. 4. Land reform—Colombia.
I. Title. II. Series: New ecologies for the twenty-first century.
HN310.P33085 2016
303.48'409861—dc23
2015032647

Cover art: Raft made of logs floating downstream, Guapi River.
Photo by Ulrich Oslender.
All interior photos by the author.

CONTENTS

ABBREVIATIONS

ACABA — Asociación Campesina del Río Baudó (Peasant Association of the Baudó River, Chocó)

ACADESAN — Asociación Campesina del Río San Juan (Peasant Association of the San Juan River)

ACIA — Asociación Campesina Integral del Río Atrato (Peasant Association of the Atrato River, Chocó)

AFRODES — Asociación de Afrocolombianos Desplazados (National Association of Displaced Afro-Colombians)

ALENPAC — Alimentos Enlatados del Pacífico (Canned Products of the Pacific); company exploiting the naidí palm hearts in Nariño since 1982

ANUC — Asociación Nacional de Usuarios Campesinos (National Peasant Association)

ASODERGUA — Asociación para el Desarrollo del Río Guajuí (grassroots organization in the Guajuí River)

ASOPEZ — Asociación de Pescadores (Association of Fishermen); aimed at improving living and working conditions in the lower part of the Guapi River

ASOPRODESA — Asociación Prodesarrollo del Río Saija (grassroots organization of the Saija River on the Cauca Coast)

AT-55 — Artículo Transitorio 55 (Transitory Article 55 of the Constitution of 1991)

CIMARRÓN — Movimiento Nacional Cimarrón (National Movement for Human Rights for Afro-Colombian Communities); one of the earliest organizations mobilizing against antiblack racism in Colombia

COADEPAL	Cooperativa Agrícola del Pacífico (Agricultural Cooperative of the Pacific); a state program established by INCORA in the mid-1960s on the Pacific Coast mainly to promote the commercialization of coconut
COCOCAUCA	Coordinación de Comunidades Negras de la Costa Pacífica del Cauca (Coordination of Black Communities on the Cauca Coast); the first regional organization on the Cauca Coast with an ethnic-territorial discourse that aims at coordinating the struggles of black communities there; born in 1993
FARC	Fuerzas Armadas Revolucionarias de Colombia (Revolutionary Armed Forces of Colombia); the largest and most powerful guerrilla movement in the country
FEDEPALMA	Federación Nacional de Cultivadores de Palma de Aceite (National Federation of Oil Palm Growers)
GEF	Global Environment Facility; a product of the Río Summit 1992, set up by the United Nations Environment Program UNEP to support, among other things, environmentally sustainable development projects; one of its first operations was the Project for the Conservation of Biodiversity in the Colombian Pacific Region
ICANH	Instituto Colombiano de Antropología e Historia (Colombian Institute of Anthropology and History)
IGAC	Instituto Geográfico Agustín Codazzi (Colombia's National Geographic Institute)
IIAP	Instituto de Investigaciones Ambientales del Pacífico (Institute of Environmental Research for the Pacific Coast)
INCODER	Instituto Colombiano de Desarrollo Rural (Colombian Institute of Rural Development); the state agency that replaced INCORA in 2003 and has since been in charge of executing agricultural policies and overseeing land tenure
INCORA	Instituto Colombiano de Reforma Agraria (Colombian Institute of Agrarian Reform); the government agency responsible for all aspects of collective land titling in the Pacific Coast region until 2003, when it was dissolved and replaced by INCODER, the Colombian Institute of Rural Development

INDERENA	Instituto Nacional de Recursos Naturales Renovables (National Institute of Renewable Natural Resources)
JAC	Junta de Acción Comunal (Committee of Communal Action); a nationwide state-driven initiative in which local committees are to watch over everyday community affairs
JUNPRO	Juventud Unida para el Progreso (United Youth for Progress); the first community organization to emerge in Guapi, mainly consisting of young professionals and former students, who are also the founding members of COCOCAUCA
OCABA	Organización Campesina del Bajo Atrato (Peasant Association of the lower Atrato River, Chocó)
PAR	participatory action-research
PCN	Proceso de Comunidades Negras (Process of Black Communities)
RMT	resource-mobilization theory
UMATA	Unidad Municipal de Asistencia Técnica Agraria (Municipal Unit of Agrarian Assistance)
UP	Unión Patriótica

ACKNOWLEDGMENTS

This book has been in the making for so long that I couldn't possibly name each and every one to whom I am indebted for support, advice, help, or simply for so generously providing their valuable time. Rather than committing the crime of omission (to which acknowledgment sections tend to fall prey), I shall refrain from mentioning individual names here, expressing my thanks to collectivities instead.

My most immediate debts are to the many people in Colombia who over the years opened their doors to me and my inquiries. In particular I want to thank the people of Guapi and the surrounding river basins on the Pacific Coast among whom I lived during 1998–99 and whom I have visited on repeated occasions since. I am most grateful to the many activists of the organizations of black communities in Colombia with whom I interacted over the past twenty years; they include the Proceso de Comunidades Negras, PCN; the National Movement for Human Rights of Afro-Colombian Communities, CIMARRÓN; the Association of Displaced Afro-Colombians, AFRODES; the Guapi-based groups of COCOCAUCA and MATAMBA Y GUASÁ; and the many community council leaders who shared their valuable time and opinions with me on the collective land titling process. Their activism, often in the face of threats to their lives, is utterly inspiring.

Very special thanks to everyone at the Colombian Institute of Anthropology and History (ICANH) in Bogotá, where I was based during my fieldwork and was appointed associate researcher. I also received invaluable support at the National Geographic Institute Agustín Codazzi (IGAC), the Colombian Institute of Agrarian Reform (INCORA), and the Institute of Environmental Research for the Pacific Coast (IIAP). I thank the staff of the biodiversity conservation plan Proyecto Biopacífico for their always open doors, thought-provoking conversations, and help with logistics of traveling in the Pacific lowlands.

The basic idea of this book began as a PhD project at the University of Glasgow in the late 1990s. I am grateful to my mentors for their unwavering commitment and to everyone in what was then the Department of Geography for their support and encouragement. For over twenty years I called Glasgow my home, and it always felt good to return after longer absences spent in the field in Colombia, in no small part thanks to my Glaswegian pals.

I have since had the pleasure of working at a number of academic institutions in the United States and have benefited tremendously from their intellectually stimulating and hospitable environments. Between 2005 and 2007 I spent time as a Marie Curie Research Fellow at the University of California in Los Angeles, where I enjoyed the privilege of working alongside true giants of political and cultural geography. I would like to thank everyone at the UCLA Department of Geography for providing an extraordinarily warm welcome during my time there.

Since fall 2010 Florida International University in Miami has been my academic home, where the Department of Global and Sociocultural Studies has proved to be a wonderful space of interdisciplinary collegiality. The generous support offered to junior faculty there included a teaching-free semester in fall 2011, which I spent writing as a visiting fellow at the University of North Carolina at Chapel Hill, where I found an intellectually inspiring atmosphere and much friendship.

Over the years I have incurred many debts to colleagues working on all things Afro-Colombian. What was a relatively small community of scholars in the early 1990s has since grown exponentially to become a dynamic field of study, and I have benefited tremendously from conversations, workshops, and collaborative research projects with colleagues and friends in Colombia and beyond.

In a more material sense writing this book was made possible by funding from several sources. As a graduate student I was funded by the Principal's Strategic Development Fund at the University of Glasgow (1997–2001). Two research grants by the Carnegie Trust for the Universities of Scotland helped offset fieldwork expenses in Colombia in 1998 and 2003. Further support was provided by an ESRC Postdoctoral Fellowship (2002–3), an ESRC Research Grant (2004–5), a Marie Curie International Fellowship supported through the 6th European Community Framework Programme (2005–8), a Summer Faculty Development Award (2011) from the College of Arts and Sciences at Florida International University (FIU), and two Morris and Anita Broad Research Fellowships awarded by FIU's School of International and Public Affairs (2012 and 2015).

A book is a collaborative effort, and it wouldn't look half as good without the committed and enthusiastic support of the wonderful editorial team at Duke University Press. I also want to thank two anonymous reviewers for their extraordinarily close reading of the initial manuscript and their sharp and insightful observations that helped to clarify some of my arguments.

Finally, I do want to mention two people in particular to whom I dedicate this book: Doña Celia Lucumí Caicedo, traditional healer and midwife from Guapi, who passed away on December 21, 2013. *¡Que la Santísima Virgen del Carmen le bendiga, comadre!* And Don Manuel Zapata Olivella, giant of Spanish American literature, who joined his ancestors on November 19, 2004. *Ekobio sabio, ya no eres prisionero.*

Black Communities in Colombia and the Constitution of 1991

In 1991 Colombia adopted a new Constitution. According to the president at the time, César Gaviria, it was nothing less than an "institutional revolution, a peace treaty, a navigation map for the 21st century" (quoted in Pizarro 1993:151). Drawn up by a Constituent Assembly that was elected in December 1990, the new Constitution was a response to a perceived state disequilibrium that had brought the country "to the brink of chaos" (Leal Buitrago and Zamosc 1991).[1] It was meant to democratize state structures, ensure increased popular participation in the decision-making processes at national, regional, and local levels, and imbue the state with a new legitimacy. Although the process of constitutional reform was not overtly aimed at "ethnic minorities," the debates on increasing popular participation opened a space for both black and indigenous populations into which issues of ethnicity and nationality could be thrust. In hindsight it is no exaggeration to say that the Constitution of 1991 marked a watershed in the relations between the state and Colombia's Afro-descendant population, providing an important new political opportunity structure for the latter to mobilize.

Whereas various articles dealt specifically with Colombia's indigenous populations, outlining their territorial and political rights, only Transitory Article AT-55 made specific reference to the country's "black communities" (*comunidades negras*).[2] This was the first official acknowledgment of the country's black population as a distinct cultural group. While the term *black community* had been used previously by black intellectuals in Colombia (Escalante 1954; Mosquera 1985), after 1991 it became specifically associated with the new Constitution and follow-up legislation. Over time other black self-identification categories would emerge, including "Afro-Colombians" and, most preferred today by black activists, *afrodescendientes*, or "Afro-descendants." In this book I use these various identity signifiers to acknowledge this process of discursive construction of ethnicity and its fluid and changing nature.

Transitory Article AT-55 was important in that it required the promulgation of a law that would, among other things, grant collective land rights to rural black communities living along the river basins of the Pacific Coast region's tropical rain forests. This legislative context set off a new dynamic and direction in the organizing processes of black communities. Until then politicization by blacks had been limited to some small urban intellectual groups on the one hand—the most prominent until today being the National Movement for Human Rights of Afro-Colombian Communities, CIMARRÓN (Mosquera 1985, 1998)—and land right struggles in the northern Pacific Coast department of Chocó on the other. There in the mid-1980s the Catholic Church was decisive in helping set up black peasant organizations that mobilized around the defense of their lands and the environment, under threat from the accelerated exploitation of natural resources by corporate interests in the region. In 1987 these first ecclesiastical grassroots groups formed the Peasant Association of the Atrato River, ACIA, which is still the strongest black peasant organization in the country.[3]

It was there that first links were articulated between a peasant identity and blackness in general, and black peasants' specific relations to territory in particular. These notions found concrete political expression in AT-55 and marked the beginning of what Colombian anthropologist Eduardo Restrepo (2004a, 2013) would later call the "ethnicization of blackness" in Colombia and what Tianna Paschel (2010) refers to as an "ethnic difference frame." Different from the "racial equality frame" of social mobilization pursued by earlier black activism such as CIMARRÓN's—denouncing anti-black racism in Colombia—the newly emerging, mostly rural-based black activist discourse of the early 1990s made claims in terms of culture, ethnic identity, territory, and the right to difference.

It is hard to overestimate the significance of AT-55. To anthropologist Michael Taussig (2004:95) it is "one of the most innovative experiments in political theory this century, [as] Artículo 55 proposes communal ownership by blacks to lands on the coast, thus granting to black ethnicity a political reality unknown in North or South America." Black communities would be the legally recognized territorial authority in these lands, and anyone interested in exploiting natural resources there would have to deal directly with the communities affected.

Once passed, intense negotiations over the extent of AT-55 ensued between government officials and black representatives in the Special Commission for Black Communities set up in August 1992.[4] These eventually led to the passing of one of the most remarkable pieces of legislation concerning Afro-descendant populations anywhere in Latin America. Adopted on August 27, 1993, Law 70, among other dispositions, laid down the legal framework to allocate five million hectares of riverine tropical rain forest lands in the Pacific lowlands—50 percent of this coastal region—to communal ownership by rural black communities.

Yet how were these lands to be allocated? According to what spatial logic would they be distributed?

As an immediate result of Law 70, black political mobilization throughout the Pacific region intensified considerably. By 1994 over 350 organizations of black communities were registered with the Office for Black Community Affairs.[5] As one of the most strongly articulated directions at coordinating these efforts on the regional and national level, the Proceso de Comunidades Negras PCN (Process of Black Communities) emerged as a network of more than 120 local organizations and a national organizational dynamic with its base in the Pacific port city of Buenaventura. PCN's strategy was consequently articulated as an "ethnic-territorial" movement based on five principles (Grueso et al. 1998):

1. *The reaffirmation of identity and the right to be black*—regarded as a cultural logic that permeates the lifeworld in all its social, economic, and political dimensions, countering the logic of domination and opposing a model of society that requires uniformity for its continued dominance.
2. *The right to territory and a space for being*—a necessary condition for the re-creation and development of an Afro-Colombian cultural vision.

3. *Autonomy as the right to the exercise of identity*—arising out of an Afro-Colombian cultural logic in relation to dominant society and other ethnic groups.
4. *The construction of an autonomous perspective for the future*—based on traditional forms of production and social organization.
5. *Declaration of solidarity*—with the struggle of black people throughout the world.

These principles address two interrelated themes: an ideological and political reflection on the part of the movement that entails a rearticulation of the notions of territory, development, and society from an Afro-Colombian perspective, and the articulation of their rights, aspirations, and dreams based on and developed through the perspective of daily life and traditional practices of black communities on the Pacific Coast.

Yet how did this movement come to express their claims in this way? How did PCN conceive of an Afro-Colombian "right to territory"? What spatial logic underlay its formulation? Or we may ask with geographers Richard Peet and Michael Watts (1996:263), what "environmental imaginaries" did this movement articulate in their project of contesting normative visions and the "imperialism of the imaginary" (268)—in PCN terms, countering the logic of domination and opposing a model of society that requires uniformity for its continued dominance?

These are some of the central concerns that I address in this book. To understand the geographies of social movements and how a movement is constituted through particular geographies on the ground, I argue, we need to fully understand not just the logic of political and economic processes operating in the particular region in which a movement operates but also the knowledge practices of place-based cultures and their environmental imaginaries as a primary site of contestation. This conviction lies at the heart of the critical place perspective that I propose in this book. It has also shaped my narrative strategy. Instead of approaching the social movement of black communities in Colombia through its diverse organizational structures, strategies, and political discourses (although I discuss these as well), I start from the situated physical, social, and cultural contexts of everyday life as framing the subjectivities of ordinary people, which subsequently become articulated as social movement discourse.

I am aware that I part from established social movement theorizing in this analytical and narrative strategy. I realize that some social movement scholars may be disappointed, looking in vain for such classic concepts as brokerage, diffusion, or scale shift in this book. Yet I am not alone in being a tad suspicious toward a routine deployment of these concepts that often reduces social movement activity to a set of generic processes and mechanisms (Castree et al. 2008; Davies and Featherstone 2013; Nicholls et al. 2013). Instead I propose an ethnographically grounded approach to the social movement of black communities in Colombia, centering my empirical inquiries on "place-making" in the Pacific lowlands as providing the "soil" out of which social movement activity arises. For this I want to draw the reader first of all in ethnographic depth into the "aquatic space" of the Pacific Coast region, the site for my ensuing examination of the growth of social movement politics.

The Geographies of Social Movements

It was the best of times; it was the worst of times. In March 1995 I traveled for the first time to the Pacific Coast region of Colombia. By then I had already spent four months in Colombia on a year-abroad study program while pursuing an undergraduate degree in geography and Hispanic studies at the University of Glasgow. As part of the program, students were sent for a year to a Spanish-speaking country in order to become fluent in their language skills. My choice fell on Colombia. Why? I am not so sure any more. Colombia is a crazed *fútbol* nation, of course. Their flamboyant style with the likes of René *el scorpión* Higuita, *el Pibe* Valderrama, and Freddy Rincón seduced many during the FIFA World Cup in 1990, when Colombia held West Germany to a dramatic 1:1 draw (with Rincón scoring the equalizer in the ninety-third minute). This surely was a convincing pull factor.

Or maybe it was the sheer exuberance of a tropical geography that attracted me. Colombia is the only country in South America with coastlines on both the Atlantic and the Pacific. The massive Andean mountain range, which runs along the western part of the South American continent, suddenly splits as it reaches Colombia. It is as if it couldn't make up its mind where to go next. This topographic indecision has resulted in three distinct mountain ranges: the Western, Central, and Eastern Cordillera. Deep valleys separate the ranges, notably those of the two great rivers, the Cauca and the Magdalena. Climatic variation is determined by this extremely diverse topography. The higher up you are in the mountains, the colder it gets. The farther down you go, the hotter it becomes. Year-round. It's not time that dictates these temperature patterns, but space.

To the east of the Andes and bordering Venezuela, the llanos orientales are a low-lying flat region made up of huge savannahs. The southeast is covered by extensive rain forests. Yet the region that would hold my fascination for the next two decades lay to the west, the far west. With a coastline of around 1,300 kilometers, stretching from Ecuador in the south to Panama in the north, the Pacific lowlands cover an area of almost ten million hectares of tropical rain forest. Sparsely inhabited by around 1.3 million people (some 3 percent of Colombia's national population), the Pacific region garnered international attention in the 1990s as one of the world's top biodiversity hotspots. Set apart from Colombia's interior by the Western Andean mountain range, the lowlands have been described as the "hidden littoral" (Yacup 1934) or the "periphery of the periphery" (Granda 1977) due to their perceived physical and economic marginality in relation to the rest of the country.

Initially of interest to Spanish colonizers for its rich alluvial gold deposits, the region's economy has been dominated by boom-and-bust cycles. During relatively short time spans, natural resources have been exploited intensively, responding to external demands, before a decline in demand led to a rapid decrease and collapse of these economies. Both tagua (ivory nut) and rubber exploitation in the first half of the twentieth century, for example, followed this boom-and-bust logic. Since the 1960s the region has been an important source of the country's timber supply. This has led to high levels of deforestation that pose a threat to traditional lifestyles of local populations in many areas. In the 1990s the region began to attract strategic attention in national development plans, with a view to conserving its biodiversity (and exploring its potential exploitation in pharmaceutical industries). This conservationist trend has recently been sharply curtailed by an aggressive return to extractive economies, such as mechanical gold mining, and agro-industrial exploitation, most dramatically seen in the sweeping plantations of oil palm monocultures. Throughout these changing development paradigms a resilient local population—made up overwhelmingly of people of African descent—has continued to practice a diversified subsistence economy in the rural areas based on fishing, hunting, agriculture, gathering, and small-scale artisanal gold panning for their everyday needs.

That was just about all I knew about this region back in February 1995, when I got off the small Satena plane at the airport in Tumaco, the Pacific Coast's most southern and third largest town. In Bogotá I had met Robin Hissong, a U.S. citizen who worked on the World Bank–funded biodiversity conservation program Proyecto Biopacífico. As a geographer-in-the-making, I was generally interested in conservation, biodiversity, and sustainable development. The Pacific lowlands seemed an exciting place, where these notions overlapped in complex ways with an emerging identity politics of the region's Afro-descendant population. Therefore I didn't hesitate when Robin extended an invitation to accompany her to Guapi, a small coastal town some 150 kilometers north of Tumaco, where she needed to deliver equipment to Proyecto Biopacífico's regional office.

This speedboat trip was a first taste of traveling through the maze of mangrove swamps that make up the southern coastline of the Pacific lowlands. Our captain suggested we should travel *por dentro*, slowly threading our way along the numerous meandering brooks and channels that cut through the mangrove landscape. He warned against navigating *por fuera*—on the open sea—as the Pacific Ocean was rough that day. Fine by me, I thought; that way I would get to see the area even better.

It was midday by the time we set off. The sky was overcast with dark clouds as we left the Bay of Tumaco. Humidity was near 90 percent. It was hot, and I didn't understand why we had waited so long. It was going to be a lengthy journey, more than eight hours. Robin had even mentioned that we might have to spend a night on the way.

"Who are we waiting for?" I asked the captain, who had said something about *esperando la marea*.

"When's Marea coming?" . . . Laughter all around. That was one of these silly gringo questions. *Marea* means "tide." Apparently there wasn't enough water in the mangrove's river channels, so we had to be patient and wait for high tide. Later I would realize how this seemingly mundane routine—the daily tidal changes—impacted everyday life patterns in a thousand and one ways. Traveling schedules are set according to the tides, calculating water availability not only in the coastal mangrove swamps but also farther up the rivers. The alluvial plains have such a low gradient that the tidal impact can be felt up to twenty kilometers upstream. High tide also pushes salt water far up the rivers, a bad time for washing clothes or fetching drinking water from the river.

Sitting at the landing steps in Guapi the day after we left Tumaco—we indeed had to spend a night in Satinga on our trip—I took in the majestic leisureliness with which the Guapi River descended to its meeting with the Pacific Ocean. The inevitableness of the encounter was marked by the calm, gracious flow of the river's waters, which veiled the underlying excited anticipation of the get-together. That first day my gaze was too caught up in the solemn grandeur and the splendid presence of *el río* to notice the sawmill on the opposite river bank. I did notice, however, a number of dugout canoes on the river, powered by the paddling strength of a single occupant, all making their way toward the landing steps from downstream. The rising tide was giving them a helping hand. They would return later that day to their hamlets downstream, when the low tide facilitated a speedier journey.

It was there, at the landing steps in Guapi, where I spent innumerable hours in the years to come, that the idea of the "aquatic space" began to take shape. Anthropologists and geographers have described the interactions of rural populations with the tropical rain forest in terms of human adaptation to an often unforgiving natural environment. In *Black Frontiersmen*, his seminal study on the Afro-Hispanic culture of Ecuador and Colombia, for example, Norman Whitten (1986) sees this adaptive process expressed in intense spatial mobility and the development of traditional systems of social organization. Colombian anthropologist Nina de Friedemann (1974) also stresses social organization as a strategy of adaptation to a changing physical environment. Fellow anthropologist Jaime Arocha (1999) describes local diverse economies, which he calls *polifonía cultural*, as adaptive strategies toward the uncertainties of the natural environment. Meanwhile, U.S. geographer Robert West's (1957:3) groundbreaking study *The Pacific Lowlands of Colombia* is an inventory of human adaptation to the myriad river basins, where "hundreds of rivers, often in flood, run through the forest from hill and mountain slope to sea. They are the pathways for human travel and their banks are the main sites of human habitation." I discuss these debates more widely in chapter 3.

Yet sitting at the landings steps in Guapi overlooking the busy activities taking place—canoes arriving, women washing clothes on the river's edge, children playing in the water, travelers awaiting embarkations to upstream locations—I felt that these were more than merely adaptive responses. The discourse of adaptation maintains those boundaries of culture and nature that seemed to dissolve in practice in front of my eyes. The idea of the "aquatic space" that was taking root then owes more to a Deleuzian understanding of these complex and changing relations between humans and nonhumans in terms of assemblages. It wants to break with the notion of exteriority of an already existing nature that culture merely adapts to and focus instead, as does anthropologist Laura Ogden (2011:28) in her landscape ethnography in the Everglades of South Florida, on "the ways in which our relations with non-humans produce what it means to be human." Beyond a mere conceptual acknowledgment of debates on "social nature" (Castree and Braun 2001; FitzSimmons 1989; Smith 1990), I am concerned here with narrative strategies of exploring how this social nature is actually experienced on the ground. For this I draw on ideas proposed under the banner of the "narratological turn" in the arts and social sciences (Daniels and Lorimer 2012) in my ways of narrating landscape and environment in the Pacific lowlands through diverse forms and genres, including storytelling.

In 1999 I would spend many evening hours in the half-covered courtyard of the house I rented on Calle Segunda in Guapi, sitting with Doña Celia Lucumí Caicedo, a traditional healer and midwife, with whom I shared this living space. As the rains pummeled the rooftops, generating a thunderous noise that drowned out all possibility of conversation, we just stared ahead, watching sheets of rainwater hammering the patio's tropical plants and quickly filling up the four barrels, one in each corner, that became a full week's household water supply. These were moments of great peace for me. There was absolutely nothing else I wanted to do but stare at the falling rain. It seemed we all became one with the rain.[1] I loved those moments of inner calm that Yemayá sent me. There was nothing I could possibly miss out on. No one in Guapi left their home during these deluges. No conversation could be had for the deafening roar of Changó's fury unleashed on the rooftops of Guapi.[2]

Doña Celia was also lost in her thoughts then. Walking along the shores of her river in her imagination—as she would later tell me—she brought to life memories of her childhood growing up along the headwaters of the Guapi River. She would rock to and fro in her rocking chair, smoking pa' dentro. A custom of many years, she would smoke with the lit end of the cigarette inside her mouth. Occasionally she would take the cigarette out and tip off the ash. This age-old custom, quite common among rural black women in the Pacific lowlands, enables them to smoke while navigating their canoes, come rain or shine. With both hands firmly holding the paddle, the lit cigarette end is safe from wind and water in the navigator's mouth . . .

"A mi río, no lo olvido," Doña Celia would murmur. "I don't forget my river." She was one with her river, as she was sitting in our patio, smoking *pa' dentro*. There, in our courtyard, it was not necessary to protect the cigarette in that way, as we were covered under a rooftop. Yet more than a mere adaptive response to an aquatic environment, Doña Celia's smoking *pa' dentro* had become part of her, no matter where she was. The concept of the aquatic space, as I develop it in chapters 2 and 3, considers these relations of "becoming" between humans and nonhumans in a landscape characterized by diverse aquatic features as dynamic assemblages. It transcends the idea of mere human adaptation to a physical environment.

So far so good, you might say. But what does this have to do with social movements? And their geographies?

Indeed these were precisely the questions that I was beginning to ask myself during those rain-drenched nights on our patio. A social movement of black communities had emerged in the early 1990s that mobilized around cultural and territorial rights newly enshrined in Colombia's Constitution of 1991. And established social movement theory seemed to have the tools at hand to examine this movement. Political process models, for example, stress the importance of political opportunity structures for creating a favorable context for movements to emerge (McAdam et al. 1996, 2001; Tarrow 1994, 2012; Tilly and Tarrow 2007; Tilly and Wood 2009). Clearly the passing of the new Constitution in Colombia provided such a new political opportunity structure. "Blackness" became a state-regulated discourse, a field of struggle, a structure of alterity (Restrepo 2013).

Resource-mobilization theory (RMT), on the other hand, proposes to examine the resources available for a social movement to draw on. It focuses above all on organizational structures, leadership, and movement goals. Resources include funding and financial support, the existence of networks, the expertise of movement leaders, and some degree of preexisting organizations on whose experience leaders can draw (McCarthy and Zald 1977; Oberschall 1973; Tilly 1978). Finally, identity-oriented perspectives that emerged in the 1980s focus on the ways actors' identities are dialectically constructed in social struggle (Escobar and Alvarez 1992; Laclau and Mouffe 1985; Melucci 1989; Touraine 1988). These approaches empha-size "the power of identity" (Castells 1997) and have become synonymous with the study of so-called new social movements. These supposedly mark a shift in collective action from class-based mobilization, such as in trade unions, toward a more identity-based contentious politics, such as ex-pressed in struggles over environmental, human rights, gender, and ethnic and racial concerns (Slater 1985).[3] Scholars examining the social movement of black communities in Colombia have drawn on these approaches to differing degrees (Agudelo 2005; Almario 2003; Asher 2009; Escobar 2008; Escobar and Pedrosa 1996; Grueso et al. 1998; Hoffmann 2004; Pardo 2001; Restrepo 2013; Wade 1995, 2002).

Yet sitting on the patio of my rented house on Calle Segunda in Guapi, with the rains pummeling the iron roof, I began to wonder how the particu-larities of this place—its year-round humidity, its water-based cultures, its river thoroughfares, its people listening to the tides—figured in the making of this social movement. What "place" did this place have in the contentious politics that began to emerge then? There was a deafening silence in the existing literature on social movements regarding the rele-vance of place in its theorizations. More broadly speaking, sociologists and political scientists had not given much thought to the spatialities of social movements. To be sure, geographers had begun to address this lacuna—Paul Routledge (1993) may have been among the first to do so (see also Pile and Keith 1997; Slater 1998)—but these early calls went largely unheard in the wider social movement literature. While I was aware of these emerg-ing debates in geography that provided exciting new ways of looking at social movements, I *felt* their necessity while listening to the rain in Guapi. In other words, my conviction that social movement theory needed to be infused with a spatial sensitivity that would account for the geographical constitution of social movement agency was first and foremost born in the field. It was not mere theoretical speculation.

In time I began to ask concrete questions. For example, how would this newly formed constitutional discourse on blackness and black cultural and territorial rights—negotiated in the faraway capital of Bogotá—be trans-lated meaningfully to local residents on the Pacific Coast? In what way would local histories of resistance (which I discuss in chapter 3) inform the structures of the emerging social movement of black communities? How would local realities on the ground be fed into mobilization processes? For example, Law 70 required the establishment of "community councils" (*consejos comunitarios*) as administrative authorities for the newly titled collective lands. How would these be formed? Based on what logic? How would the particularities of place in the Pacific region inform and guide the formation of these community councils? How would local environmental knowledges (which I conceptualize and discuss as "local aquatic epistemologies" in chapter 2) be mobilized by the movement?

Beyond these immediate empirical concerns lay the wider question of how to feed them into a better conceptual understanding of social movements. If theory and practice are regarded as a dialectical unity, as Marx pointed out long ago, and theory is derived, at least partially, from practical experience, then there was a need to transcend the empirical specificity of my case study in the Pacific region to construct a theory of social movements that would account for these experiences more widely. In other words, the geographies of social movements had to be theorized.

Based on this understanding, I propose in this book a "critical place perspective" on social movements. With the focus on place I do not intend to privilege a particular spatiality at the expense of another, as some may impute (e.g., Leitner et al. 2008:166). But I do want to recover the significance of place as a corrective to the increasing trend on seeing the transnational as the "master spatiality" in social movement research. In this I share Arturo Escobar's (2008:7) concern that "there is a need for a corrective theory that neutralizes this erasure of place, the asymmetry that arises from giving far too much importance to 'the global' and far too little value to 'place.' "

Place and Social Movement Research

Roughly since the mid-1990s geographers have attempted to show how geography matters in social movement research. Whereas Routledge (1993) stresses above all the importance of place in his book *Terrains of Resistance*, Byron Miller (2000) focuses on scale variations in political opportunity structures in his attempt to elaborate a geographical model of social movement mobilization. These examples may illustrate what Leitner et al. (2008:158) describe as "shifting fashions of socio-spatial theory [and the] tendency to privilege a particular spatiality—only to abandon that in favour of another." Since 1995, they argue, there has been a tendency to focus on the politics of scale in social movement research, in particular examining a movement's multiscalar strategies, or "scale-jumping."[4] More recently the focus has shifted toward examining networks and mobility. In particular a fascination with the transnational scale of mobilization has dominated recent social movement research and publications. This can be seen in book titles such as *Coalitions across Borders* (Bandy and Smith 2004), *Transnational Protest and Global Activism* (Della Porta and Tarrow 2005), *Transnational Social Movements and Global Politics* (Smith et al. 1997), and *The New Transnational Activism* (Tarrow 2005), to name but a few (see also Featherstone 2008; Keck and Sikkink 1998; Routledge and Cumbers 2009; Smith 1998).

While this focus is understandable, given important developments in the way social movements increasingly organize globally—successfully "jumping scale" and engaging global resistance networks such as the World Social Forum (Fisher and Ponniah 2003; Sousa Santos 2006)—it also reflects an enthusiasm on the researchers' part that may easily gloss over other important spatialities that make up social movement mobilization. In other words, the transnational has evolved into the hegemonic scale of analysis in social movement research or, as Leitner et al. (2008:158) refer to it, a "master spatiality." These accounts focus on the connections that movements make, on the commonalities between them, and on the discourse that is produced at these transnational intersections.

All of this is important, of course. But what does this transnational fixation say about an individual movement and its inner workings? Or about the "mobilization within movements," as geographer Wendy Wolford (2010) puts it in her insightful analysis of the landless peasants' movement MST in Brazil. Is there not a real danger of distortion in research that focuses almost exclusively on the well-elaborated discourses of social movement leaders as they are enounced in various transnational settings (to which the researcher can comfortably travel without having to get dirty in the field), if it does not at the same time examine how these discourses can be traced in the everyday, on-the-ground realities of the far-flung places of which a particular movement talks? Often, it may seem in these accounts, "the movement" is little more than the movement leaders' discourse, or rather the researcher's interpretation of the latter.

Longtime social movement scholar Robert Benford (1997:421) critiques this "tendency to focus on the framings of movement elites to the neglect of rank-and-file participants":

Much of the literature is written as though participant mobilization were simply a matter of movement activists pushing the appropriate rhetorical button. . . . This bias is in part a reflection of the ways in which researchers typically study social movements. We tend to study movements either by interviewing people identified as key activists, via media accounts (most frequently newspaper stories), or by analyzing movement-generated or related documents. In all three cases, we obtain data that tend to reflect the views of movement leaders and extra-movement elites. In short, our analyses of framing processes often have a built-in, top-down bias. (Benford 1997:421)[5]

Moreover I argue that "place," or the complexity of the places out of which these movements emerge and of which they talk, often merely becomes a backdrop in these accounts.[6]

In my approach place is not just one of many spatialities of mobilization. On the contrary, I argue that place implicates space, scale, and territory. Leitner et al. (2008:169) are surely right in affirming that "no single spatiality should be privileged since they are co-implicated in complex ways, often with unexpected consequences for contentious politics." If they are co-implicated, however, then it might not make much sense to regard them as separate in the first place. Therefore the authors' effort to come up with a framework of five distinct "co-implicated spatialities of contentious politics" seems counterproductive for two principal reasons. First, they rather haphazardly choose these co-implicated spatialities: scale, place, networks, socio-spatial positionality, and mobility. One may ask, for example, where is territory? Or argue with John Agnew (1987) that place implies scale. Second, it is not clear how their empirical case study—the Immigrant Workers' Freedom Ride (IWFR) in the United States—shows the co-implication of these spatialities or illustrates "the complexity of these inter-relations" (Leitner et al. 2008:166). Place, for example, is remarkably absent from their account. In other words, co-implication is shown by undertheorizing place. While their general approach may be useful to show "how geography matters in contentious politics" (158), I argue that it is something altogether different to show *how social movements are constituted through particular geographies on the ground*. That is the focus in this book.

There have been other recent attempts reflecting on the organization of sociospatial relations in multiple forms. Jessop et al. (2008), for example, replicate in part some of Leitner et al.'s framework, adding territory. In their argument "territories (T), places (P), scales (S), and networks (N) must be viewed as mutually constitutive and relationally intertwined dimensions of sociospatial relations" (389). In their "TPSN framework" they identify these four distinct spatialities as framing principles of sociospatial relations. In my view both these frameworks fall into what we may call "the spatial trap."[7] By this I mean that the ever more complex language of spatialities may trap and ultimately limit the empirical usefulness of what is offered. In other words, geographers hold each other prisoner in ever more complex conceptualizations over the spatiality of social life that do not necessarily have much empirical purchase any longer.

For example, how do we show empirically what each "part" in these frameworks contributes to the whole? The argument for distinct yet co-implicated or mutually constitutive spatialities has led Leitner and colleagues (2008) and Jessop and colleagues (2008) to search for polymorphic frameworks in order to account for the totality of relations between and among these co-implicated spatialities. In the end, however, the mind-boggling complexity of this venture gets reduced to multinodal frameworks that are both inclusive, in that they explicitly draw on certain spatialities, and exclusionary, in that they leave out others. Call it SPNPM, as Leitner et al. (2008) could have called it, or TPSN, as Jessop et al. (2008) do call it—the result is the same: a conceptual reduction of the complexity of sociospatial relations that only works (or seems to) by undertheorizing one or several of its key components.

Not surprisingly maybe, that undertheorized component is place, associated by many with notions of traditional, unmoving, backward, and fixed, whereas "mobility," "transnational," and "space" are considered dynamic and progressive (although see Massey 2005 for an impassioned argument against this simplification). One may feel that the abstract dancing around has not paid off much in terms of throwing light on real-world political questions. Maybe "middle-range" theorizing is more useful here than that which often remains distant from empirical concerns.[8]

From this viewpoint my proposal of a critical place perspective unashamedly recovers the progressive notion of place; one that acknowledges multiscalar connections in place and between places and that grounds networks, however momentarily, in place. It is not a one-dimensional methodological place-centrism that neglects other spatialities. On the contrary, a critical place perspective co-implicates scale, territory, and networks. Its aim is to account more fully for the multiple, multiscalar, rooted and networked experiences *within* social movements. At least that is the way I envision it deployed.

Narrating Place and Social Movements in the Colombian Pacific Coast Region

Drawing on my ethnographic fieldwork among Afro-Colombian communities over the past twenty years, I examine how "local aquatic epistemologies"—the place-based and culturally specific ways of knowing a profoundly aquatic environment—have informed political organizational processes in the Pacific region. The book explores these relationships through interviews and participant observation (I discuss methodological implications in the interlude following chapter 1). In my narrative I draw extensively on perspectives of many of the people who accompanied me on my travels throughout the Pacific Coast region. Voices of fishermen, traditional healers, midwives, political activists, miners, poets, schoolchildren, peasant farmers, government officials, priests, and teachers are woven into my account. These help me unfold a deeply spatial understanding of the Pacific lowlands. I also describe how these voices and bodies move through this space, drawing on recent work in narratology to "redeem narrative as a theoretically powerful and complicated form of explanation, a precise cognitive instrument, taking many forms, genres, tropes, tenses, including various kinds of storytelling" (Daniels and Lorimer 2012:3).

As such my approach differs from most studies of social movements, in that my narrative starts from a close examination of the river- and landscapes of the Pacific lowlands, before I turn to the political aspects of social mobilization. This analytical strategy allows me to map the ways specific environmental experiences have been fed into social movement agency and, crucially, what difference they have made in the political organizing processes. This becomes apparent above all in my discussion of the community councils as newly established territorial authorities in the Pacific river basins (chapters 4 and 5). So far the community councils have mostly been sidelined in existing scholarship on black resistance in Colombia. While important contributions have been made in relation to racialization processes (Agudelo 2005; Arocha 1999; Hoffmann 2004; Restrepo 2013; Wade 1993, 2000), to the imbrications of development and black resistance (Asher 2009; Escobar 1995, 2008), and to territorial conflicts (Ng'weno 2007b; Villa 2013), there are to date no larger ethnographic studies of the community councils on the Pacific Coast. I hope to fill this void by mapping the experiences of some of these community councils in ethnographic detail and by examining the discourses that emerge from these new political actors.

A Note (or Two) on Difference
A First Difference: Difference Within

When writing about social movements, it is important to acknowledge that these are rarely homogeneous entities following a single logic in which all participants share the same goals all the time. Instead they should be seen as spaces of debate, difference, and even dissent. They are multiplicities, in the sense that an array of interests usually underlies their formation, and a range of often quite diverse tactics may be deployed, while they still articulate a more or less coherent strategy of an overall unifying goal.

From this viewpoint the social movement of black communities in Colombia is made up of different sectors, which at times pursue different aims. For example, responding to the human rights crisis in the late 1990s in the Pacific Coast region, the Association of Displaced Afro-Colombians, AFRODES, was formed in 1999 in order to support thousands of Afro-Colombian families who live in conditions of forced internal displacement (more on this in the epilogue). AFRODES, it may be argued, deploys above all a "displacement frame" that constructs their claims in terms of a defense of Afro-Colombian rights and their cultural identity in the face of violent upheaval. The National Movement for Human Rights of Afro-Colombian Communities, CIMARRÓN—one of the earliest expressions of black mobilization in Colombia and still an important part of the social movement of black communities (Mosquera 1985, 1998)—also deploys this "displacement frame" nowadays in its wider struggle for racial justice and equality.

Clearly the changing situation in the Pacific Coast region starting in the late 1990s has led to new framing strategies by black activists. The movement is heterogeneous, constantly evolving and responding to these changing circumstances. Social movement scholars argue that movements are most effective when they achieve an alignment of their interpretive orientations (Snow et al. 1986), and we may be seeing such a "frame alignment" around movement discourse on displacement and violent upheaval today, in which the various sectors of the movement come together to focus on a common goal. (This has not always been so.)

Yet in this book I am more interested in examining the particular geographies out of which the movement emerged in the Pacific Coast region in the 1990s and how these are reflected in the movement's framing strategies. Thus my analysis and narrative focus above all on the ethnic-territorial aspects of the struggle of the social movement of black communities in the Pacific region in a historical perspective. While acknowledging the possibility of different readings of the movement and the diverse expressions of black mobilization in Colombia—the "difference within," so to speak—I am mostly concerned in exploring what I call the "ethnic-territorial frame," the ways in which the movement has managed to bring together concerns about ethnic identity and difference with a particular territorial vision, expressed through an Afro-Colombian cultural logic intrinsically linked to the right to territory. That is why I focus in my analysis on those sectors of the movement that work directly on issues concerning ethnicity and land rights—in particular the Process of Black Communities (PCN)—and less on those who mobilize around human rights and displacement, such as AFRODES (which does figure prominently, however, in the epilogue).

A Second Difference: Difference without Romanticizing

In writing this book it was my desire to offer a cultural geography of Colombia's Pacific lowlands as a lens through which to view and understand the social movement that has mobilized in that region. To achieve this I chose to slowly unravel in front of the reader, in ethnographic detail, the cultural difference of the region in relation to the rest of the country. I realize that this insistence on difference—absolutely necessary in my eyes to understand the region and its political mobilization—might be read by some as an inside-outside dichotomy, or modernity-versus-tradition frame of thinking. Others may read into it a tendency to homogenize or even romanticize the region, its people, and political movements. Such critiques are quite common and frequently launched against accounts of social movements that organize politically around the notion of difference (see, for example, certain political economy critiques of postdevelopment theory). I find that these debates have become increasingly entrenched and little productive.[9]

Instead we should acknowledge diverse politics of reading across positions. In my narrative I do not appeal to a totalizing difference. (Some movement activists indeed do that—the well-known "strategic essentialism.") On the contrary, throughout the book I point to the many ways rural black populations in the Pacific Coast region are indeed entangled in modernity (most obvious in the lengthy discussion of community councils in chapters 4 and 5). Locals are part of larger logging operations; many work on oil palm plantations; some employ dynamite while fishing; others use mercury or mechanical dredgers in gold mining; many are now involved in illegal coca cultivation; much river travel today is by engine-driven speed boat. All of these things do happen. Rural black populations are modern too, and locals are often deeply entangled as agents in modern technologies and processes.

At the same time, traditional production practices and local subsistence economies are still central to rural lifeworlds and form the backbone to both the definition of "black communities" as expressed in Law 70 and subsequent legislation, and the visions of alternative life projects promoted by sectors of the social movement of black communities. It is necessary, then, to move beyond the all too facile dichotomy of traditional versus modern. In a more nuanced understanding, based on an assemblage approach that I advocate here, one would acknowledge that most people on the Pacific Coast are both modern and traditional to differing extents. This seems a productive way to conceptualize the entanglements of locals with modernity and tradition.

Yet I am unapologetic for my narrative strategy in this book: I need to stress and examine the existing cultural difference of the Pacific Coast region in order to understand the social movement discourse based on difference, while still keeping a critical distance from it. Such is the politics of reading (and writing) across positions. While some observers only briefly acknowledge difference to then emphasize entanglements—thereby often taking the wind out of social movement discursive strategies, even if involuntarily so—I choose to spell out and document in ethnographic detail existing differences on the ground that can explain these discourses. I'd like to think about this narrative strategy as documenting difference without romanticizing.

Overview

In chapter 1 I develop what I call a critical place perspective on social movements. This also means an engagement with space. I make a sustained theoretical argument as to why space and place matter in social movement research, and how they influence, shape, enable, or otherwise constrain resistance practices. In particular I draw on Henri Lefebvre's (1991) spatial triad that he developed in his book *The Production of Space*, and on John Agnew's (1987) threefold approach to place as optics through which to examine social movements. Following Lefebvre I examine how "representational space"—encompassing the subjectivities of everyday life—can be regarded as a (re)source for the "quest for a counter-space" that social movements often articulate. Tying these insights into an analysis of Agnew's threefold concept of place, I show how "location," "locale," and "sense of place" provide the pillars for the framework that I term "critical place perspective on social movements."

These theoretical elaborations are followed by methodological reflections in the interlude. Here I describe the moment I met Don Agapito Montaño, a respected *decimero* (practitioner of oral poetry) for the first time in 1995 in his house in Guapi. Our conversation was dramatically interrupted that day when three young Afro-Colombians burst into the room demanding explanations as to my motives for interviewing Don Agapito. It turned out the "intruders" were local activists upset that I had not consulted them before. This incident serves to reflect on methodological and ethical considerations of conducting ethnographic research in a politically charged context. I also outline how my prolonged presence among Afro-Colombians in Guapi led to a dialogical engagement, in which I drew on a rich tradition of experimental ethnographies and activist methodologies proposed by paradigmatic figures such as Paulo Freire and Orlando Fals Borda.

In chapter 2 I develop the concept of the aquatic space to theoretically and methodologically focus the book. The aquatic space refers to an assemblage of always shifting relations in which everyday life patterns in the region are deeply entangled with a range of aquatic elements, such as the physical and symbolic presence of the sea, intricate river networks, streams, waterfalls, mangrove swamps, high levels of precipitation, significant tidal ranges, and frequent large-scale inundations. Prominent in this chapter are the perspectives of two important people I mentioned already: Don Agapito and Doña Celia. Their experiences and stories provide the individualized, personal keys through which I unlock a more analytical account of the sense of place in this part of the world. Here I engage recent anthropological scholarship on the performative qualities of storytelling as a way of practicing knowledge (Blaser 2010). I then show how the various expressions of local aquatic epistemologies have been mobilized in the political project of black communities in Colombia. Drawing on James Scott's (1990) work on resistance, I argue that the oral tradition functions as a "hidden transcript of resistance" that is turned public in the articulation of an Afro-Colombian identity politics that reclaims cultural and territorial rights.

Chapter 3 closely examines location and locale on the Pacific Coast. It elaborates on the concept of the aquatic space and its manifestation both in the physical environment of a rain forest crisscrossed by intricate river networks and mangrove swamps and in the spatialized social relationships along river basins (settlement patterns, landownership, kinship ties, and transport). These contexts for social interaction are further channeled through the "logic of the river," a notion with which I frame the flow of life in the Pacific lowlands and the specific forms of spatial mobility organized around river basins.

Chapter 4 brings us into the field of politics proper, examining the ways the aquatic space is reflected in a new political context. In particular I show how that context has been drawn upon in the formation of community councils along river basins. The river remains a key resource here for political mobilization—both materially and symbolically. Yet I also show how ethnic-territorial politics in the region has been mediated by capital and the state, highlighting the complex entanglements between state discourse, capital's profit-seeking drive, and local organizing processes. Crucially I maintain that the community councils—far from being mere administrative bodies—are complex spaces of negotiation between these various actors.

In chapter 5 I describe in more detail the actual formation processes of the community councils, as well as their practices and ideals. I examine the legislation that created these organizing figures as part of the state's conservationist strategy toward the Pacific lowlands and its attempt to extend its reach into this region. I then explore the role that leadership and previous organizational experience played in the newly emerging community councils as important resources for mobilization.

The epilogue brings the analysis to the present. I begin by outlining the geographies of terror that have been produced in the Pacific Coast region since the late 1990s as a result of an aggressive return to extractivist economic practices, specifically oil palm cultivation and mechanical gold mining. I have published elsewhere on these changing economic, social, and political relations in the region that have led to selected killings of activists, massacres of entire communities, and massive forced displacement (Oslender 2007b, 2007c, 2008a, 2008b, 2012). I draw on these insights in this epilogue to juxtapose the current dehumanizing condition and relentless environmental destruction to the progressive spirit and winds of hope that blew across the Pacific lowlands in the early 1990s. I insist that to continue imagining an alternative future for the Pacific Coast region with its people, we need to turn back our gaze and reengage with the seeds of hope that were sown then.[10] For this we need to fully understand not just the logic of political and economic processes in the region but also the knowledge practices of place-based cultures and their vision for an alternative future. This book's critical place perspective hopes to ensure the latter is not forgotten.

ONE

Toward a Critical Place Perspective on Social Movements

A whole history remains to be written of *spaces*—which would at the same time be the history of *powers*.

—MICHEL FOUCAULT, *POWER-KNOWLEDGE*

Social movements emerge out of specific places at particular times. This may be an obvious claim, a truism, but rarely is a spatial alertness to social movements spelled out analytically. Emphasis is most often placed on the temporal dimensions of social change, a trend powerfully reflected, for example, in one of the key concepts of established social movement literature: cycles of protest. As Charles Tilly and Sidney Tarrow (2007:183)—among the leading social movement scholars—keep stressing, the civil rights movement in the United States of the early 1960s must be seen as "the most important American cycle of contention of the twentieth century." Whereas temporality is given preference in such an analytical approach, spatiality is often left by the roadside.

This focus has been challenged by geographical scholarship in social movement research (Miller 2000; Routledge 1993; Wolford 2010) and by anthropological concerns that recognize the construction of collective identities in social movements as intricately linked to place (Escobar 2008; Moore 1998). To understand an identity-based movement, for example, we have to understand the specific *places* where social movement agency evolves and where these identities are constructed and physically acted out. There are concrete questions arising out of the interactions between social movement agency and place: How do the particularities of a place impact on people who form into a social movement? How do they constrain or otherwise enable individuals to get involved in collective action? How far does the experience of living in a place, and the subjective feelings that this generates, influence an individual actor's choice of engaging in social movement activity? Do the particular local histories of a place play a part in understanding how locals think about their participation in collective action? But also how do the wider and more objective characteristics of a place, as inscribed in the political and economic macro-order of things, account for the organization and articulation of resistance in a particular place? What are the implications of a particular physical environment in local organizing processes?

In the case of social movements that mobilize around land struggles, the material physical space is at the center of their activities. Their struggle for land is at the same time a contestation of space, and of the interpretations, readings, and representations of this space. In the case of the Process of Black Communities (PCN) in Colombia, which defines itself as an ethnic-territorial organization, their struggle for territorial rights in the Pacific lowlands is explicitly linked to a reinterpretation of space. In effect, in PCN discourse the region becomes a site of struggle over representations of space.

These developments in practice should be fed into theoretical reflections on how place and space impact on social movement agency, articulations, and strategies. It is not possible (or desirable) to radically separate space and place in these considerations, as if space constituted a more abstract idea of the things that surround us, whereas place would refer to a more tangible notion of things we can touch, see, feel, and smell. Instead space and place can be thought of as conceptually melting into one another, as Andrew Merrifield (1993:520) attempts to show in outlining a "Lefebvrian reconciliation" of space and place: "Space is not a high level abstract theorization separated from the more concrete, tactile domain of place which is frequently taken as synonymous with an easily identifiable reality such as specific location or 'locality.' . . . Both space and place have a real ontological status since they are both embodied in material processes—namely, real human activities. Their distinction must, therefore, be conceived by capturing how they melt into each other rather than by reifying some spurious fissure."

Debates have been raging in human geography over the place-space distinction and won't end any time soon. John Agnew (2005), for example, identifies three principal approaches in these debates: they either privilege place over space or space over place, or they do away altogether with the distinction. One of geography's most beloved space-place theoreticians, Doreen Massey (2005:6), somewhat provocatively proposes the last option at the beginning of her book-length reflection on space and place (although her book is simply titled *for space*, it clearly deals with both concepts): "And what if we refuse that distinction, all too appealing it seems, between place (as meaningful, lived and everyday) and space (as what? the outside? the abstract? the meaning*less*)?"[1] I too believe it is necessary to disentangle some common misconceptions over the often proclaimed abstractness of space vis-à-vis the supposed concreteness of place. Clearly I *do* see place as something tangible that I can picture in my mind. Yet while space certainly enables us to make abstractions from particular places, it also has its concrete "moments." Rather than adding more conceptual oil to this fiery theoretical debate, however, I want to show how both concepts can be usefully deployed to examine an actual empirical scenario. Thus in chapters 2 and 3 I approach the Colombian Pacific lowlands through the concept of the "aquatic space." This will enable me to examine the spatial articulations of everyday life forms in place and how they are mobilized and fed into particular political organizing forms.

In this chapter I will arrive at an account of why space and place matter in social movement research by drawing on Henri Lefebvre's (1991) often-cited threefold spatial theory (distinguishing between spatial practices, representations of space, and representational space) and Agnew's (1987) approach to place as constituted of three elements (location, locale, sense of place). Although on first sight these may appear to be incompatible theoretical frameworks, they interact on the empirical level by doing slightly different work in this book. Whereas Agnew's concept of place enables us to outline both the objective and the subjective aspects that make up the "place" that is the Colombian Pacific Coast region, Lefebvre's spatial theory opens up ways of contextualizing these place aspects and of imagining the construction of an alternative life project in this place, as articulated by sectors of the social movement of black communities (what Lefebvre would call "the quest for a counter-space"). The "melting into each other" of space and place thus occurs in a real empirical scenario, while a conceptual distinction is still preserved. I therefore discuss these theoretical concepts from the outset with their practical applicability in mind. Their apparent abstractness must be regarded as a "concrete abstraction," one that is "embodied in a social process that creates abstract forces that have concrete and personal effects in daily life" (Harvey 1985a:1).

Lefebvre and the Production of Space

In the 1970s the French urban sociologist Henri Lefebvre elaborated his vision of a politics of space. For him space was both the source and the objective of political conflict. From this viewpoint the multiple resistances against the global neoliberal order today can be considered struggles over space, or, in Lefebvre's (1991:349) words, a quest for a "counter-space in the sense of an initially utopian alternative to actually existing 'real' space." In his 1970 article "Reflections on the Politics of Space" (the English-language version appeared in *Antipode* in 1976), Lefebvre (1976:31) states:

> Space is not a scientific object removed from ideology or politics; it has always been political and strategic. If space has an air of neutrality and indifference with regard to its contents and thus seems to be "purely" formal, the epitome of rational abstraction, it is precisely because it has already been occupied and used, and has already been the focus of past processes whose traces are not always evident in the landscape. Space has been shaped and molded from historical and natural elements, but this has been a political process. Space is political and ideological. It is a product literally filled with ideologies.

In other words, space is not only the material site of struggle but also the symbolic site of conflict over interpretations and representations. To think about space critically, therefore, is not merely a conceptual exercise but a critical tool for the construction of a progressive politics of space. To Lefebvre (1991:40) the abstract model always needs to have practical implications for the everyday. This is how we should understand the conceptual triad, or the three interconnected "moments" that Lefebvre proposes in the production of space: spatial practices, representations of space, and representational space.[2]

Spatial Practices

Generally speaking, *spatial practices* refer to the ways people generate, use, and perceive space. More specifically spatial practices "take on their meanings under specific social relations of class, gender, community, ethnicity or race and 'get used up' or 'worked over' in the course of social action" (Harvey 1989:223). On the one hand, therefore, they affect the processes of commodification and bureaucratization of everyday life, a phenomenon symptomatic and constitutive of modernity, which has effectively colonized an older, historically sedimented "concrete space." (A similar argument has been made by Habermas [1987], who refers to these processes as "colonization of the life world.") On the other hand, these spatial practices are intimately linked to the experience of everyday life and the memories and residues of older and different life forms. They bear therefore a potential for resisting the colonization of concrete spaces. These are crucial insights for the case study of the Pacific lowlands, where traces of a historically sedimented concrete space can be found, especially in the more remote and less accessible parts of this region. This may be most evident in everyday cultural practices such as traditional healing, the performance of oral tradition, and funeral rites. It is precisely *these* spatial practices that social movement leaders evoke in their political project, intent on resisting the further penetration of capital into the region.

Representations of Space

Representations of space are derived from a particular logic and from technical and rational knowledges. They refer to the "conceptualized space, the space of scientists, planners, urbanists, technocratic subdividers and social engineers" (Lefebvre 1991:38). Their expert knowledges form part of the scientific discourse of modernity in health, education, family planning, and so on, which invades the spheres of social life through institutionalization (Foucault 1972). Lefebvre refers to these knowledges as *savoir*: knowledges that are connected to an institutional apparatus of power and to dominant representations generated by a hegemonic logic of visualization. These knowledges are presented as readable spaces, as, for example, in maps and statistics. Such readability produces particular normalized visions that reduce space to a transparent surface and obscure struggles and existing ambiguities while laying claim to a truthful representation of space.

Lefebvre argues that in "traditional" societies spatial practices preceded representations of space, whereas in today's postindustrialized societies the opposite is true; that is, before we experience space through spatial practices, it has already been represented to us. In my view the teleology implied in this argument is too deterministic.[3] I see the relation between spatial practices and representations of space as more contingent and subject to all kinds of contestations and reappropriations by human agency in general and by social movement agency in particular. Nevertheless what is important here is the ever-increasing significance of representations of space and the underlying logic of visualization. The growing importance of information technology and new ways of dynamically modeling social life, as for example in geographical information systems (GIS), present another "leap forward" in these hegemonic forms of representations of space. Their effect is one of increasing abstraction and decorporealization of space, always backed by scientific claims to truthful representation. There hence emerges an "abstract space," in which "things, acts and situations are forever being replaced by representations" (Lefebvre 1991:311). This abstract space is precisely the space of contemporary capitalism, where the law of commodity exchangeability as the dominant economic rationale of modern capitalism has led to an increased commodification of social life.

Rather than a homogeneous, closed space, though, abstract space is the site of contestation. According to Lefebvre (1991:365), "Socio-political contradictions are realized spatially. The contradictions of space thus make the contradictions of social relations operative. In other words, spatial contradictions 'express' conflicts between socio-political interests and forces; it is only in space that such conflicts come effectively into play, and in so doing they become contradictions of space." These contradictions will ultimately give rise to a new kind of space, a "differential space," "because, inasmuch as abstract space tends towards homogeneity, towards the elimination of existing differences or peculiarities, a new space cannot be born (produced) unless it accentuates differences" (52).

It can be argued that this is precisely what we are witnessing today: a proliferation of differential spaces as a result of the contradictions inherent in an abstract space that seeks to homogenize and create conformities. Identity politics that mobilize around issues of class, race, ethnicity, gender, sexuality, and so on have led to an accentuation of differences that are articulated in myriad resistances and contestations of dominant representations of space. Thus, according to Lefebvre (1991:383), the contradictions inherent in abstract space lead to a "quest for a counter-space." Differing from Lefebvre, however, I do not see these processes as teleologically determined, as if at some point a differential space will replace the abstract space altogether. Rather both spaces must be seen as existing parallel to one another, side by side, always in dialectical struggle.

Representational Space

To Lefebvre *representational space* refers to the directly lived spaces in which less formal and more local forms of knowing (*connaissances*) are produced and modified over time. These spaces are dynamic, symbolic, and saturated with meanings. They are rooted in experience and constitute a repertoire of articulations that are not bound by some overarching logic but are characterized by their flexibility and capacity of adaptation without being arbitrary. As Lefebvre (1991:41) argues, "Representational spaces . . . need obey no rules of consistency or cohesiveness. Redolent with imaginary and symbolic elements, they have their source in history—in the history of a people as well as in the history of each individual belonging to that people."

These spaces find their articulation in everyday life, where they embody complex symbolisms. They are neither homogeneous nor autonomous. They are constantly involved in a complex dialectical relationship with dominating representations of space, which intervene, penetrate, and attempt to colonize the lifeworld of representational space. Representational space therefore is also the dominated space that the imagination seeks to change and appropriate. It is both subject to domination and the source of resistance.

From these reflections it should be clear that the three moments in the production of space (spatial practices, representations of space, representational space) must be regarded as interdependent. In other words, there exists a dialectical relationship within the triad of the perceived, the conceived, and the lived. Such a conceptual understanding has direct implications for empirical research: we cannot treat these moments independently one from another, a conduct that Lefebvre (1991:41) accuses some social scientists of: "Ethnologists, anthropologists and psychoanalysts are students of representational spaces, whether they are aware of it or not, but they nearly always forget to set them alongside those representations of space which coexist, concord or interfere with them."[4] I shall heed that advice and pay attention in the following chapters to the manifold imbrications of the two.

However, let me briefly point toward a departure from Lefebvre's teleo-logical predictions in my approach. To Lefebvre counter-spaces emerge as a result of political struggle; they are spaces to be constructed in a politics of resistance. Counter-spaces may form when a differential space emerges in opposition to an abstract space. Lefebvre thus centers his analysis on sce-narios, in which a differential space as actively lived experience can come into existence. That is to say, he conceives of differential space as a pro-cess, not a fact. I would argue, however, that there are in fact already exist-ing, fully fledged differential spaces that have functioned as such through time. As I suggest in this book, the Pacific Coast region in Colombia can be conceptualized in these terms. The local aquatic epistemologies that I elaborate on in chapter 2 are a testament to this differential space. Empiri-cal evidence for such an interpretation comes mainly from ethnographic observations in the field, but it can also be found in activists' published statements. As PCN states with regard to their vision of the Pacific Coast region, "In the setting that the Pacific presents today, the ethnic-territorial organizations of black communities do not only plan the appropriation but also the defense of the territory from a perspective past-present-future, which understands, assumes and develops the tradition and the history of resistance of Afro-Colombians and their *aspiration to maintain, develop and re-alize a different and alternative life project*" (PCN 1999:2, my emphasis). Whereas the desire to "*maintain* . . . a different and alternative life project" points to the already existing differential space in the region, the "aspiration to . . . *develop and realize*" it expresses the movement's quest for a counter-space.

At the same time, what is at stake here is a defense of *place*. As Merrifield (1993:525) points out in his attempt at a Lefebvrian reconciliation of place and space, "Social practice is place-bound, political organization demands place organization. . . . Equally place is *more* than just lived everyday life. It is the 'moment' when the conceived, the perceived and the lived attain a certain 'structured coherence.' " Thus place may be seen as contextualizing and grounding Lefebvre's conceptual triad (the conceived, the perceived, the lived).

A Critical Place Perspective on Social Movements

Marxist geographer David Harvey (1996:208) notes that "place has to be one of the most multilayered and multipurpose keywords in our language." He strikes a chord here that hints at the myriad ways in which place has been embraced to explain all sorts of phenomena. Some have concentrated mainly on the material and territorial qualities of place, as reflected, for example, in certain strands of economic geography (Massey and Allen 1984). Others have focused on the meanings and inner connections inhabiting place, or the "sense of place," a key concept in the 1970s in the development of a humanistic geography that proposed to investigate the micro-episodes of everyday life and their embeddedness in specific contexts or milieux (Ley and Samuels 1978; Tuan 1976). Place was also central to structuration theory, which argued that place was both constituted *by* social practices and constitutive *of* these very practices (Giddens 1979; Pred 1984).[5] In the 1990s Entrikin (1991) suggested examining what he called the "between-ness of place," by incorporating both the totality of the concept through an objective pole of scientific theorizing and its contextuality through a subjective pole of empathetic understanding. In his approach Entrikin drew on earlier phenomenological approaches to place as "comprising both the objectivity of the map and the subjectivity of experience" (Ley 1977:509). This tension between the objective and the subjective has been at the heart of much thinking about place, as can be seen, for example, in the experiential perspective drawn up by humanistic geographer Yi-Fu Tuan (1975:152): "Place is a center of meaning constructed by experience. Place is known not only through the eyes and mind but also through the more passive and direct modes of experience, which resist objectification. To know a place fully means both to understand it in an abstract way and to know it as one person knows another. At a high theoretical level, places are points in a spatial system. At the opposite extreme, they are strong visceral feelings." There hence emerges the full complexity of the concept, in that it stresses the interactions between the very material aspects of physical location and the experiential dimensions of a subjective understanding that derives from living in a place.[6]

More recently, authors have pointed to the relationality of place. As one of the best-known proponents of these ideas, Doreen Massey (2005:141) has argued that place is "open and internally multiple . . . not intrinsically coherent . . . [resulting from] the coming together of the previously unrelated, a constellation of processes rather than a thing." Her emphasis on the relational aspect of place is in many ways an extension of her earlier formulation of what she termed a "global sense of place" (Massey 1994:146–56). Instead of regarding place as a neatly bounded unit, it should be seen "as an ever-shifting constellation of trajectories" (Massey 2005:151).[7]

While I agree with the general thrust of these arguments—my own assemblage approach to the aquatic space is testament to that—I am concerned that an almost fetishized insistence on relationality in some accounts may go too far, in that it appears to skew an analytic approach to place toward those "ever-shifting constellations of trajectories," toward those moments of becoming, while often having little to say about in-place lived experiences that may be just a little bit too rooted (*arraigado*) for relational comfort. In other words, has all that conceptual fear of seeing place as too parochial, too bounded, too essentialized driven us away from paying closer attention to those characteristics of place that may explain its peculiarity, its relative uniqueness? A serious engagement with ethnography, I argue, can help to strengthen relational accounts by tracing in-place constellations in ethnographic detail.

In order to disentangle the concept of place, I turn to Agnew (1987), who identifies three main elements in his perspective on place: location, locale, and sense of place. (Agnew has revisited his original framework many times [e.g., Agnew 2005, 2009:36], yet with only minor revisions.) Broadly speaking, *location* refers to the physical geographical area and the ways it is affected by economic and political processes operating at a wider scale. *Locale* refers to the formal and informal settings in which everyday social interactions and relations are constituted. More than merely the physical settings of activity, locale implies that these contexts are actively and routinely drawn upon by social actors in their everyday interactions and communications. Anthony Giddens (1979) suggests that certain locales can be identified as the typical physical settings and interactions that compose collectivities as social systems. As I argue in this book, the aquatic space can be seen as the typical locale for rural black communities in the Colombian Pacific lowlands: an assemblage of relations in a tropical rain forest environment in which everyday social interactions are imbued with an aquatic logic. This is not to essentialize certain settings and practices as unchanging and fixed in space and time, nor does it suggest a typography or specific "codex" of organizational traits. Rather it allows us to theorize the mobile practices of local communities and their spatialized embodied interaction with a physical environment as a more or less durable and locally meaningful network of actively forged connections. Relevant for social movement theorizing, the locale in general—and the aquatic space in particular—can be thought of as providing the place-based context in which social movement agency is generated.

Finally, *sense of place* refers to the ways human experience and imagination appropriate the physical characteristics and qualities of geographical location. It captures the subjective orientations that are derived from living in a particular place as an outcome of interconnected social and environmental processes. Phenomenological approaches to place, for example, tend to emphasize the ways individuals and communities develop deep attachments to places through experience, memory, and intention (Relph 1976). They often highlight "the dialogical nature of people's relationship to place" (Buttimer 1976:284), which draws on and constructs both personal and collective memory. As I show in this book, the "aquatic sense of place" among rural black communities in the Pacific lowlands holds a pivotal role in the social movement discourse that draws on and mobilizes collective memory in an identity politics as defense of their particular constructions of place.

Meeting Don Agapito

Reflections on Fieldwork

A phenomenologist must tell everything.
—GASTON BACHELARD, *THE POETICS OF SPACE*

It was already getting dark as I climbed a wooden ladder that led to a small platform from which I entered the house of Don Agapito. He was waiting for me, rocking back and forth in his wooden armchair. It was a hot and humid afternoon in the tropics. I was only just beginning to get used to this climate. "Buenas tardes, Don Agapito," I greeted my host and stretched out my hand to shake his, immeasurably larger and firmer, as befits a peasant farmer and fisherman who at eighty-plus years old still seemed fit and strong.

I had come to talk with Don Agapito about his life growing up along the riverbanks of the Pacific lowlands. Law 70 and subsequent legislation had triggered widespread political mobilization in the region, and discussions regarding the territorial reordering often concerned how the lands to be titled should be demarcated. In countless meetings and workshops the collective memory of local populations was mobilized to reflect on past ways of occupying their territories and what these might hold for future strategies of territorialization. The elderly—traditionally respected in those communities—were seen as rich sources of knowledge about land, customs, and history. Most of these *conocimientos tradicionales* were passed on in the oral tradition, and this was precisely what I wanted to explore with Don Agapito: his relationship to land and river and what he thought about the exciting new political opportunities that were opening up and around which a growing social movement of black communities was forming in Colombia.

I sat opposite Don Agapito, a cup of *agua de panela* in my hand,[1] which his wife had offered me during her brief appearance, after which she disappeared again behind a curtain that presumably led to the kitchen. As Don Agapito kept rocking back and forth in his armchair, he began to tell me about his life as a boy fishing in the rivers and accompanying the elderly, *los viejos*, on their long trips into the hinterland, *el monte*, where they went hunting. On these journeys in their dugout canoes, they spent their time challenging each other in ritual storytelling, which often took the form of a *décima*, a poem with a fairly complex rhyming structure (more on this in chapter 2). Don Agapito loved to perform these décimas throughout his life. I was fortunate, as he still remembered many of them and was quite happy for me to tape them on my rudimentary recording device.

I was thrilled at this opportunity that had come up quite by chance. A few days earlier I had visited the local office of the biodiversity conservation program Biopacífico, where they had mentioned Don Agapito as one of the recognized elders in town and a respected *decimero*, or poet of the oral tradition. Two days later I sat in his living room, enchanted by the wealth of his stories, his ability to recite long poems, and in general his gusto in talking about days past (not without frequently complaining about the state of his health). All of a sudden three young people burst into the room and questioned me in no uncertain terms about who I was, what I was doing there, and who had authorized my presence. I was flabbergasted. Who were these people? And what right did they have to storm into Don Agapito's house and ask me all these questions? I didn't know what to say or how to react. I looked over at Don Agapito. He kept rocking back and forth in his armchair as he had done for the past hour. The expression on his face did not change a bit. I was shell-shocked . . . It was then that one of the gang of three stepped forward and explained that they were members of the regional community organization of black communities, that they should be informed if anyone wanted to do "research" in their community, that all those gringos had wreaked enough havoc already in the region, that times were changing . . .

I immediately realized my mistake. I really should have known better. I knew of a number of community organizations active in town and should have contacted them beforehand. In fact I had intended to do so but was so thrilled by the opportunity to talk to Don Agapito that I had put this concern momentarily aside. What followed was my attempt to explain my situation: who I was, where I was coming from and with what objectives—doing ethnography—and that no, I was not one of those dodgy gringos coming to exploit local knowledge to sell on. It was an awkward situation.

However, the slightly aggressive tone underlying our conversation quickly subsided. Don Agapito's wife had entered the room again and brought more cups of agua de panela for the visitors. Suddenly I found myself talking to them about the University of Glasgow (where I was doing my PhD studies at the time). They were particularly interested in hearing about the growing signs of devolution in Scotland and if that was the first step toward independence from the United Kingdom. In return they told me of attempts to push for the devolution of the Pacific Coast region from the Colombian state, an argument based on the region's cultural specificity and its overwhelming Afro-descendant population. In sum our initially awkward encounter turned into a friendly and animated discussion, exploring common links and experiences, connecting local realities in the Pacific lowlands (territorial reorderings and cultural politics) to wider global processes of political change. My interlocutors were young and educated former university students themselves, keen on understanding the intersections of local and global processes to better place their own lucha in the wider history of minority rights, land, and peasant struggles.

It was in this first discussion—which was followed by many others in the days to come—that the idea of doing a more collaborative kind of research emerged. I felt that my own research questions seemed to have potential relevance for the communities' project of a "recovery" of their collective memories that I had not foreseen until then. The initial encounter with these three activists clearly forced me to rethink my fieldwork strategy, but it also opened up new and exciting channels of doing research.

There exists a strong tradition of collaborative research in Colombia, which I felt I could draw on, almost always linked to the pioneering work of the sociologist Orlando Fals Borda and others in what is known as participatory action-research (PAR), or *investigación acción participativa* (IAP) in Spanish. Surprisingly perhaps, much collaborative research elsewhere today often reinvents itself without even referencing this groundbreaking work.[2] Referring to a large gathering in Cartagena, Colombia, in 1997

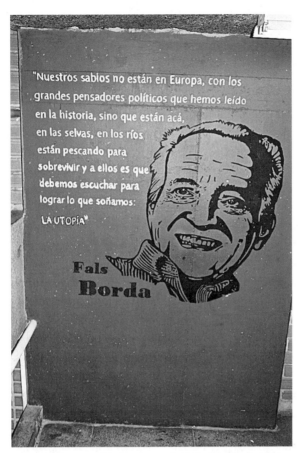

FIG. INTER.1. Mural in homage to Orlando Fals Borda on the campus of Universidad de Antioquia, Medellín, April 2012. The inscription reads, "Our wise people are not in Europe, with the great political thinkers who we have read in history. No, they are here, in the forests, fishing in the rivers to survive, and it is to them that we need to listen in order to achieve what we dream of: Utopia."

that celebrated the twentieth anniversary of the global launching of the PAR movement, Escobar (2008:365) tellingly states that "these more third world–oriented gatherings tend to go unreported in northern accounts of the global justice movement." In light of this "trend to forget" and these southern absences in northern accounts, it is useful to briefly review PAR here and to reflect on reengaging some of its central proposals. While this book should not be seen as an example of "doing PAR," I refer throughout to some of its principal insights and how they are echoed in my research methodology.

Participatory Action-Research

In its most basic ideal, Fals Borda (1987:336–37) regards "the participatory action-research approach as . . . a dialogical research oriented to the social situation in which people live." Another of PAR's leading figures, Mohammed Rahman (1991:23), describes the theoretical stance of PAR in these words: "The basic ideology of PAR is that conscious classes and groups, those which at present are poor and oppressed, will transform their environment progressively via their own praxis. In this process other people can play a catalytic and supportive role, but they will not be able to dominate the process."[3]

Until 1977 PAR was characterized by activism and even antiprofessionalism. The Mexican intellectual Gustavo Esteva (1987:128) stresses the ambiguous positionality of activist and researcher and promotes the idea of a "de-professionalized intellectual" as the only way of working with oppressed groups and against established academic models and paradigms. Many of the early activists actually renounced their academic posts as they became more deeply involved with PAR projects.[4] The early efforts of PAR were strongly influenced by other participatory research methodologies, such as *intervention sociologique*, proposed by the French sociologist Alain Touraine (1988), or the concept of *conscientização*, conceived by the Brazilian educator Paulo Freire (1971). Freire in particular provided the basis for a more clearly articulated methodology, in which the traditional division between researcher (as subject) and the researched (as object) was to be substituted by a subject-subject relation, wherein a horizontal dialogue between the two was to take place (38–39).[5] Such a process often implied the "rebirth" of the researcher herself (47), a notion that was further developed by Gayatri Chakravorty Spivak (1996), who insists on the need to unlearn one's own privileges when conducting research, and Esteva (1987:141), who stresses the need for unlearning the language of domination.

In 1977 the International Symposium on Research Action and Scientific Analysis (held in Cartagena, Colombia) provided an important formal space of reflection on the theoretical and methodological advances of PAR, as well as a first measurement of its practical implications. As Rahman and

Fals Borda (1991:40) retrospectively state, "We began to understand PAR as a research methodology with an evolution towards a subject/subject relation in order to form symmetrical, horizontal and non-exploitative standards in social, economic and political life, and as a part of social activism with an ideological and spiritual commitment in order to promote (collective) popular praxis." These aims were further developed during the Tenth International Congress of Sociology in Mexico in 1982, where a wider field of action was explored, transcending the initially somewhat restricted peasant and communitarian questions to include dimensions of urban life.

PAR was now seen as a "revolutionary science [that] becomes a real possibility, not only a felt necessity" (Fals Borda 1987:330). Ultimately Fals Borda conceived of PAR as a catalyst for generating a "people's power," a "countervailing power exercised against exploitative systems" (331). This was to be achieved by stimulating "the capacity of the grass-roots groups . . . to articulate and systematise knowledge (both their own and that which comes from outside) in such a way that they can become protagonists in the advancement of their society and in defence of their own class and group interests" (330).[6] The outsider/researcher was regarded as crucial in setting off and guiding these processes of self-reflection: "Catalytic external agents play a crucial role in linking up the local dimension to regional and, at a later stage, to the national and the international levels" (334).

To briefly summarize PAR's four principal strategies:

1. *Collective research on a group basis.* This process implies a conscious dialogue between the researcher and the people. It takes the form of meetings and workshops, which the researcher organizes and where locals are encouraged to engage in articulated self-reflexivity. This is intended to raise awareness and consciousness of their situation. The researcher acts as the catalytic agent to stimulate and contribute to this debate.
2. *Critical recovery of history.* The collective memory of communities is constructed in the oral tradition. Stories, poems, and legends are rich in symbolism, metaphors, and place-specific references. The recovery of a community's collective memory is seen as a "grass-roots corrector of official history" (Fals Borda 1987:341). The aim is to articulate new visions and alternative projects based on a people's historical experiences.[7]

3. *Valuing and applying folk culture.* Aspects of folk culture such as traditional music, dances, storytelling, and religious beliefs are drawn upon in the articulation of a people's struggle. According to Fals Borda (1987:343), "All these elements of oral culture may be exploited as a new and dynamic political language which belongs to the people. . . . Feelings, imagination and the sense of play are apparently inexhaustible sources of strength and resistance."

4. *Production and diffusion of new knowledge.* As a final step there has to be a systematic dissemination of the knowledge derived from dialogical research. Fals Borda (1987:344) stresses, "There is an obligation to return this knowledge systematically to the communities and workers' organisations because they continue to be its owners."[8]

Reengaging Participatory Action-Research and "Failures" in the Field

I don't intend to go into the various critiques that PAR has been confronted with over the years.[9] Of course for some its very language may seem to pertain to a different age, rooted in structuralist thought that didn't give a damn about postmodern uncertainties. Others may find a perceived hierarchy troubling, in which the external researcher as "catalytic agent" seems to play a deterministic, possibly patronizing role. What was most relevant for my own research and my reengaging with some of PAR's aims was its serious and systematic engagement with local knowledge (the "folk culture" in Strategy 3 above) and the critical role played by collective memory in the articulation of alternative visions and projects (Strategy 2). It was clear that I could not stamp a PAR project out of the ground like that. Particularly Strategy 1—collective research on a group basis—requires an enormous amount of preparation and discussion before embarking on a formal PAR project. However, on a more informal basis, it became apparent in the conversations with community activists that our respective interests overlapped and could be mutually beneficially pooled together. My research thus became more collaborative as it went on. I accompanied movement leaders on their trips to river communities. I held workshops on "social cartography" (exploring territorial perceptions with local communities that were drawn upon in the demarcation of lands to be titled collectively). We had hours and hours of meetings and discussions.

One of my concerns was over what I perceived to be a lack of cooperation between the various community organizations active in the region. Clearly there were divisions between these groups, and I increasingly felt this to be a real hindrance in the advancement of what seemed to me the principal political goal: the territorial empowerment of local communities vis-à-vis the state. Such divisiveness at the local level was not unique to the organizations in Guapi. I observed this phenomenon in other river basins as well (see my discussion of community council leadership in chapter 5), and it is important to acknowledge these "differences within" so that we don't paint a romanticizing picture of the movement's supposed unity and harmony. Yet I felt this lack of cooperation in Guapi to be extremely counterproductive, and I addressed these concerns with the various groups. I realized that personal issues between movement leaders played a part in the animosity with which they confronted each other. I got increasingly desperate with what appeared to be petty divisiveness. As a last act of trying to help to reconcile the different groups—what made me think that I could do that in the first place?—I invited movement leaders to a dinner at my house. Alas, no one showed up . . . This situation was no doubt the greatest frustration in my attempt at collaborative research, as it quite painfully showed up the limitations of my potential as an "external catalytic agent" (in PAR-speak).

For a long time I hesitated to write about this frustration. After all, what good could come of it? Would it not be harmful to the movement to be portrayed in my writing as one where internal bickering took precedence over the "real" issues of representing community interests in relation to the Colombian state? Would my story of divisiveness not be counterproductive to the construction of a people's power that Fals Borda claimed is one of the central objectives of PAR?

Time went by, and now, some fifteen years later, I am less traumatized by what happened. Was it really as bad as it felt at the time? (Yes, it was.) Is it not natural for differences to occur in all social mobilization processes? (Yes, but did they have to be so destructive?)

So what could be learned from this *fracaso*, this failure? First, it taught me to be humble in my approach to fieldwork. To accept the limitations. To not see myself as a catalytic agent but rather a friend who accompanies the political process with whatever modest contributions are at my disposal. Being a friend to the process also means accepting the imperfections of political mobilization—to work on them, yes, but to despair over them? No. Quite to the contrary, the limitations and failures themselves can be mobilized in future collaborative work in order to better define expectations

FIG. INTER.2. Airport Julio Arboleda in Guapi before its name was changed.

and possibilities. Second, it taught me to recognize the process of political mobilization for what it is: a process. A process that goes through various phases. Today, fifteen years later, new alliances have built in the region; previously antagonistically opposed movement leaders work together (God knows how they got it sorted out) and have moved on. They always do. With or without me. Again humbleness helps.

In one particular incident, what felt like a frustration at the time has turned into a positive outcome—with time. In March 1999 I suggested to a group of activists that they change the name of the local airstrip, which was then called Aeropuerto Julio Arboleda. Most Colombians, if they have heard of him at all, think of Julio Arboleda as a well-known poet. Yet he was also one of the country's most cruel slave owners. His origins are in the town of Popayán, and he owned a number of gold mines in the Pacific lowlands. Shortly before the official abolition of slavery in 1851, he sold 99 adult slaves and 113 child slaves for 31,410 pesos to Peru (Mina 1975:40–41), thereby not only defying the idea of abolition but also acting illegally since it was then already against the law to sell slaves abroad.[10] It seemed incomprehensible that the local airport was named after this man, in a town whose population was over 90 percent Afro-Colombian. Julio Arboleda had entered official history as a respected poet, and his blood-stained hands and heart had been whitewashed by collective amnesia. It seemed time for a "grass-roots corrector of official history," Fals Borda might have said (Strategy 2).

As we sat around the patio of my house in 1999, some proposed to name the airport after a local female educator. The next day we painted a banner with her name that we would drape over the "letters that said slavery" at the airport. We agreed on a time for the event to take place and arranged for the local radio station to cover the direct action live. However, at the last minute some leaders retracted their support and argued that it might be better to discuss the issue with the mayor first. It was probably a wise decision not to go ahead with the planned action, as an already nervous police force, alert to the presence of guerrilla forces in surrounding river basins, might have reacted in a hostile manner. Nevertheless I felt frustrated over what I perceived at the time as a failure to make a potentially significant statement in the "critical recovery of history" (Strategy 2). Catalytic agent or not, I was very happy to hear from my friends that in 2005 the incoming municipal administration made the name change of the airport one of their priorities. Today the airport is in fact named after the local historian and practitioner of folk culture Juan Casiano Solís. It seems that PAR's Strategy 3—valuing and applying folk culture—has been adhered to in the renaming process.

TWO

Mapping Meandering Poetics and an Aquatic Sense of Place
Oral Tradition as Hidden Transcript of Resistance

Local poets and *cantadoras* (women singers) of the Pacific are more likely guides to a phenomenology of the place.
—ARTURO ESCOBAR, *TERRITORIES OF DIFFERENCE*

RÍO GUAPI
Desde las cumbres viajas altanero,
pero esclavo en el riel de tus orillas,
desciendes hasta el mar de ondas sencillas

a tributar tu arroyo placentero.
Cuando estoy lejos, tierno yo te quiero,
con todo el potosí de aguas tranquilas;
con tu fauna de sábalos y anguilas
y con tus noches plenas de luceros.
—GUILLERMO PORTOCARRERO, *SONETOS EN EL PUERTO*

GUAPI RIVER
From the summits you travel aloof,
yet a slave to the bends of your river banks,
toward the sea you descend in plain waves

paying tribute with your pleasant stream.
When I am far away, I love you tenderly,
with all the fortune of calm waters;
with your fauna of perch and eel
and with your nights full of bright stars.

Of a Despairing Scientist and a Fisherman

A story in Colombia tells of a scientist who, over the course of a week, observes a fisherman stretched out in his hammock slung between two coconut trees on a beach.[1] The scientist makes careful notes of the man's moves, which do not seem to be many. He just rises now and again to pick up a coconut that has fallen onto the beach. With his machete he cuts the coconut open and gulps down the refreshing water. After seven days of observation the scientist gets restless with the lazy fisherman who doesn't make the slightest move to catch any fish. He finally decides to enlighten him on the enormous potential that the sea's resources hold, if only he was willing to exploit them. "Look," the scientist begins, "why do you spend the entire day in your hammock, when the sea is full of fish that just wait for you to go and catch them?" The fisherman seems bewildered by the question, so the scientist continues: "The more fish you catch, the more you can sell on the market, and the more money you make." Still not getting an answer, the scientist explains, "You can then build a refrigeration unit and increase profits." The fisherman finally responds, "Why would I want to do that?" Despairing over the seeming incomprehension of his interlocutor, the scientist bursts out, "You can then employ other fishermen who do the fishing for you. Then you don't have to work anymore, and you can spend the entire day lying in your hammock!" At this the fisherman smiles and answers, "Well, this is what I am already doing." The scientist looks at the object of his study and, shaking his head in disbelief, leaves the beach to finish writing up his fieldwork notes, in his head already planning the layout of his upcoming publication on the lost causes of developing Colombia's fishing communities. He would never find out that the fisherman, whom he had observed so intensely, rose at midnight that week to go fishing according to the rhythm of the tides and that his working day was finished by 8 a.m., when he returned from sea to rest. But this, of course, is another story.

To tell these other stories of fishermen who act according to the rhythm of the sea, of shellfish pickers who make use of tidal changes when traveling to mangrove swamps, and to explore the implications of these life forms for the political organizing processes of black communities in Colombia's Pacific lowlands, I introduce the concept of the *aquatic space*. By this I mean the particular assemblage of spatial relations that results from human entanglements with an aquatic environment characterized by intricate river networks, significant tidal ranges, labyrinthine mangrove swamps, and frequent inundations. I begin by exploring the ways the aquatic space is reflected in the *sense of place* on the Pacific Coast among rural black populations—to the extent that we can talk of an "aquatic sense of place." In particular I draw on the rich Afro-Colombian oral tradition to map an elaborate geographical imagination that activists have evoked in the political mobilization in the Pacific lowlands.[2] Drawing on James Scott's (1990) work, I suggest that the oral tradition functions as a hidden transcript of resistance, which becomes an important political tool when strategically drawn upon in public discourse, or, as Scott would phrase it, as it is turned into a public transcript.

At the same time, I examine ways in which the aquatic space is meaningful beyond language. Sense of place is also related by how people
move through landscapes and how these movements are affected by water,
weather, time, and sound. In other words, I show how place is embodied,
enacted, and practiced through discourses of non-verbal communication
(Bateson 1972): movements, gestures, dance, music, rituals, smell, laughing,
and silences. As Afro-Colombian writer Manuel Zapata Olivella (2000:8)
liked to say, "Body-language preceded the word."

Structures of *Sentipensamiento* and Local Aquatic Epistemologies

> These odors of damp earth, sea, rivers, swamps, cascades, . . . odors they
> are of earth fertilized by the waters of Mother Yemayá, after giving birth to
> the Orichas, her fourteen children, in a single stormy delivery.
> —Manuel Zapata Olivella, *Changó, the Biggest Badass*

Afro-Colombian intellectuals sometimes point out that rural black populations in the Pacific lowlands differ from Western norms of rationalization
in that they allegedly show no interest in capitalist accumulation or fre-
netic consumption (Arboleda 1998; see also Restrepo 2001:60).[3] Anthropologists have argued that local epistemologies entail relations to time and
space that differ from those in the West (Arocha 1999:148). While these
statements, standing alone, may appear to be essentializing generaliza-
tions, I want to explore their assumptions in ethnographic detail through
what I call "local aquatic epistemologies." By this I mean the particular
ways of knowing a profoundly aquatic environment and how these both
produce and are produced by specific temporal and spatial relations with
that environment.

Temporal relations among rural black populations on the Pacific Coast
have sometimes been expressed through the notion of tranquility. Colombian anthropologist Jaime Arocha (1999:149) explains, "Tranquility forms
part of the ways in which the *ombligados de Ananse* [Afro-Colombians] relate
to their environment and, therefore, of the creativity with which they get
around the difficulties that the latter poses."[4] This tranquility is argued to
be a constitutive part of the *ecosofía*, or ecological philosophy, with which
rural black populations embrace the realms of fauna and flora: "The relation that [Afro-Colombians] created with their rivers, their streams and

forests was not only one of respect, but one of sisterhood. . . . So that . . . amongst Afro-Colombians neither plants nor animals exist *per se*, but further complemented and qualified through the word, through people's minds" (155–56). In other words, animal and plant worlds come into being through the assemblage of human and nonhuman relations. They do not exist outside of these relations.

The river plays a central role in this assemblage. It is a constant reference point, both in its material presence and as a source of people's creative imaginations and mythological constructions. We may think of this assemblage as a structure of *sentipensamiento*. This is how Orlando Fals Borda (1978) documented for the Caribbean Coast the ways feelings and emotions (*sentir*) on the one hand and thinking and reason (*pensar*) on the other amalgamate into a culturally and place-specific logic that does not fit easily into Western ways of reasoning and as a result is often regarded as superstitious or magical. Arocha (1999:142–47) regards the funeral rites on the Pacific Coast as the synthesis of Afro-Colombian sentipensamiento. During death wakes (*velorios*), the dead person is accompanied by yearning chants (*alabaos*) or by playful songs (*arrullos*) in the case of the *chigualo* when the dead person is a young child under seven (*angelito*).

I attended numerous velorios in Guapi. These were moments when I most clearly felt the cultural difference between me and my hosts. I remember the first time I attended a chigualo. A young girl of about four had died, and her open coffin was on display in a corner of the living room of her parents' house. As people filed past the coffin, they bent over to kiss the dead little girl on her forehead. All the while musicians played joyful tunes and children's songs on the traditional percussive instruments *cununo*, *bombo*, and *guasá*. This was a way of accompanying the dead child on her journey with sounds she was accustomed to. The idea in these chigualos is to create a cheerful atmosphere and to keep public mourning at bay.

When my turn came to kiss the girl good-bye, I froze up. There she was, beautifully robed in a white dress, her hair meticulously made up, her eyes closed, and her tiny hands folded over her belly. She truly was an angelito, a little angel. I stared at her and at what seemed pure innocence lost to me. I sensed my heart break with sorrow, while percussive beats filled the air. I felt dizzy, in shock. Someone gently pushed me in the back and I moved

FIG. 2.1. *Velorio* of Don Agapito Montaño, Guapi, January 1999.

forward so that the person behind me could pay her respects to the little girl. It was then that her father, who I hadn't noticed before, stormed over to the coffin and flung himself over it with a terrible wail. He was immediately pulled back and admonished by a number of guests and family members. Religious beliefs dictated that parents were not allowed to publicly mourn the death of their daughter. Her wake was meant to be a celebration of her life.

I have often looked back on this episode, my first experience at a child's death wake. As I am writing these lines, I still sense a lump in my throat. I remember that I felt completely out of place at the time, as I had real problems joining in with the joyous spirit on display. I had seen corpses before, just not under these circumstances. My own reasoning and feelings were profoundly challenged on these occasions.

Figure 2.1 shows a scene from the death wake of Don Agapito Montaño, the first decimero I interviewed in Guapi. As is common on these occasions, it was held in his house. His wife, on the left, had asked me to come and take photos, which I would later give to the family. The velorio was a social occasion, the main room filled with relatives, neighbors, friends, and in the first row facing the altar, the *cantaoras*, the women chanters. Doña Celia was among them, with her *botella curada* (cured bottle) full of herbs and *viche* by her side to help her intone the arrullo chant.[5]

Of the role of religion Fals Borda (1987:343) writes, "Feelings, imagination and the sense of play are apparently inexhaustible sources of strength and resistance among the people. These three elements have a common basis which cannot be ignored in the struggle to promote mobilisation and people's power in our countries: religious beliefs." Beliefs are just one aspect of the sentipensamiento that I explore when "valuing and applying folk culture" (PAR Strategy 3) in relation to emerging political mobilization. For this I dive now into the local aquatic epistemologies of black communities, as they were revealed to me by two of the region's *sabios*, who so generously gave me access to their sentipensamiento and to their discourses of nonverbal communication. The local voices in this narrative act as personal keys to unlock a more analytical understanding of the sense of place. Following recent anthropological scholarship on the performative qualities of storytelling, I conceive of these as "a way of practicing knowledge [that] always has a purpose" (Blaser 2010:xv).

Doña Celia Lucumí Caicedo and the Rivers of Her Pacific

I was born in Balsitas, in the upper parts of the Guapi River, three streets below the village of Balsitas, in a place called La Corriente. I was still a little girl when my mother sent me to Balsitas to run errands. Even though I didn't know how to swim. When the current came, I took my little dugout canoe, and splash, splash, splash, on foot, I pushed it to the top of the current. Then I sat down in my canoe, and plap, plap, plap [making the sound of a paddle in the water], that's how I went up all three currents. The one near the house was street, street, street, until one got to another street. And then there was a little stream. I went up on the right side, and when I was already quite high up, poom, I crouched down. Little devil since small; smart, but I didn't know how to swim. My mother wasn't afraid, though. That I could perhaps wrongly place the paddle and turn over in the water. That's how I got to Balsitas.[6]

The notion of a street (*calle*) in this quote requires an explanation here. In the rural areas of the Pacific lowlands there are very few streets. The often inundated environment, with its myriad rivers and smaller streams, is highly inappropriate for the construction of roads. When Afro-Colombians talk about streets in this context, they apply urban descriptive parameters to a rural landscape. What they measure with the denomination *street* is in fact the distance between two points on a straight line when looking ahead along a meandering river. This line finishes at a river bend, where again one looks ahead on a straight line to the next river bend. The distance between these visible reference points is measured in streets. When Doña Celia talks about traveling three streets upstream, this means navigating three river bends before reaching her destination. Therefore, the street is a flexible measurement, as the metric distance between river bends changes. As a reference that assumes that one knows the river section in question, it is a specific characteristic of the local aquatic epistemologies in the Pacific lowlands.

Doña Celia continues:

In Balsitas I went to the now deceased Joaquín Ledesma, father of Andelmo Ledesma. He was a good friend of my father and my mother. My mother put something into a handkerchief and then she sent it with me to the late Joaquín. Then he put something in my bag and said, "Take this, my child, take it to Ms Lucha. And tell Ms Lucha not to send you anymore, because you cannot swim. Sit down, child, you hear me!" There, comfortable and well sent I was, I put my things in the prow of the canoe, and then I took my little paddle and, proom, I sat down on the bottom of the canoe. [laughing] Look, when one is growing up, hmm . . . And now, pay attention: I arrived home faster than running the errand. When my mom thought that I was just arriving at Balsitas I was already back home. So I arrived and gave her what I had. And I told her, "Mom, the day you go to Balsitas, you should go and see Don Joaquín." Because I told her what he had asked me to. "The day you go to Balsitas you should go and see Don Joaco."

It is said that children in the rural areas of the Pacific Coast move around in small dugout canoes well before they actually learn how to walk. The river is not just the place where they play; it is also the main road that connects them to neighbors, friends, and relatives who live along the same river. From an early age children are incorporated into adult life.

FIG. 2.2. Doña Celia Lucumí Caicedo smoking *pa' dentro*,
Guapi, April 1999.

Girls help their mothers in the household, wash clothes, clean dishes,
and look after their smaller brothers and sisters, while boys go fishing
to supplement the family's meals. Doña Celia, like many other young
girls, also worked alongside her mother and grandmother in the gold
mines, panning sands and gravel in her *batea* when she was only eight
years old.[7] As Doña Celia tells us here, her mother used her as a kind of
"fluvial messenger" to send information or goods to friends, neighbors,
and relatives. The river in this context functions as the main road that
little Celia had to navigate, an action in which she acquired considerable
skill.

FIG. 2.3. Doña Celia with one of her great-grandsons on the porch of her house, Guapi, December 2004.

Figure 2.4 shows a little girl traveling in her *potrillo*, a dugout canoe. I took this photo in the middle section of the Guapi River on an overcast but dry day. Torrential rainfall the day before had caused the river to break its banks and led to significant flooding. In the foreground to the right we can see a tree submerged that would be standing in dry soil otherwise. The little girl oozes confidence as she steers her potrillo on the swollen river, her short paddle directing the canoe along the river bank. Traditionally women and girls sit on small wooden, carved chairs in their potrillos when navigating (men do it standing up). The photo is a snapshot of how the aquatic space as an assemblage of relations is coming together at this particular

FIG. 2.4. A "fluvial messenger": little girl in a *potrillo* (dugout canoe) on the Guapi River.

point in time. The girl has learnt to steer her potrillo in adverse conditions. It might not be clear in the photo, but it was a tough current that day. The girl's composure shows the routine nature of the action. She is completely in control of the situation. This is her river, her home, her playground, her road. Some seventy years earlier this could well have been little Celia.

Celia, the fluvial messenger on her aquatic road to the upper reaches of the Guapi River, remembers:

One day something happened. My mother liked her bad habits more than anyone. She never took the pipe out of her mouth. When we were eating, and I hadn't finished yet, she had already her second pipe lit. And big pipes these were, because the tobacco she put in was a piece this big, sticking out of the pipe. . . . [laughing] She smoked it, and immediately, chac, the next one. And it so happened that she ran out of tobacco. It was pouring down with rain, thunder and lightning. Ay, my brother, it was still light, around six o'clock in the afternoon, when my dad gave her some of his tobacco, because my dad had less of a bad habit. He smoked, well, when he remembered. So he gave her some tobacco. . . . When it was seven o'clock at night, and my mom realized that she would be without tobacco for the night, she said, "Alejandra, Celia, get dressed and go and buy me some tobacco in Balsitas!" The waning moon seemed to swallow us up, but we couldn't say, "We're not going to the river." It was raining cats and dogs. And lightning that seemed to strike us, and thunder crashing. . . . [laughing] As good as I could, I threw myself into the prow of the canoe. I wasn't that small anymore, I had already small tits. And then, pum, pum, pum [sound of the paddle in the water], till we got to Balsitas.

From the moment she was born, Celia's life revolved around a fluvial landscape where the only means of transport was her potrillo and where it rained frequently and heavily.[8] Helping in the household also meant looking after her grandfather, who was living nearby, separated from Celia's grandmother:

One day my mother sent me to my granddad Juan Gregorio on an errand. So I took my little canoe and left. I arrived at my grandfather's, greeted him in the name of God, he gave me his blessing, and I told him, "Granddad, here, my mom sends this for you."[9] He was a fisherman catching mojarra [a perch-like river fish]. Many a time when I brought him his lunch, I found him sitting there on the beach. He caught mojarra, he caught sábalo, he caught sabaleta [other common river fish]. They grow as big as this [measuring the fish against her arm]. This sabaleta is delicious! And maybe he had already caught two fish, when he would tell me, "Take it up to my house!" And I would take the lunch that I had brought him up to his house. After that I returned with a container to take the fish he had caught. My granddad Juan Gregorio, the father of my father. It was he who fished. . . . He loved my mother, and she also came to love him, so my mother cooked the food at home and sent it to his house with us. We lived one street apart. For example, we lived here in this street, and in the street above lived my grandfather. Around the corner. One had to take the canoe. There was no path. Where we lived, it was all very steep. And over there, on the other side, it was all cultivated fields. And I tell you, when my granddad had already caught some fish, "Look, my child, take this fish, there in the basket, and take it to your mom." So I returned, and immediately my mom prepared the fish. If it was midday, she prepared the meal, and again sent it to my grandfather. I was a little girl when she prepared this fish. And I also went to my grandmother, taking food to her too, to my grandmother Juana María. Well, my grandmother lived farther away; she lived much higher up with her other sons. She came down to my mother only occasionally. Because my grandfathers, I knew them all divorced from their women.

In Doña Celia's account, the river is the site providing dwelling, shelter, and a living space, and also the site for performing family. Relations to family members are enacted in the daily movements around the riverscape. Young Celia, in her function as fluvial messenger, acts as the connection between relatives who live quite dispersed along the riverbanks. She remembers her childhood spending time with her grandfather, watching him while he was fishing, and with her grandmother in the gold mines or observing her when she prepared infusions of medicinal herbs to alleviate illnesses. Those observations would be useful to Celia when, later in her life, Felix, her second son, fell seriously ill with what she judged to be the "evil eye." El ojo is a frequent diagnosis for a sick, feverish child, often attributed to the malevolent influence of a jealous adult. It is traditionally treated with infusions of medicinal herbs and prayers. Modern medicine is deeply suspicious of both the diagnosis and the treatment. However, among Afro-Colombians the evil eye forms part of the magic-religious relations of everyday life:[10]

My son Felix was three months old. He could just about sit upright. One day I went to the upper reaches of the Guapi River to a stream called Calle Honda [Deep Street]. That's where they threw an evil eye on my son. Ay, I hadn't learned a thing yet! I had the wisdom, from listening to the conversations of the old folks, but I hadn't done anything like this. There was a certain Juan Eugenio, and he knew how to cure the evil eye. So I went upstream and called on him, "Compadre Juan Eugenio!"—he was the husband of an aunt of mine—"Compadre Juan Eugenio, do me a favor![11] Please, cure my boy of the evil eye, he is ill with a fever that doesn't go away." "I'm going upstream to see a girl of comadre Polenia" [Doña Celia imitates the voice of an old man here]. "Okay, when you come down again, come to see us, to have a look at my boy, maybe he has the evil eye, maybe not. I haven't got the money to pay you. But if you travel, you will come across the father, you know the father. And I know that he will pay you. Because he is a responsible man. He is not one of those irresponsible men," I told him. The man did not listen to me. He passed by downstream and did not stop at my house to do me the favor.

Facing this dilemma, Celia had no alternative but to try out the knowledge that she had acquired by observing her grandmother practicing traditional healing methods. The distance to the hospital in Guapi was too great, and

Celia did not have the money anyway for her son to be seen there. So she started preparing a medicinal infusion, rubbed her son with it, and said the necessary prayers:

Finally, the next day I gave him the other two rubbings, and the other two infusions. And since then, I always did this with my son. Because that man had played a bad trick on me. Well, I say "bad trick." He made me remember the knowledge that I had learned. And ever since then it was healing espanto [another illness, affecting babies in particular], healing evil eye, healing espanto, healing evil eye, right up to today. And here it so happened that I healed that man's grandchildren—such is life [laughing].

As Doña Celia's account reveals, all her life she moved routinely along the fluvial thoroughfares. Just as Laura Ogden (2011:74) has shown for the Florida Everglades, in the Pacific lowlands too "landscapes are experienced by *bodies in motion.*" It is through Doña Celia's routine movements that place is imbued with meaning. Indeed, as Christopher Tilley (1995:27) has argued, "daily passages through the landscape become biographic encounters for individuals, recalling traces of past activities and previous events and the reading of signs." We can conceive of the aquatic space as being coproduced through Doña Celia's biographic encounters with the river, her canoe, and the folks she meets while navigating. Her daily passages are socially produced movements saturated with cultural meanings. Tim Cresswell (2006) refers to these time- and place-specific movements as "mobility," and we can usefully think about the aquatic space as being practiced and embodied through mobility.

Mobility in the Pacific lowlands creates emotional attachments and a sense of belonging to particular river basins. The North American cultural geographer Robert West commented as early as the 1950s on this close and intimate relationship between the individual and the river. He observed that the river was a central point of reference in identity formation and everyday discursive practices: "People living on a given river consider themselves as a single community. . . . Negroes and mixed bloods speak of 'nuestro río,' or mention, for example, that 'somos del Río Guapi,' or 'somos Guapise-ños' [sic], indicating their social attachment to a given river" (1957:88).

Today the river is still the most immediate geographical reference for the people of the Colombian Pacific Coast. Rather than referring to a settlement or village, when asked about their place of origin Afro-Colombians name the particular river where they live. The poet Alfredo Vanín from Guapi, an authority on local history and oral tradition, told me, "If someone asks, 'Where are you from?,' then the answer would be, 'I am from the Chagüí River,' here in Nariño, or 'I am from the Saija River,' in the Cauca Department. Rather than talking of the village, first is the river." The river is not merely the route on which to traverse the forests—a fluvial thoroughfare. It is also the source of emotional attachment and of a particular sense of belonging, what I call an "aquatic sense of place."

The rivers are in fact considered the places out of which individuals emerge and in which they submerge again when the time has come for the final voyage, returning in body if possible, but always in spirit, to the river of origin the moment that death approaches. Such was Doña Celia's imaginative journey, when some years back she suffered from high fever and felt that the time had come for her body to leave this life. Reflecting "the dialogical nature of people's relationship to place" (Buttimer 1976:284), she returned to her river of origin in her imagination, as her life was coming full circle:

There I went to all the places of my river where I grew up. I was walking them the very moment I was dying.

I was not by her side when this moment finally did come, on Saturday, December 21, 2013. But I have no doubt that Doña Celia's last "biographic encounter" took her to her birthplace at Balsitas on the upper reaches of the Guapi River, maybe panning for gold one more time or navigating upstream in her potrillo to take a big, fat sabaleta to her *abuelo*.

Don Agapito Montaño, Poet of Faraway Journeys and Nostalgic Farewells

> In Africa, when an old man dies, it's a library burning.
> —Amadou Hampâté Bâ[12]

The attachment to a particular river of origin remains with one for life, no matter if one leaves the river basin temporarily to migrate to other parts of the Pacific or to the cities in the interior of the country. Don Agapito

Montaño was living in the town of Guapi when I met him in 1996. He was a *decimero*, a poet of the oral tradition, well known and respected not only locally but mentioned in anthologies (Pedrosa and Vanín 1994:13). He died in January 1999 and took with him an enormous wealth of *décimas*, poems, stories, and local wisdom before historians, anthropologists, linguists, or leaders of black organizations, who so rightly call for the need to value the collective cultural memories of black communities in the Pacific region, paid Don Agapito a visit to record his life history. I managed to tape only a fraction of his oral poetry, and Don Agapito remains today, together with so many others, one of the great unpublished poets of the Pacific lowlands.[13]

Although he lived in Guapi most of his adult life, as a native of the Guajuí River (see map 2.1), where he still owned lands that he cultivated, he never forgot his river of origin:

I am guapireño [from the Guapi River]. *One changes. Temporarily, or the terrain. Well, this is a change in terrain. Obviously I don't forget my river. There I cultivated plantain and made a living, because it is a river of much food. I killed a lot of rabbits there, sábalos, all these things. When I was young and healthy, I made a living there. A lot of rabbits, ay! I killed up to twelve rabbits in one night there in Guajuí. With my shotgun. At night. Bang! . . . And we cultivated plantain, rice, corn, coconut. There were large rice-hulling machines here in Guapi. Ships loaded with rice left from here to Buenaventura. Eggs, hens, all of this left from here. These days nothing leaves from here anymore.*

In these lines Don Agapito hints at the capitalist long-term presence in the region, in particular at the changing patterns of agricultural production and consumption (more on this below). He also refers to the city of Buenaventura, whose name can be translated into English as "good adventure," *Buen Aventura*, or "good luck," *Buena Ventura*, depending on the capricious mood of the beholder. Buenaventura is Colombia's largest port, with a population of some 350,000. Cali, the capital of the Valle del Cauca Department, can be reached by road in two to three hours. Small cargo ships operate between Buenaventura and Guapi to the south, a journey of about twelve hours on the open sea. Since the late 1990s speed boats have begun to run this route, taking about four hours on a choppy sea.

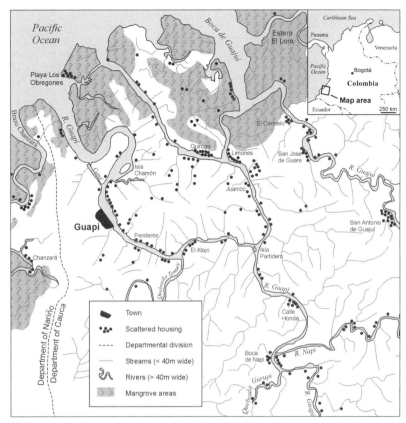

MAP 2.1. Guapi and surrounding rivers in the Cauca Department. *Source*: Adapted from Instituto Geográfico Agustín Codazzi, Departamentos de Cauca y Nariño—Guapi, sheet no. 340, 1994.

Locals regard Buenaventura as the gateway to the rest of the world, as large cargo vessels leaving the port to neighboring Panama and the United States nurture strong images of the American Dream. Many young men try to embark illegally on these vessels. Known as *polizontes*, they are often simply thrown overboard on the open sea by a ruthless crew when found in their hiding spots on the vessel. Nevertheless some of the polizontes reach the United States in this way and manage to survive there, although rarely in ways they had dreamed of. The occasional letters sent back home, together with money and often suggestively posing photographs, contribute to the myth of the American Dream being reproduced back home in Buenaventura and in the surrounding river basins.

The son of a neighbor of mine in Guapi had made it to the United States as a polizonte. One day his mother walked around the neighborhood proudly displaying a letter from her son, now supposedly successful in the United States. He had included a photo, in which he could be seen standing in front of a wardrobe full of nice suits and shirts and countless pairs of shoes. His handwritten note on the back of the photo read, "I can't decide what to wear today!"

Not surprisingly Buenaventura features prominently in Don Agapito's poetry. He explains:

Everyone must have been in Buenaventura. One goes to Cali, to Medellín, to the United States; you have to have been in Buenaventura. It's a sea port.

These lines reveal Buenaventura as the relational space per se in the Pacific lowlands, oriented toward the outward world beyond itself, as most ports are (see Massey 2005:149–51 on the German port city of Hamburg), yet also an important destiny in its own right:

El puerto de Buenaventura,
un puerto bien venturoso,
donde apegan los navíos
y los hombres de reposo.

El puerto de Buenaventura,
¿cuándo estaremos allá?
Viendo muchachas bonitas
que bajan del Anchicayá.

(The port of Buenaventura,
a very fortunate port,
where vessels land
and men of leisure.

The port of Buenaventura,
when will we be there?
To see the beautiful girls
who descend from the Anchicayá.)[14]

Buenaventura clearly holds a central role in Don Agapito's geographical imagination. When he says that "these days nothing leaves from here anymore," he deplores the drastic decline in agrarian productivity in the area around Guapi. Whereas in the 1950s and 1960s rice, plantains, and bananas were shipped to Buenaventura, they embark on a reverse journey these days, as Guapi now needs to import these agricultural products. Once an export destination for Guapi's agricultural output, Buenaventura is today the provider of essential food staples.

This change of fortune can partly be explained by the large-scale introduction of coconut cultivation in the river basins around Guapi, which was encouraged by the Colombian Institute of Agrarian Reform (INCORA) in the 1960s and which led to a decline of subsistence agriculture in the region. The failure of the coconut as a viable export commodity, linked to the lack of efficient commercialization and the disastrous effect of a plague known locally as *anillo rojo*, meant that campesinos were unable to repay INCORA the loans they had received and thus fell into debt with the institution. To make things worse, many campesinos had lost food self-sufficiency and had to import and pay for the very agricultural products that they cultivated themselves before the 1960s.

While the state-led coconut experiment was a huge blow to small-scale peasant farmers, the negative effects were somehow absorbed by the particular land tenure relations in the region. The lands of any one farmer can be quite dispersed at times, in different river basins even, and many farmers keep their smaller fincas planted with staples. Traditional land tenure frequently lacks formal documents such as title deeds to serve as evidence of ownership. Yet property relations are known and accepted in the wider community, as information on landownership is handed down from one generation to another. Rather than defined by a Western cartographic logic of lines fixed in space (and on paper), a richly textured geographical imagination underlies the ways territories are delimited in space and boundaries are drawn between lands pertaining to individual farmers. Don Agapito explains:

This land of mine, it's from my ancestors, from my grandfather and my great-grandfather. My grandfather worked there, my father worked there, and now I am working it. That's how things are. And there I am going to die, and onwards it goes to the next generation.

Question: *How much land do you have?*

Well, since it is not measured . . .

Question: *Well, in how many places do you have land?*

I have lands along a small stream called La Plata. This land, I received from my mother-in-law, the wife's mother. We took the land in La Plata, and we worked it. The land in Guajuí is from my father's side. Here in Penitente I also have large plots of land, from my mother's side. Through heritage, as they say. I have in Guajuí. I have in Quiroga. But they have not been titled, like today. And there weren't any problems before. Because one feels that this land here is mine. And then comes another person claiming a title over it; how am I going to allow this? Because now they only respect titles here. What is titled is respected more. But it is only now that they don't respect those without title. Before, the old folks used to respect each other. For example, I was going to work here. And you over there. We put this post over there as a limit. And I got to my side of the post, and I cleared my side, and you cleared yours. Everybody accepted this. But today not any more. Today they only respect titles.

Don Agapito hints here at tensions in changing land property relations. Traditionally land demarcation takes the form of natural boundaries, such as certain trees, brooks, or rocks. Raquel Portocarrera, a local historian and schoolteacher in Guapi, explains, "Although the land is not titled, we know the boundaries. Even though there are no fences. Natural boundaries are the fences. As they say, the peach palm, the breadfruit tree; these are the references. A small brook; these are the references to draw boundaries."[15]

These boundaries are highly respected within the community, and they are marked by showing someone around and pointing them out. Teófila Betancourt, a community leader in Guapi, remembers how she found out about the lands she would inherit: "When my grandfather died, and I was tiny then, the very community told me, 'From this pumpkin to there is yours, because it was your grandfather's,' and no one crosses from there to here, no one trespasses. This is sacred and was respected. Well, it was like a title deed, you see. But it was visible, it was a tree, a ditch, an opening in the land, something like that, and it was highly respected. This was sacred."[16]

These patterns of traditional landownership were ignored and made invisible by national legislation in 1959 that declared rural untitled lands in the Pacific lowlands as *tierras baldías*, or unoccupied state-owned public lands. This enabled the government to increase the number of concessions handed out to companies that wanted to exploit the natural resources in the region. In particular sawmill owners increasingly appropriated lands that traditionally had belonged to black communities. Territorial conflicts ensued as a result. When Colombia's new Constitution of 1991 opened up legal mechanisms that would guarantee collective land rights to rural black communities occupying these tierras baldías, it was through recourse to the oral tradition that knowledge about traditional land property relations was channeled into formal land titling procedures. In other words—and invoking Lefebvre's spatial triad—the oral tradition was mobilized in the political processes that sought recognition of a differential space that hitherto had been held invisible by dominant representations of space and state legislation.

An important vehicle in the oral tradition is the décima.[17] As Álvaro Pedrosa and Alfredo Vanín (1994:12) write in their authoritative investigation:

> There is no doubt that the décima is the most important poetic structure in the Pacific. . . . The decimero works with history or with everyday life, with the specific or with the symbolic. Themes deal with the "divine" (religious aspects) or the "human." . . . The "human" décimas deal with disputes, the rules of generational and interpersonal relations, seduction, stories of historical events, tales, social critique and protest. . . . The decimeros are in a certain way a kind of collective conscience, critics and historians of local, national and sometimes international events, tale-tellers and praisers of love, loss of love, fortune, and setbacks of fortunes.

With all these characteristics, the decimeros are a creative source of collective memories, local history, and aquatic epistemologies. We may think of them as the voices of the sense of place.

One of the remarkably consistent tropes in décimas is the farewell, not surprising in a migrant society. Farewells can be both temporary, for example when someone embarks on a journey, or final, when one remembers a lost love or friend. It was one of Don Agapito's favorite themes:

Adiós adiós amigo
Hasta el alto fuimos juntos,
comunicando los dos.
Aquí fueron los desmayos,
donde nos dijimos adiós.

Donde nos dijimos adiós,
fueron grandes mis tormentos,
porque no pude sacar
lágrimas de sentimientos.

Sentimientos puse en tí,
prenda querida del alma.
Cómo querés que navegue,
si tu amor me tiene en calma.

Si tu amor me tiene en calma,
cómo no me lo dijiste,
para yo haberte sacado
d'esa cama en que dormiste.

Esa cama en que ti duermes
es una hiel para mi,
estos son los ayes-ayes,
cuando me acuerdo de ti.

Cuando me acuerdo de ti,
me dan ganas de llorar,
de ver las puertas abiertas
cerradas en tu voluntad.

(Farewell my Friend
To the top we walked together,
talking one to another.
Here we nearly fainted,
as we said farewell.

As we said farewell,
immense was my anguish,
because I could not shed
tears of sorrow.

Love I invested in you,
my dear sweetheart.
How do you want me to carry on,
if your love has deserted me.

If your love has deserted me,
why did you not tell me,
so I could have thrown you
out of this bed in which you slept.

This bed in which you slept
is like bile to me,
these are the sorrows
when I remember you.

When I remember you,
I just want to cry,
seeing the open doors
closed in your will.)

Sorrows over the leaving of a beloved person are often drowned in alcohol consumption, which at the same time is indispensable fuel for poetic license. Don Agapito learned from an early age to take a good drink:

When I was young, I liked to have a drink with the old folks, well, the really old folks. I drank a lot with them. The old folks said . . . Is that recording? [referring to my tape recorder] . . . Get lost you! [to his grandchildren who surrounded him, listening to his story] . . . The old folks said, "Look, we have run out of drink." [So I said,] "Well, give me the money; I'm going to buy some." It could be ten or twelve o'clock at night; I went to get the drink. And since these old folks, their pleasure was drinking, because they always told me, "Drinking is a pleasure. A guy has no reason to quarrel with his friends when they are drinking. Why would you quarrel?" They were five, six, seven, eight, ten of them, drinking and rhyming, and eating, because drinking is a pleasure. They taught me to drink, and I learned it.

For Don Agapito this drink would mostly have been the rurally distilled unrefined sugarcane spirit called viche (also spelled biche). Not surprisingly, heavy drinking (and its effects) is another familiar trope found in décimas:

Vení, tomemos hermano,
le dijo el desdichado.
Tomemos mucho trago,
tomemos sin cesar.

Yo también como tú,
soy otro desgraciado,
que a la taverna vengo
mis penas a aliviar.

(Come here, my brother, take a drink,
the wretched one told him.
Let's get drunk,
let's drink without stopping.

I, as well as you,
am just another poor devil,
and I come to the bar
to relieve my sorrows.)

While the decimero may also reflect on the negative effects of high alcohol consumption, at the end of the day a good drink is simply considered part of social life and the indispensable spirit for rhyming sessions to the beat of the rain and the flow of the river:

Voy a dejar de beber
el aguardiente diez años,
porque estoy viendo
que me hace daño;
y esa enmienda voy a hacer.

Yo no fuera sido de bebedor,
sería un hombre acaudalado,
porque sé que un hombre pasado
de grosero e insolente,
él tomó un susto de repente,
y todos prueban que así fue,
y por eso hoy en día
he dicho que voy a dejar de beber.

Pero ¡caramba! pico, adelante digo,
he pensado beber mi bebido.
Mi mujer no pare un hijo;
¿para quién diablo trabajo?

(I will stop drinking brandy
for ten years,
because I can see,
that it does me harm;
so I will mend my ways.

If I wasn't always drinking,
I'd be a rich man,
because I know that a man
overly rude and brazen,
suddenly got a fright,
and everybody testifies to that,
and therefore on this day
I say that I will stop drinking.

But, damn it, come on, I say,
I'd rather take another drink.
My wife won't bear me a child;
who the heck am I working for, then?)

When I interviewed Don Agapito, he was seventy-seven years old and remembered these décimas just as in his youth, although he complained that
in his old age he was beginning to forget a lot of them:

---

*When I was young, I knew seventy-nine décimas. But not anymore. Since I had this
accident* [a heart attack, as a result of which the doctor forbade him alcohol
consumption], *I live very bored. So, these things, well, one remembers these things.
There are other decimeros here. There was a primo hermano* [a relative of second
or third degree] *who always came to my house. And in the afternoon we were
throwing rhymes between us.*

The notion of "throwing rhymes" (*echar décimas*) expresses well the often
competitive character of these social gatherings. One person starts by
composing a few rhymed verses that he challengingly directs at someone
else in the group, who then has to improvise by rhyming to the same structure and pass it on. In this way verses are "thrown" from one to another,
accompanied by laughter, clapping, cheering, and, of course, serious viche

intake. The most original improviser in the art of rhyming gains the highest reputation.

While such performances are common to other oral cultures, these good-natured poetic exchanges should not be confused with the altogether more aggressive popular word games in Mexico City that the Mexican poet and essayist Octavio Paz (1961) comments on in *The Labyrinth of Solitude*. There, Paz remarks, "each of the speakers tries to humiliate his adversary with verbal traps and ingenious linguistic combinations, and the loser is the person who cannot think of a comeback, who has to swallow his opponent's jibes . . . full of aggressive sexual allusions; the loser is possessed, is violated, by the winner and the spectators laugh and sneer at him" (39–40). In the Pacific lowlands these word games are a raucous but rather jovial affair.

I found Don Agapito's ability to remember these stories, poems, and décimas, which he narrated repeatedly, utterly impressive. Most decimeros can neither read nor write, a common phenomenon in a society with high levels of illiteracy, estimated to be around 40 percent (DNP 1998:18). Don Agapito himself laments not having gone to school because his mother was too poor to afford him a place, and because of the conventional assumption in the countryside that children should help in the household and work rather than go to school. It is still common for children to attend school only outside of the harvest season or when their parents do not need their help in some productive activity:

I didn't go to school, because my mother was very poor. My mother was abandoned, my father left her. I mean, I didn't have a father; my older brother was my father. And the old folks said, "Go to work." If I had gone to school, I think I would have learned something. Because when some old man threw a décima, I was paying attention. And the next day I already knew it by heart. That's the way I learned.

Oral Tradition as Hidden Transcript of Resistance

As Don Agapito illustrates, knowledge has traditionally been passed on to the next generation in the oral tradition, the vehicle that holds past and present in tension.[18] I understand oral tradition as a set of cultural practices that contains and constantly reconstructs the collective memory of a population group by means of the spoken word. "Tradition" in this dynamic process is neither stable nor fixed in time and space. Rather it should be understood as a process marked by improvisation and characterized by variation. Oral tradition has also been said to be "contaminated" by written practices, as Walter Ong (1982) has shown with the penetration of oral discourses by literacy. Crucial in the continued reconstruction and performance of oral tradition is its collective character and its practitioners' dialogical relationship that goes beyond the borders of individual creation and single performances (Bakhtin 1986).

Despite rich debates over the dynamics of oral traditions, surprisingly little has been said about their relevance to politics.[19] The oral tradition among Colombia's black communities, for example, has mainly been analyzed for its folkloristic significance (Vanín 1996; Velásquez [1959] 2000). Much less space has been dedicated to an examination of the role that it plays, or could play, in Afro-Colombian political mobilization. To redress this imbalance, I draw in this section on James Scott's (1990) conceptual framework elaborated in his study *Domination and the Arts of Resistance*. In particular I examine the oral tradition among black communities on Colombia's Pacific Coast as passing *from a hidden transcript* of discourses and practices, generated and performed mainly within the communities themselves, *to a public transcript*, in which these discourses are geared at external consumption. By doing so I extend the meaning of the term *hidden transcript* beyond its restricted use in Scott's original conception, where it is mostly reduced to a dialectical relation vis-à-vis public discourses of domination. By focusing on the *transition* from hidden to public transcript—or from backstage to frontstage, to use Goffman's (1972) metaphor—such an ethnographic approach offers new insights for debates over domination and resistance, highlighting the specific workings of micro-level politics.

In his book Scott examines how processes of domination generate a hegemonic public conduct and a backstage discourse—a hidden transcript—by both dominant and subordinate groups. Of relevance for the latter, he argues, "Here, offstage, where subordinates may gather outside the intimidating gaze of power, a sharply dissonant political culture is possible" (1990:18). Different from the public transcript, which represents the open interaction between subordinate and dominant groups, the hidden transcript constitutes a "privileged site for nonhegemonic, contrapuntal, dissident, subversive discourse" (25; also in Scott 1992:60). It is within the space of the hidden transcript that acts of resistance are imagined and take on shape.

In his earlier work, *Weapons of the Weak*, Scott (1985) explored such a conceptualization of resistance as located in the everyday. There he examined the politics of resistance by poor Malay peasants to disadvantageous changes in rice production. Notably he analyzed peasant actions such as subterfuge, poaching, and foot dragging in agrarian communities as a source of positive resistance. His focus on such seemingly "trivial" acts as everyday resistance within an explanatory framework of the rationality of political action and revolutions has been commented on widely, albeit not always favorably.[20] Some have gone as far as to critique Scott's approach as "conceptual confusion [that] only stretches the concept of 'resistance'" (Tarrow 1994:219).

Yet I argue here that this conceptual "stretching" allows a more wide-ranging understanding of the multiple ways in which resistance is acted out. Rather than restricting our analysis of resistance practices to the more spectacular and widely visible and recognizable acts—such as demonstrations, rebellions, and revolutions—we should indeed stretch our analytical vision to include other, more low-key manifestations. As Carolyn Nordstrom and JoAnn Martin (1992:7) point out, cultural practices have not always been understood in relation to their potential for political challenge: "Practices that anthropologists might once have viewed as a survival of 'tradition,' when analyzed in relation to structures of domination, emerge as nonessentialist forms of resistance. . . . Resistance may be encoded in a wide range of cultural practices that are meaningful by virtue of their opposition to a dominant culture." As a study into identity construction on Colombia's Pacific Coast concludes, for example, resistance there should not be seen as acts of total confrontation but as a way of life (FUNCOP 1996:50).

The concept of the hidden transcript is reminiscent of bell hooks's (1991:41–49) notion of "homeplace," a social space free from control and surveillance in which feelings of safety, homecoming, and solidarity are produced: "Historically, African-American people believed that the construction of a homeplace, however fragile and tenuous (the slave hut, the wooden shack), had a radical political dimension. Despite the brutal reality of racial apartheid, of domination, one's homeplace was the one site where one could freely confront the issue of humanization, where one could resist" (42). It is precisely in these spaces of homeplace that the hidden transcripts are produced as "a critique of power spoken behind the back of the dominant" (Scott 1990:xii). Yet Scott (1992:78) restricts the meaning of the hidden transcript to those discourses, practices, and gestures that are produced "offstage" *as a reaction* to dominant discourses of the powerful. In fact, he argues, the public transcript *produces* the hidden transcript in dialectical fashion. This interpretation seems too restrictive to me, as it does not account for the myriad cultural practices of subaltern groups that are enacted in the safety of the homeplace, relatively autonomous from dominant script and speech acts yet carrying within them the seeds of resistance.

Take the case of the Pashtun women of Afghanistan and their poetic expressions known as *landays*. On the surface it may appear that these women suffer quietly their fate as subjugated second-class citizens in a male-dominated society with an extremely masculinized tribal and clannish structure. Yet, as the celebrated Afghan poet Sayd Bahodine Majrouh (2003) argues, it is through the poetic two-liners of the landay (which literally means "the short one") that Pashtun women feed their indignity and inner rebellion.[21] According to Majrouh it is "from this *deep-seated and hidden protest* that grows more resistant with every passing day, [that] she comes out with only two forms of evidence in the end—her suicide and her song" (xv, emphasis added). Future historians will tell us if the oral tradition among Pashtun women as hidden transcript inspired an emancipatory women's movement against male domination in Afghan society. Yet it would be short-sighted not to take seriously the "deep-seated and hidden protest" of the landay as a significant site and a hidden transcript where resistance broods and may boil over.

As a social movement scholar I am particularly interested in this transition from sources and sites of resistance to overt political action. In other words, whereas Scott (1992:58) is interested in "assessing the discrepancy *between* the hidden transcript and the public transcript," I want to focus on the *transition* of the hidden transcript to a public transcript. This implies both a spatial displacement of the discourse from backstage to frontstage and an epistemological shift in which previously hidden discourses and cultural practices are turned public as crucial reference points with empowering effects on subaltern groups. The emergence of identity politics in Latin America, for example, articulated by indigenous and

Afro-descendant populations, has at its heart an epistemological shift to-ward other (ethnic) ways of knowing that is informed by a rich history of decolonial thought (Escobar 2008; Mignolo 2005). These ideas, I argue, are reflected in Colombia in the official recognition of a black ethnicity as a differential cultural fact that makes up the nation. That explains why it is so important for black activists to defend the legislative changes that have made this possible. As I show in chapter 4 in detail, the oral tradition that existed as hidden transcript within Colombia's black communities has indeed "stormed the stage," as Scott (1992:78) might say.

The concept of the hidden transcript is useful in the analysis of forms of resistance in the Afro-Colombian case for a number of reasons. First, Scott focuses in his study on forms of slavery, colonialism, and racism, all conditions that Colombia's black populations have experienced likewise. Racism, however covert in its manifestations, still prevails in much of Colombian society (Wade 1993). In particular the importance that Scott gives to interpreting rumors, gossip, folktales, curses, and magic as a critique of power and an "infrapolitics of the powerless" opens an interesting path of inquiry into the rich oral traditions of black communities in Colombia.

Second, much of the histories and geographies of Afro-Colombia flows together in a semantic field around the notions of invisibility, marginality, and the hidden. Geographically separated from Colombia's interior by the Western Andean mountain range, the Pacific region has been described as the "hidden littoral" (Yacup 1934) and as the "periphery of the periphery" (Granda 1977) due to its physical and economic marginality in relation to the industrializing interior of Colombia. Moreover, since the mid-1980s anthro-pologists have drawn attention to the "invisibilization" of Afro-Colombians in studies of the country's history and anthropology (Friedemann 1984; Frie-demann and Arocha 1986). The notion of the hidden, then, is suggestive of the wider geographical, historical, and sociopolitical context. Rather than a mere spatial metaphor, it provides an epistemological opening into the so-cial world of the Pacific Coast region by inviting us to "unhide" and "dig into" the rich invisibilized cultures and their ways of knowing and understanding.

Third, by analyzing cultural practices such as the oral tradition in terms of resistance we put flesh on the concept of cultural politics, a key element in postcolonial and social movement studies, which is too often discussed in abstract terms without concrete links being made to the everyday prac-tices of (political) cultures that nurture it (Alvarez et al. 1998).

If remembering is an act of resistance against processes of forgetting and oblivion, then the articulation of local history—as practiced by decimeros such as Don Agapito—can be an important tool in challenging representations of space that homogenize and make a historically sedimented differential space invisible. While Don Agapito's décimas and verses have previously been regarded as part of Afro-Colombian folklore, they now get mobilized by social movement agency, as they are seen to hold testimony to a form of life that is under threat yet considered to hold the keys to possible future lifeworlds. Engaging these hidden transcripts is therefore not merely an ethnographic exercise that celebrates a rich folkloric tradition; it is a strategic move to foreground local epistemologies as a political tool in Colombia's evolving cultural politics.

"Myth-Poetics of the Thriving Shore": Engaging the Hidden Transcript

> No language dies whilst its last speaker is alive who monologues with the ancestors.
> —Manuel Zapata Olivella, "Omnipresencia africana en la civilización universal"

The oral tradition of black populations in the Colombian Pacific is a hybrid form characterized by aspects of the heritage of both African cultures and certain literary structures from Castilian Spanish.[22] The latter has been of interest to linguists and historians, who have shown the influence of the Don Quijote and of the Spanish poetic forms of the décima and the copla of the Golden Age literature (Granda 1977).[23] Although the Spanish language was imposed on the enslaved during colonial times, Afro-descendants adapted it to their own needs and desires. They effectively reworked linguistic structures and vocabulary to create a kind of "counterlanguage." As the Afro-Colombian poet and expert on oral traditions Alfredo Vanín (1996:47) explains, "In a world of oral tradition and shamanism, the spoken language acquires a magic dimension that reaches unsuspected limits. . . . Colonization by way of language generated in the Pacific a kind of counter-language; the language was imposed but, as a cultural reaction, another one was created, because the desires for freedom or for belonging are linked to the language we share" (emphasis added).

This counterlanguage can be thought of as a hidden transcript of resistance, in that it articulates (echoing Lefebvre) the lived, representational space of black communities on the Pacific Coast against hegemonic representations of space. The social importance and status of the decimero, the public voice of this counterlanguage, is a heritage of West African cultures in which the griot assumes the function of conveyor of history and morality (Pedrosa and Vanín 1994:14). Indeed today's Afro-Colombian decimeros can be considered the inheritors of the West African griot.

Of Faraway Geographies and Imaginary Journeys

> Now that we have examined manuscripts and tired pages, it is useful to return to the non-written metaphors, to those which stroll along the shores of the Pacific with their lavishness and shortages, their tenderness and violence, their cataclysms and origins.
> —Alfredo Vanín, "Mitopoética de la orilla florida"

As conveyors of local history, the decimeros reflect individual and collective experiences of the aquatic space. Prominent features in these stories are real and imaginary journeys to distant places and the exploration of faraway geographies. A popular décima in this respect is "La Concha de Almeja" (The Cockleshell), wherein the poet imagines his experience of traveling the world and the seven seas in a cockleshell, a journey of magic dimensions and encounters:

La Concha de Almeja
Yo me embarqué a navegar
en una concha de almeja
a rodiar el mundo entero
a ver si hallaba coteja.

Salí de aquí de Tumaco
con rumbo a Buenaventura
yo no embarqué un cargamento
porque la mar estaba dura.
Pero embarqué quince curas
un automóvil pa'andar
a Guapi dentré a embarcar
cien tanques de gasolina
cargando en popa una mina[24]
yo me embarqué a navegar.

Desde Cristóbal Colón
salí con rumbo a la Europa
con una tripulación
como de cien mil en popa.
Con viento que a favor sopla
atravesé a Casa Viejas
y muchas ciudades lejas
las visité en pocos días
navegando noche y día
en una concha de almeja.

Con un grande cargamento
como de cien mil vitrolas
me atravesé a Cabo de Horno
y no me dentró una ola.
Llevaba quinientas bolas
sobre cubierta un caldero
cuatrocientos marineros
una gran tripulación
hice la navegación
a rodiar el mundo entero.

Cuando los náuticos me vieron
que iba navegando al norte
cien vapores se vinieron
que los llevara a remolque.
Cuarenta mil pailebotes
llenos de arroz y lenteja
todos los pegué a la reja
y puse rumbo a la Europa.
Y navegué a Constantinopla
a ver si hallaba coteja.

(**The Cockleshell**
I embarked to sail
in a cockleshell
to travel around the whole world
to see if I found my match.

I left from Tumaco here
heading for Buenaventura
I didn't stow a cargo
because the sea was rough.
But I embarked fifteen priests
a car to move around
I entered Guapi to take on board
one hundred tanks of petrol
weighed with a mine in stern
I embarked to sail.

From Cristóbal Colón
I set off heading for Europe
with a crew
of one hundred thousand in stern.
Helped by a blowing wind
I passed through Casa Viejas
and many distant cities
I visited in a few days
sailing day and night
in a cockleshell.

With an impressive cargo
of one hundred thousand gramophones
I passed through Cape Horn
and not a wave washed into my shell.
I carried five hundred balls
on deck a boiler
four hundred sailors
an impressive crew
thus I made the voyage
to travel around the whole world.

When the naval officers saw
that I was sailing north
a hundred steamers came
for me to tow them.
Forty thousand pilot boats

full of rice and lentils
I tied them all to the railing
and I set course for Europe.
And I sailed to Constantinople
to see if I found my match.)
(transcribed in Pedrosa and Vanín 1994:15–17, my translation)[25]

This version of "La Concha de Almeja" was recorded in 1976 with a farmer in the Saija River basin on the Cauca Coast. Since décimas in general do not adhere to a definitive authorship, one may hear the same décima in other parts of the Pacific region with slight changes in structure or vocabulary. As it is reproduced orally on countless occasions and in different places, each decimero may add to or change certain vocabulary. The décima thus effectively turns into collective authorship, a characteristic of all forms of oral literature among black populations in the Pacific region (Pedrosa and Vanín 1994:13).

The same décimas can be heard on the northern part of Ecuador's Pacific Coast (Rahier 1986, 1999), a region that shares much of the ecological, ethnic, and cultural characteristics with the Colombian Pacific region. Which is why Norman Whitten (1986:xii) has subtitled his pioneering study of the black frontiersmen *Afro-Hispanic Culture of Ecuador and Colombia*, allowing him "to cut back and forth across the national borders." Clearly the decimeros don't give a flying hoot about national borders either. They are a testimony to the oral tradition as transborder space that laughs indifferently at Westphalian territorialized nation-state thinking. Laura Hidalgo (1995:281–83), for example, recorded and transcribed two versions of "La Concha de Almeja" in Esmeraldas, Ecuador. Her collection also features the décima "El Capitán Pirata" (305–6), which I recorded with Don Agapito and transcribe here:

El Capitán Pirata
Cuando el capitán pirata
me convidó a navegar
para que fuera escuchar
lo que pasaba al mapa.
Dijo que me cuidaría
con mucha delicadeza,

pagándome al mes cien pesos
y tres comidas al día.

Que el viejo diablo me veía
luciendo buena ropa
él me pondría en Europa
dueño de casa y hacienda.
Me enseñaba toda lengua
desde los números general
y cuando el capitán pirata
me convidó a navegar.

Salimos de Punto Areno,
de Barcelonia [sic] un día.
Echamos sesenta días
para hondear en Cartagena.
A mi me valió la pena
caminar el mar d'Europa
con chico comiendo en popa
mandando mis oficiales
y luciendo de buena ropa
me convidó a navegar
el capitán pirata.

(**The Pirate Captain**
When the pirate captain
invited me to sail
so I would see
what was happening in the world.
He promised to look after me
with great subtlety,
paying me a hundred pesos a month
and three meals a day.

So the old devil would see me
sporting fine clothes
he would make me in Europe
owner of house and estate.

He taught me all languages
from the basic numbers
when the pirate captain
invited me to sail.

We left from Punto Areno,
from Barcelona one day.
It took us sixty days
to unload in Cartagena.
To me it was worthwhile
traveling the seas of Europe
with boys eating in the stern
ordering my officers
and sporting fine clothes
as he invited me to sail
the pirate captain.)

Dealing with a similar theme as in "La Concha de Almeja," Don Agapito evokes in this poem a journey that he never embarked upon to places he never got to see. Yet these imagined faraway geographies and places, known only through the circulation of these poems and stories, become meaningful through the grounded experiences of black communities bound up with their aquatic space. The references to rivers, ports (Punto Arena, Barcelona, Cartagena), and the sea reveal an everyday aquatic vocabulary that speaks of the routine engagement with the water-based environment in the Pacific region. In this sense the expression *caminar el mar*, literally "to walk the sea," is characteristic of the ways black communities refer to their travels on sea. It is central to their geographical imagination.

Of Farewells and Encounters with Aquatic Spirits

> There were kings without power and glory, princes transformed into
> unbearable animals . . . and powerful sorceresses who were able to alter
> space-time and dematerialize realities.
> —Alfredo Vanín, "Mitopoética de la orilla florida"

The décima also reflects another important feature of black communities on the Pacific Coast: their intense spatial mobility, both short term within the region and as long-term migration in search of education and employment outside the region.[26] Each voyage implies a separation from people and places that one leaves behind. Not surprisingly many of Don Agapito's verses are around the *adiós*, the farewell to friends, family, and places. Associated with the notion of leaving is a strong melancholy, as a return is never guaranteed, although always sworn to:

> *El que se va no se aleja*
> *ni deja ningún sentido*
> *porque la paja se va y vuelve*
> *a su mesmo [sic] nido.*[27]

> *Él que se va se divierte*
> *a lo lejos del camino*
> *él que se queda se queda*
> *con el pesar del continuo.*

> *Quiero ser la cuchara de plata*
> *para echar el oro cocido*
> *adiós alumbren mis ojos*
> *nunca te echo yo en el olvido.*

> (The one who leaves does not really do so
> nor does it make any sense
> because the hen leaves and returns
> to her same nest.

> The one who leaves finds joy
> along the way
> the one who stays, stays behind
> weighed down by routine.

> I want to be the silver spoon
> that throws the cooked gold
> my eyes shine farewell
> I shall never cast you into oblivion.)

Leaving a place and people behind is in itself not problematic. One is expected to leave home at some point to experience other places. This rite of passage is reflected in the common expression *salir a caminar*, "to leave and go walking," but without breaking bonds with the place of origin. Place attachment and a strong sense of belonging are central characteristics of the sense of place in the Pacific, and they could not be better expressed than in these verses by Don Agapito.

Migration and return also have an important effect on today's political mobilization in the Pacific region, as an Afro-Colombian activist explained to me in an interview in November 2004 in Bogotá, while making a casual reference to the décima "The Cockleshell": "There are many cases of people who were economic migrants, who left the Pacific region, traveled the world, in the cockleshell, and then returned with this outside knowledge to play a mobilizing role and become community leaders who know what's going on inside [the communities] but also outside, and this is how they can bring a new dynamic to things." In chapter 5 I discuss the cases of several of these "economic migrants" who returned to the Pacific region to take on leadership roles in the newly emerging community councils.

While the aquatic space is often drawn upon for the source material or *content* of the oral tradition (rivers, sea, harbors), it frequently also provides the physical setting and *context* in which these traditions are practiced. A distinct spatiality is associated with the performance of the oral tradition. Women traveling in the solitudes of the rivers and mangroves, for example, often sing rhythmically to the sound of their paddles in the water. These songs are known as *cantos de boga*, or rowing songs. Some of them may be voice games, imitating the sounds of the embarkation, whereas others are about the fortunes of love and loss of love (Pedrosa and Vanín 1994:64). The river is the site of performance here, as it was for Don Agapito, when he used to tell stories and compose décimas traveling with male friends in his canoe:

We chatted wonderfully when we were traveling. So one said, "My friend, when are you going to travel?" Because in those days there was no engine; everything was by paddle. "Well, I will be leaving at midnight." "So let's go together." And then one spoke to the other, and he to another, and so we all went as a crowd. And we went chatting, rhyming, talking, well, about life.

In an environment where people are surrounded by water—the sea in front, the rivers all around, and torrential rain from above—it is not hard to imagine that the aquatic plays a crucial part in local mythologies. Legend has it, for example, that the town of Tumaco is built on an island that formed when three whales came to rest on shore. As time went by, sand accumulated on their backs until it covered them completely. It is said that one day these whales will shake the sand off their backs and dive into the sea again, taking every living soul with them (Vanín 1998:270–71).

Another marine mammal, the dolphin, figures prominently in a mythological story set on the island of Gorgona, located some fifty-six kilometers off the Pacific Coast west of Guapi. A small landmass of 1,600 hectares, Gorgona is thought to be the summit of a fourth Andean chain that was gradually submerged during the present interglacial period. As a result of this separation from the continent, the island is home to diverse fauna, including a number of highly poisonous snakes. The island's name is derived from ancient Greek mythology. The Gorgons, three sisters who favored snakes over hair as their headgear of choice, turned anyone who looked at them to stone, or so it goes. This must have been on the mind of the conquistador Francisco Pizarro, when he set up camp on the island in 1527 to replenish his water supplies on his way south to what is today Peru. So many of his men died from poisonous snakebites that Pizarro hurriedly broke camp, naming the island Gorgona. Between 1959 and 1984 the island was a high-security prison. It would no doubt have matched Alcatraz in fame if only the Birdman, or at least Capone, had set up camp there. Escapes from the prison often ended fatally, with the escapee bitten by one of the numerous venomous snakes, just as the conquistadors were 450 years earlier.[28]

No wonder the island is "impregnated with legend" (Taussig 2004:271–81). Local lore has it that one day an underwater volcano erupted and threw the entire population of the island of Gorgona into the sea, where they were transformed into dolphins. According to received wisdom, that is why dolphins live as marine mammals whose young cry as children do and why they like to follow boats to protect their human crew and to save the shipwrecked (Vanín 1998:275).

In these stories the aquatic space is not merely the surrounding environment—a contextual space—but a socially produced space that becomes meaningful through the practice of storytelling. These stories are often spiced up in the Pacific lowlands with references to mythical characters such as the *riviel*, a danger-spelling "vision" that solitary fishermen may have on sea at night, or the *maravelí*, a maritime apparition with a crew of satanic spirits and skeletons that passes by every village at midnight to call upon those who have made a pact with the devil.[29] Both *visiones* have social control functions: the riviel acts as a warning to fishermen not to stray alone on the sea late at night, while the story of the maravelí is meant to deter people from being malicious.

These stories and myths reveal the power of the spoken word, often performed in intimate settings and everyday life. We should not view them as finite components of a supposedly bounded cultural canon but rather as vital traces of the interconnectedness among animate and inanimate bodies, spaces, and narratives. They are the vehicles through which the aquatic space is embodied and performed. Yet they also often hold the seeds of resistance that may get mobilized to defend certain cultural practices against the colonization of a differential space. Religious beliefs in general and the saints in particular play a crucial role in the imagination of such acts of resistance.

Navigating Saints Who Have Come to Stay

> Throughout the Pacific, the saints navigate alone, going to their festivities, where they are celebrated (in the mind of men and women) and their statues are paraded on adorned rafts until they reach the place of the arrullo, death wake or worship, where people have prayed and sung for nine nights, to be celebrated in style, until the musicians are "penetrated by the saint" through their heads or their instruments. The Virgin of Carmen, San Antonio, the Immaculate of Guapi; they are long-standing navigators.
> —Alfredo Vanín, "Mitopoética de la orilla florida"

Not only the aquatic spirits navigate endlessly at night on the open sea in search of lost souls. The saints on the Pacific Coast are also linked to the aquatic space. Most of them are said to have arrived by sea or river, which effectively makes them *santos navegantes*, or "navigating saints," as Vanín (1998) calls them. Each village has its own patron saint that is celebrated on a particular day each year. Guapi's patron saint, the Purísima, or the Virgin of the Immaculate Conception, is honored every December 8. The festivities start the night before with a spectacular water celebration, when the Guapi River is illuminated by countless torches on numerous *balsadas*, or rafts, which are adorned with palm thatch and colored lightbulbs, as they approach the town's landing steps. The crew on these rafts frenetically play the traditional instruments of the region—cununo, bombo, and guasá—and sing *arrullos* in honor of the saint. With this ceremony the people of Guapi re-create the way the Immaculate Virgin is said to have arrived in town, a legend that has been passed on through generations:

> One day, a sailing boat was caught in a heavy storm on the open sea south of Guapi. As the sailors feared for their lives, they began to pray to the statue of the virgin that they carried with them. They promised to take her on land and worship her in the first village they would reach, if only she extricated them from the danger. As dawn broke, the storm miraculously calmed down, and the sailors arrived unharmed in Guapi, where they took the statue to a small chapel to worship her. However, as they were about to leave, the statue was impossible to lift, as it suddenly weighed too much. Maestra Rita Tulia Perlaza, a school teacher in Guapi and life-long observer of the festivities, explains: "A lady called Orobio, member of one of the most distinguished families, offered to buy the virgin paying her weight in gold. But when they weighed her, the virgin became suddenly very light and only weighed six kilograms. From that moment on she became our patron saint. . . . Since she came here over water, we re-enact this event with the rafts each year."[30]

Even more revered is the Virgen del Carmen, considered protector of sailors, fishermen, and anyone else who travels by sea. The festivities every July 16 are renowned in Guapi. As Maestra Rita Tulia Perlaza told me in an interview in July 1999:

The Virgin of Carmen is the savior of the shipwrecked. She is their protector. They get stranded because sometimes these boats don't carry the virgin with them. They don't know her prayer. And they run aground. But if you know the prayer to the Virgin of Carmen, you don't drown. You can swim four, five days. Here we once lost some young women, two young girls and a young man. They went to Gorgona, and coming back they went off course. They were navigating for twenty days. But they didn't drown. Nor did they die of hunger. Because the boat's engineer knew the prayer to Carmen, and he said that when he called on the virgin, the waves somehow calmed down. Until they were found. Of course they looked almost dead. But they didn't die. Here they are today, one of them lives in Cali, and the other one in Popayán.

FIG. 2.5. Procession through the streets of Guapi in honor of the Virgen del Carmen, Guapi, July 16, 1999.

The Saints Are Always with the People

> The eyes of the Lord of the Sea of Salahonda are the eyes of a shipwrecked
> —Alfredo Vanín, "Mitopoética de la orilla florida"

Few would doubt the powers of the saints. In Salahonda, near Tumaco on the southern Pacific Coast, the patron saint is said to have saved the village from destruction by the tsunami of 1906. As the giant sea wave threatened to submerge the population, he raised his hands and stopped it. He is said to have done the same on December 12, 1979, during the most recent terrible seaquake. Amid the general chaos and confusion, the statue of the saint suddenly appeared outside the church without anyone having put it there. The saint faced the great wave and stopped it from washing the settlement away (Vanín 1998:267).[31]

The Lord of Calle Larga on the Napi River arrived at his village in a similar way as Guapi's Immaculate Virgin. A group of pilgrims is said to have rested at Calle Larga, and as they were about to leave, they could not manage to lift the heavy statue anymore and had to leave it behind. The saint must have liked the place and become attached to it. Since he was used to moving around and could not stay still for long, he wandered along the riverbanks at night. His power asserted itself one day in an act of defiance to the Catholic Church. The bishop in Guapi wanted to close the doors of the church in Calle Larga because no priest was available at the time to be appointed for the village. The saint knew, of course, that the bishop was worried about the "pagan" worshipping of the saints, a social reality that the Catholic Church still considers far too excessive in the Pacific region. The saint was on the people's side, however, and one night, at midnight, he broke down the church doors so locals could have continued access to him (Vanín 1998:268).

Similarly some years ago in Guapi the bishop ordered the removal of all saints' statues from the church because he felt that people's worshipping of the saints distracted them from the holy trinity of God the Father, the Son, and the Holy Spirit. Resisting the bishop's intentions, some of the believers advised him that they would no longer go to mass if he took their saints out of the church building. After some reflection the bishop gave in and decided to leave the statues in their place. After all, the saints are always with the people . . .

It would be easy to dismiss these stories as mere lightheaded narratives that are more myth than reality. Too easy. And too lazy. These stories do in fact reveal at least two important facets of social life in the Pacific lowlands. First, the aquatic space should not be regarded as mere contextual space, a kind of container in which social activities simply take place. Rather it is constituted and becomes meaningful through social practice, including popular narratives and storytelling. As such it constitutes the central or main spatiality of social interaction in this region—if we understand spatiality, as Edward Soja does, as socially produced space.[32] It is worthwhile reflecting with Soja (1980:209–10) on this difference between contextual and socially produced space:

> Contextual space is of broad philosophical interest in generating discussion about its absolute and relative properties, its character as "container" of human life, its objectifiable geometry, and its phenomenological essence. But it is an inappropriate and misleading foundation upon which to analyze the concrete and subjective meaning of human spatiality. Space itself may be primordially given, but the organization, use, and meaning of space is a product of social translation, transfor-

mation and experience. Socially produced space is a created structure comparable to other social constructions resulting from the transformation of given conditions inherent in life-on-earth, in much the same way that human history represents a social transformation of time and temporality.

This distinction between contextual and socially produced space lies at the heart of Soja's (1989) concern in outlining a sociospatial dialectic, with which he hopes to unsettle the often taken-for-granted assumptions about dead spatiality found in a "tradition of historicism which reduces spatiality . . . to the stable and unproblematic site of historical action" (130).[33] In this understanding the aquatic space, with its "objectifiable geometry" (the "location" that I discuss in the next chapter), comes into being only through "social translation, transformation and experience." The saints wandering along the riverbanks or stopping tsunamis from destroying villages are part of this social translation and transformation of the aquatic space into meaningful, socially produced space.

This leads us to the second point revealed in the stories just told. Spatiality is always dynamic and often imbued with conflict. The saints are always with the people, as the representatives of the Catholic Church in the stories had to realize, suspending their dogmatic attitudes. The potential power for change lies in the hands of a populace determined to fight for their saints.[34] Rural black populations in the Pacific lowlands are a very spiritual and religious people and worship their saints with fervor. Catholicism is the official religion in Colombia, originally imposed by Spanish colonial rule. Yet Afro-Colombians on the Pacific Coast have embraced it by adapting some of its structures along the way and making it their own religion—in processes not unlike those discussed earlier in the appropriation of the Castilian language. The rhythmic clapping and the use of traditional instruments during mass, for example, distinguish a religious service in the Pacific region from one in the interior of the country. This has always been viewed with suspicion by the Catholic Church and has often led to conflict.

In fact inquisitionary practices against black music and dance in Colombia have a long history and can be traced back at least to around 1730 (Wade 1997a:331). It is said that the most resistant of the Afro-Colombian

FIG. 2.6. Marimba, "instrument of the devil and played only by men."

traditional instruments is the marimba, a type of xylophone made of bamboo and slats of the hard chonta wood. "Instrument of the devil and played only by men" (Taussig 2004:73), it was the target of a campaign by the Catholic Church against its "diabolical" dances at the beginning of the twentieth century, when a particularly fervent priest ordered all instruments to be burned (Friedemann and Arocha 1986:418). But a local *marimbero*, Francisco Saya of the Chagüí River, is said to have saved one marimba from the onslaught of Padre Mera and thus guaranteed the instrument's survival. Not only did Francisco Saya have to fight against the fervor of Padre Mera, but he also had to fight off the devil, which he did by playing the national anthem. This legend has been reenacted on numerous occasions, such as during the carnival of Tumaco in February 1998, where the "return of the marimba" was celebrated (Agier 2002).

Collective memory and storytelling are evoked in this way as a conscious strategy in the construction of resistant identities among rural black populations on the Pacific Coast. As I have argued in this chapter, these identities are shaped by a sense of place that is characterized by local aquatic epistemologies, myth-poetics, and cultural memories. As I show in chapters 4 and 5, this "aquatic sense of place" has been mobilized as a key resource in the ethnoterritorial organizing processes of black communities.

THREE

Historical Geographies of Resistance and *Convivencia* in the Pacific Lowlands

Guapi,	Guapi,
tierra querida donde respira	beloved land where we breathe
aire con ternura;	air with tenderness;
porque en tí, la tranquilidad	the peacefulness
de tu vivir	of your way of life
es la mayor fortuna de tu nombre.	is the greatest fortune of your name.
Y en la aurora de tus hermosos días	And at dawn of your beautiful days
cuando el sol refleja	when the sun is reflected
en aguas de tu río	in the waters of your river
que sube y baja,	that rises and descends,
con la tranquilidad	with the tranquility
que tus hijos pasan	that your sons spend
aquellos días de inolvidable frenesí.	those days of unforgettable frenzy.
Guapi que lindo eres	Guapi, how beautiful you are
tierra bendita donde yo nací	blessed land where I was born
Guapi que vas al mar	Guapi, as you descend to the sea
Yo en mi potrillo junto de ti.	by your side in my canoe, that's me.
En las tardes cuando el sol declina	In the afternoon when the sun sets
se va hacia el mar	we row toward the sea
a la bocana de tu nombre	to the river mouth of your name
con las tristezas y las alegrías	with the sadness and the joys
que se ahogan con la furia de las olas.	that drown in the fury of the waves.

—EUSEBIO ANDRADE BAZÁN, "GUAPI, TIERRA QUERIDA"

In his pioneering work *The Pacific Lowlands of Colombia* (1957:3) North American geographer Robert West, in a passage typical of cultural geographers working in the Carl Sauer tradition at the time, portrayed the region in the following words:

> Seen from the air the canopy formed by the giant trees resembles a sea of green, overlapping umbrellas, broken only by streams and occasional clearings. Hundreds of rivers, often in flood, run through the forest from hill and mountain slope to sea. They are the pathways for human travel and their banks are the main sites of human habitation. . . . If the area has any physical unity, it is to be found in the hot, humid climate and the vegetation cover of dense tropical rain forest. Colombia's Pacific lowlands are the rainiest part of the Americas, with average annual totals from 120 to over 400 inches. The area's position between 1° and 8° north of the equator gives it high year-round temperatures and contributes to an almost continuous relative humidity above 90 per cent. But the most striking physical feature of the area is the rain forest.

More than half a century later, and in spite of increasing deforestation rates, West's description would still be an accurate impression from a bird's-eye view over large parts of the Pacific lowlands (figure 3.1). The region extends from the Western Andean slopes and the border with Ecuador in the south, to the Darien gap on the Panamanian border in the north, including the vast delta of the Atrato River that flows into the Atlantic Ocean on the Caribbean Coast (map 3.1). It covers an area of over ten million hectares, some 6.2 percent of Colombia's total land surface, with 1,300 kilometers of Pacific coastline and extending between eighty and 160 kilometers toward the Andean foothills.

The region is situated within the Intertropical Convergence Zone, a low-pressure belt of weak converging air masses loaded with humidity, which are responsible for high levels of precipitation. In some areas, such as Tutunendo in the northern Chocó Department, precipitation reaches annual averages of over ten thousand millimeters, making it one of the zones of highest rainfall worldwide. Today the region is considered a "biodiversity hotspot," with only an estimated 50 percent of its plant species having been identified to date (Proyecto Biopacífico 1998).[1]

The Pacific lowlands are characterized by an expansive network of rivers that quite literally carve up these lands. Originating on the western

FIG. 3.1. Aerial photograph of the southern Pacific lowlands around Guapi.

slopes of the Occidental Andean range and meandering toward the Pacific Ocean, these rivers are joined by numerous tributaries, which create web-like structures that cut through the alluvial plains. As they approach the coastline, they often create vast river deltas, such as the Patía Delta in the southwestern department of Nariño, which extends over three thousand square kilometers. The rivers constitute the arteries of life and death of the Pacific Coast. Everything and everyone travels along this vital fluvial infrastructure. Yet the rivers are also subject to frequent flooding, especially during and immediately after periods of high precipitation, often bringing with it destruction and loss of life.

Nearly eight million hectares, or 80 percent of the region, are covered in tropical rain forest. The forest cover guarantees the availability of nutrients in the otherwise poor soils of this fragile ecosystem. Afro-Colombian architect Gilma Mosquera (1999:59) describes the area's forest, lands, and sea as a "spatial trinity." This expresses quite well the "togetherness" of the various ecological elements forming a holistic environment. I would replace "lands" with "rivers" maybe, thereby further stressing the aquatic nature of this spatial trinity.

We can distinguish between two coastal types of the littoral: a high mountainous coast that extends northward from Cabo Corrientes just

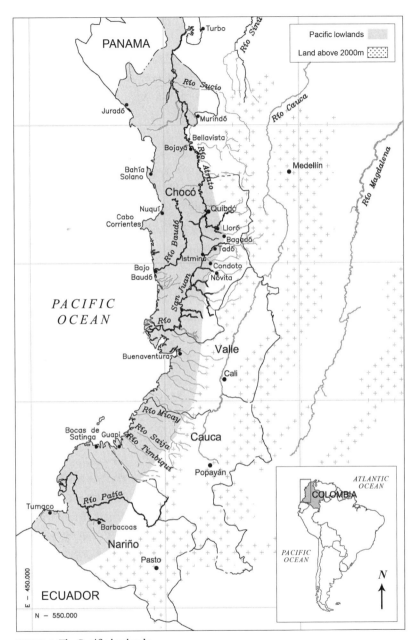

MAP 3.1. The Pacific lowlands.

south of the Gulf of Tribugá to Panama, and a low alluvial coast fringed by dense tidal forests and sandy beaches that stretches south of Cabo Corrientes for more than 650 kilometers right into the province of Esmeraldas in Ecuador (West 1957:52). Tidal ranges along the coast can reach up to 4.5 meters, which produce significant impacts up to twenty kilometers upstream, with the river channels widening twice a day in response to the tide.[2]

The southern half of the Pacific coastline is characterized by extensive and labyrinthine mangrove swamps. West (1957:53) identifies four geographic belts in this zone, arranged in sequence from the sea inland: (1) a belt of shoal water and mudflats immediately off the coast; (2) a series of discontinuous sand beaches, interrupted by tidal inlets, estuaries, and wide mudflats; (3) a zone of mangrove forest, usually 0.5 to 5 kilometers wide; and (4) a belt of freshwater tidal swamp. Behind the tidal swamp, on slightly elevated ground, the equatorial rain forests begin.

Searching for Access to the "Hidden Littoral"

Access to the region has always been difficult, which was one of the reasons the Spanish never effectively colonized this part of South America (Aprile-Gniset 1993; Romero 1995).[3] There are still only three main roads leading into the region from the interior of the country.[4] Instead the rivers are the main arteries of transport and communication. As expressed in a government report on a visit by agro-economists to the Napi River on the Cauca coast:

> Due to the geographical location of the communities that form the Napi River Community Council, they can only be reached by river. One sets off from the town of Guapi and changes onto the Napi River at its mouth. The means used up to the community of San Antonio [on the lower parts of the Napi River] are speedboats powered by large engines (60 and 70 hp or more). There, one changes to smaller dugout canoes (made out of wood), powered by small engines (9, 15, 25 and 40 hp), to reach the community of San Agustín. Access to the interior of the communities is along paths and small streams, which are the only form of penetration. (INCORA 1998d, point 1.2)

A similar journey must be undertaken to reach the communities on the San Francisco River:

Leaving the town of Guapi, the only communication route is by river. One has to travel along the Guapi River up to the mouth of the Napi River [Boca de Napi], and then keep on traveling upstream on that river until one reaches the mouth of the San Francisco River [Boca San Francisco]. The most commonly used means of transport are the wooden dugout canoes with outboard motor, or the smaller canoes with paddles and *recatón* (a paddle with an iron cover at its point). (INCORA 1998c, point 1.2)

The region's population of some 1.3 million is around 93 percent Afro-Colombian, an estimated 2 percent indigenous, and 5 percent mestizos who migrated from the interior of the country.[5] French Colombian architect Jacques Aprile-Gniset (1993) identifies two cycles of settling processes in the Colombian Pacific region. First was an Indo-American or Amerindian cycle, on the origin of which we have few data and which entered into decline at the end of the sixteenth century as a result of the Spanish conquest and colonization. Combing through archives and secondary literature in search of documented evidence of indigenous presence in the southern Pacific Coast region between Buenaventura and Tumaco, for example, Colombian historians Francisco "Pacho" Zuluaga and Mario Diego Romero (2007:112) can merely affirm that "at the time of conquest, the Patía River valley was settled by indigenous groups such as the Sindagua, Bamba and Patí, who lived along the river banks, and, sharing similar cultural characteristics, produced fairly homogenous ceramics."

Aprile-Gniset identifies the second, Afro-American cycle starting in the seventeenth century. Within this cycle he further distinguishes two phases: a partial settlement phase around the gold mines at the end of the seventeenth century, driven by processes of colonization and slavery, and an extensive drive of agrarian colonization and independent mining on the part of maroons, or runaway slaves (*cimarrones*), and self-liberated blacks, which involved intense circulation and the expansion of territorial appropriation. Both settlement phases followed an aquatic logic: colonial gold mines were located in the upper and middle sections of the rivers, where auriferous sands and gravels were deposited, and agrarian colonization and territorial appropriation by free blacks extended along the riverbanks, with the river invariably being the central axis of orientation. I discuss these settlement patterns in more detail below.

The Transatlantic Slave Trade as a Bridge between
Africa and the Americas

During the transatlantic slave trade beginning in the sixteenth century, an estimated twelve million Africans of various ethnic groups were kidnapped from their lands and kept in atrocious conditions in the prisoner camps along the West African coast, before being transported to the Americas and enslaved. Those who arrived at the slave port of Cartagena, on what is today Colombia's Caribbean Coast, were sold and moved to the gold mines of Antioquia (1580–1640), later to the Pacific Coast (1690–1810), and to a lesser degree condemned to work on haciendas and in domestic services. Some three thousand Africans, mainly Wolof and Biáfara people from the Guinea River region (in today's Senegal and Sierra Leone), entered through Cartagena between 1533 and 1580 (Del Castillo 1982:38). Between 1580 and 1640, the period of the first gold cycle in the Zaragoza Medio area of Antioquia (Colmenares 1976), 169,371 Africans, mostly from the Congo Kingdom, were officially imported through the port of Cartagena (Del Castillo 1982:18, 160–62). The real number is likely to be much higher, considering the importance of contraband in the slave trade at the time (Maya 1998:27). Both phases were controlled by the Portuguese.

The second major gold cycle was initiated around the end of the seventeenth century in the Chocó region. It corresponded to a Dutch hegemony of the slave trade (1640–1703), after the Spanish Crown had lost control over it around 1640 due to the political and economic decline of its empire and the war against Portugal, which until then had provided the bulk of enslaved Africans. This rupture resulted in a sharp decline in the introduction of new *bozales* (enslaved persons directly brought from Africa) between 1640 and 1662 (Maya 1998:31) and contributed to a "profound crisis [of the mining economy] during which the *reales de minas* of the 16th century practically disappeared" (Colmenares 1994:35).[6] Most of the Africans who arrived at Cartagena during this time were kidnapped from the Gold Coast, today's Benin. Yet a particularity of this phase was the fact that most Africans first passed through the Caribbean island of Curaçao, which was in Dutch hands, before arriving at Cartagena. Curaçao acted as a stopover before further distribution in the Americas. It thus also became a point of contact among different ethnic groups from Africa. Here the Akán mixed with the Yoruba, the Fanti, the Ibo, and the Ewe-Fon peoples, among others.

Following the Dutch hegemony, the French held a relatively short monopoly over the slave trade, from 1704 to 1713, and then the English until 1740. During these two periods the number of bozales who arrived at Cartagena dropped significantly, to thirty thousand, while a contraband slave trade from Jamaica became important (Del Castillo 1982:126). From the mid-eighteenth century until 1810, which marked the end of Cartagena as a significant slave port (Maya 1998:43; Sharp 1976), relatively few bozales were imported. Instead the owners of gold mines searched for a supply of enslaved labor largely in local markets.

The use of such an economic and dehumanizing vocabulary when discussing the slave trade is not coincidental. It echoes the historical realities at the time and the fact that African prisoners were regarded and treated as mere merchandise, a process of depersonalization that was also reflected in the jurisdiction of the colonial laws (Leyes de la India). However, it also reveals the analytical language that researchers applied when discussing this period. As Colombian historian Adriana Maya (1998) points out, the works of Germán Colmenares (1976), William Sharp (1976), and Robert West (1952, 1957), through their focus on the gold mining industries, reduce the enslaved in their analyses to their economic functions and regard them as parts of the colonial machinery. Thus they fail to treat them as the protagonists of their own history, positioning them merely as an appendix to the history of the slave system writ large.

This trend is also evident in historical accounts that represent the Republican state as the agent of freedom for the enslaved rather than the enslaved themselves as agents. West (1957), for example, refers throughout his seminal work on the Pacific lowlands to free blacks as "freedmen" (as in "those who were freed"), emphasizing with this expression—possibly involuntarily?—the passive nature of the enslaved in this process. Throughout this book I use the nongendered Spanish term *libres*, which includes both "free men" and "free women," thus stressing black agency in the self-liberating experience.

The date associated with the end of slavery in most accounts is 1851, the year its abolition was decreed in Colombia by Liberal president José Hilario López.[7] Prior to this legislation the Free Womb Law (Ley de Libertad de Vientres) was passed on May 28, 1821, which declared every newborn by an enslaved mother after this date a free person. It also introduced in Article 18 a fairly progressive notion at the time to do with land redistribution, in that libres were granted the right to work empty and uncultivated lands as their property. Owners who had abandoned their lands would thereby lose their rights over them.

Yet even earlier, libres appealed to laws of colonial justice to defend their rights. In 1798, for example, a libre named Ybarguen living in the San Francisco River basin near Guapi complained about the attempt of a slave owner to expel him from the territory and mines he had been working for two years (Romero 1993). Not surprisingly the judiciary system in such cases favored the slave owner, who was frequently the judge as well. Nevertheless it is important to bear in mind that libres were already making use of colonial legislation some fifty years before the abolition of slavery in 1851. There were also multiple forms of resistance in which the enslaved themselves acted as agents in the pursuit of their freedom. Many escaped the slavery system by running away from the mines or haciendas, a process known as *cimarronaje*. Others bought their freedom by making use of the judiciary system, a process referred to as *automanumisión*.

Aunque mi amo me mate, a la mina no voy: Embodying Resistance

"Even if my master kills me, I shall not go to the mine." So go the lyrics of a popular song in the Pacific lowlands. They serve as a reminder of black resistance during slavery times in this region. By withdrawing their bodies—essential tools of capital accumulation in the alluvial gold mines—from the production process, the enslaved hit out at the very source of their oppression. Relatively little is known—and even less documented—of these embodied experiences of resistance in the gold mines. Why is that so?

Resistance formed part of the slavery system from the beginning. As Norman Whitten and Arlene Torres (1998:17) put it, "Wherever slavery existed, self-liberation began." In fact the Pacific lowlands can be regarded as a territory of resistance, dating back to the early stages of colonization, which was confronted with bitter and long-lasting indigenous resistance. Alonso Valencia (1991) regards the Spanish attempts at conquest as a failure, considering that for nearly two hundred years the indigenous populations were never conquered. The first conflicts took place in Urabá on the northwestern Caribbean Coast in 1510, and Valencia registers major resistance as late as 1687 without the Spanish Crown able to establish central, colonial control over the Pacific lowlands. The lowlands consequently became known as a "war frontier" (*frontera de guerra*), with indigenous resistance proving a major obstacle to the exploitation of the region's gold resources. West (1957:98) observes, "Although Spanish mining activity in the Chocó began on the upper Tamaná in the 1570s, Indian hostility prevented intensive placering and the importation of many Negroes for more than a century."

Indigenous groups in the southern part of the Pacific lowlands became known as *indios de guerra*, or warring Indians, for the ferocity with which they attacked the *conquistadores*, so that Spanish settlements were mainly restricted to the Andean axis of Quito (in today's Ecuador), Popayán, and Cali. Rebellions in the gold mines too were quite common. Mateo Mina (1975:32; aka Michael Taussig) documents one such in Zaragoza, Antioquia, in 1598, which involved four thousand enslaved laborers. In another incident, on January 15, 1684, Citaraes *indios* massacred miners and Spanish missionaries in the town of Neguá (in today's Chocó Department). This incident spread like a fire and gripped the whole region, as towns and churches were destroyed (FUNCOP 1996). The Chocó rebellion forced Spanish miners and enslaved laborers to retreat to the highlands, thus preventing the exploitation of the gold placers for more than four years (West 1957:229). According to Valencia (1991), it is only from 1690 onward that we can talk of an authentic conquest, and even then resistance remained a daily practice for both indigenous and Afro-descendant populations.

Resistance took on a variety of forms, including escapes, rebellions, killings, and suicides (Friedemann 1998:83). Abortion and infanticide were frequent forms of female resistance, as enslaved mothers denied the slave owner control over their children, who would have been appropriated as labor (Spicker 1996). However, many acts of resistance either are not documented or are misrepresented in official history. The reasons for such omissions are quite obvious. According to Sabás Casamán (1997:64), an Afro-descendant elderly political leader of the North Cauca region, "Colombia's history has not been written . . . for a very simple reason. Because history is always written by the winners; the losers, we have no part in it, as long as we have this condition of losers." Remembering a verse passed on in the oral tradition, Casamán reflects on the impossibility of meaningful speech in a context of oppression (72). Here he refers to the slave owner Julio Arboleda, who was renowned for his cruelty toward the enslaved (briefly discussed in the interlude):

Aquí, aunque más se habla,
no habla sino quien pueda,
el dueño de la propiedad,
señor Don Julio Arboleda.

(Here, no matter what you say,
only speaks who can,
the owner of this property,
Mr. Julio Arboleda.)

Historical documents on black resistance, if they exist at all, are often plagued with a racist vocabulary. Black rebellions are not represented as liberating processes by historical subjects but as criminal acts that betray the enslaved people's lack of gratitude toward their masters, who saw themselves as having brought Christian redemption to ignorant pagans. According to Arocha (1999:48), these are "documents in which the Spanish never cease to be heroes while the blacks rarely are anything but cowards and traitors."

This unequal power relationship is also at the heart of the extraordinary Afrocentric novel *Changó, el Gran Putas*, written by the Afro-Colombian novelist, ethnographer, and intellectual Manuel Zapata Olivella (2010). In this unrivalled literary masterpiece—still to be fully acknowledged in literary history as such for its sheer mesmerizing narrative power and sweeping vision—in a section dedicated to the rebellion of the enslaved on Haiti at the end of the eighteenth century, the author addresses the relation between dominant history and intentional oblivion: "For the Wolf's forgetful scribes, the history of the Republic of Haiti will always be the fanaticized and hate-crazed blacks' massacre of their white brothers, never the slave owners' genocide against a defenseless people" (175; the "Wolf" being a metaphor for the white man in Zapata's account).[8]

It is important to document the myriad historical experiences of rebellion for a number of reasons. First, such documentation challenges dominant versions of history by ascribing agency to the libres that is often missing in the accounts of the "Wolf's forgetful scribes." Second, and most important to today's organizing processes of the social movement of black communities in Colombia, such a focus on agency allows for empowering connections to be made to historical resistances from today's perspective. The Pacific lowlands, once considered a territory of indigenous resistance against the colonizers of the Spanish Crown and of black resistance against slavery, is now seen by PCN activists as a territory of Afro-Colombian resistance against dominant development models fueled by the logic of displacement-inducing modernity.

Some observers will be keen to point to a homogenizing trend here in PCN discourse. They will affirm that the Pacific lowlands are instead a much more heterogeneous region with a host of varied positions in relation to the logic of modernity and capitalism. To be clear: I acknowledge the heterogeneity both in life experiences in the region and in social movement positioning. In my politics of reading the activist discourse, however, I choose to engage with the *vision* that this sector of the movement has for the region, a vision based on a notion of difference that has historically evolved in relation to various forms of oppression by dominant society that enslaved, exploited, or employed Afro-descendants in ways that those activists condemn. (Slavery obviously was an oppressive system, but, they argue, so are extractive industries such as gold mining and timber exploitation and state-led development projects today.) The fact that this is above all a political *vision* rather than a homogenously rolled-out on-the-ground reality, is unfortunately lost on commentators who, in their politics of reading, choose to foreground the many ways black communities partake in the very modernity and development projects that PCN activists denounce.

From a social movement perspective, there are no ambiguities or paradoxes in this engagement. That is quite simply what social movements do: they form in order to change realities on the ground. They do not need to represent everybody in the group for which they make claims, not even a majority. Social movements produce visions for change that often transcend the banal, the immediately obvious. As social movement scholars, it is our task to engage these visions, critically for sure, but with an understanding that goes beyond merely observable "facts" in the field. Utopias are social spaces under construction that require imagination and faith. They look forward with a profound awareness of the past. Examining the moral economies and everyday resistances that have shaped Afro-Colombian society's difference in the Pacific lowlands over the past four hundred years and making connections hitherto unseen (by the dominant gaze) is a project not only of uncovering hidden histories of resistance but of meaningfully interpreting the current moment with a view to possible futures. In many ways the Pacific lowlands still are, in Escobar's (2008) conceptualization, "territories of difference." Or, as I argue throughout this book, applying Lefebvre's ideas to the region, they may be seen as constituting a "differential space," which PCN activists see in opposition to modernity's logic of capitalist accumulation.

Palenques as Homeplace

Colombian anthropologist Nina de Friedemann (1974, 1979, 1984, 1985, 1989, 1992, 1998) has made it her lifelong work to lead historical black resistance out of its "invisibility" in academic literature and sociopolitical life in Colombia. She does so by documenting the myriad rebellions and escapes, but also the consequent attempts at social organization in *palenques*, those communities that embodied for the maroons the "homeplaces" that bell hooks (1991) talks about: places liberated from the control and the surveillance of the white man.

Palenques were fortified villages built by maroons, often located in areas difficult to access. They functioned as autonomous spaces within the colonial territory from which the inhabitants resisted colonial rule and slavery. There were frequent military confrontations between colonial armies and palenques, some of which were destroyed, while others persisted.[9] In a number of cases the Spanish Crown was forced to negotiate and acknowledge a palenque's existence. Whereas two palenques were officially registered during the sixteenth century, by the end of the seventeenth twenty palenques had been established, mainly in the Caribbean Coast region near Cartagena.

Friedemann (1998:85) documents in some detail the "numerous occurrence of palenques on the territory which today is Colombia." One of the most important of that time was the Palenque de La Matuna, founded in 1600, with its legendary leader, Benko Bioho.[10] In 1603, after a series of failed military excursions, Spanish governor Gerónimo Suazo signed the first peace agreement with the inhabitants of La Matuna. Other palenques formed in the foothill area known as the Sierra de María. They became a real threat to colonial territorial authority, as their inhabitants launched frequent attacks on garrisons and haciendas and granted safe haven to fugitives.

The most famous of all is without doubt the Palenque de San Basilio. Located some seventy kilometers southwest of Cartagena, it still exists today and has become something of a celebrity in studies of slave rebellion. It has also experienced what linguist Armin Schwegler (2012:115) calls an "ethnohistoric reinvention" since the 1970s. Historical fact, myth, and legend entwine in the story of San Basilio in not always easily discernible ways.

The first to write on San Basilio was Colombian anthropologist Aquiles Escalante (1954), who did fieldwork there in the 1950s. He detected a spoken language among residents, *palenquero*, that was entirely original. It consisted of Spanish and African languages.[11] Many of San Basilio's four thousand inhabitants still practice it today. According to Escalante, San Basilio was founded in 1713 by an entente cordiale. This pact of mutual concessions was signed between the inhabitants of San Basilio and the bishop of Cartagena, Antonio María Casiani, after attempts by Spanish colonial troops to subdue its rebellious population had consistently failed. In this pact the palenqueros committed themselves to refuse entry to more maroons who had escaped haciendas and domestic services. In return the colonial administration acknowledged San Basilio's right to self-government.

We do not know how closely the palenqueros adhered to this agreement, and if they indeed turned away newly arriving maroons. Yet they certainly applied this pact to demand their rights, as happened in 1774, for example, when they refused entry to their palenque to Coronel Antonio de la Torre Miranda, who wanted to conduct a census. To this day Palenque de San Basilio remains one of the most visible symbols of black resistance in the Americas, and its inhabitants have been referred to as the "first free peoples of the Americas" (Arrázola 1970). In 2005 UNESCO declared San Basilio a Masterpiece of the Oral and Intangible Heritage of Humanity.

Interestingly, in the popular imagination the Palenque de San Basilio has acquired a legendary status that does not shy from bending historical facts. It is common today to associate the rebel leader Benko Bioho with San Basilio, even though Bioho lived one hundred years earlier in the Palenque de La Matuna. In 1621 he was caught by colonial authorities, and hanged on March 16 that year. The international recognition of San Basilio by UNESCO seems to have further inscribed the myth of Benko as its founder. A monument to Benko in the town's central square shows the rebel leader's bust on a column stretching out his right arm to the skies, with a broken chain dangling from his wrist. For a while an inscription at the bottom of the column read, "Benkos Bioho, Fundador de Palenque, 1603."[12] Just a historical error?

Colombian historian María Cristina Navarrete (2008) has tried to shine a light on the conundrum. According to her archival research, the seventeenth century saw much maroon activity in the province of Cartagena and the establishment of a number of palenques. After the execution of Bioho and the destruction of La Matuna at some point in the 1620s, the remainder of maroons formed into new palenques. One of them was the Palenque de San Miguel Arcángel, which was renamed in January 1713 Palenque de San Basilio (171). The origins of San Basilio can thus be traced back to the second half of the seventeenth century as a result of the destruction of other palenques (Schwegler 2012:120). Naming Benko Bioho as founder of San Basilio, however, seems a bit of a stretch. Yet apart from some die-hard historians and linguists, not many people seem to be too bothered about this historical inaccuracy. Benko Bioho and San Basilio are simply the perfect couple that embody and emplace resistance in time and space.[13]

Invoking this peculiar mix of memory and myth making, Zapata Olivella (2002:97–103) beautifully brings to life the story of King Benkos in his book *Freedom's Magic Tree* (El Arbol Brujo de la Libertad). Benkos had identified a huge ceiba tree as a strategic gathering place. Following his death, it was there where maroon leaders assembled, "under the magic tree, where the sacred drums' thunderous beats would be heard by the dead no matter where they slept. . . . The choir of a thousand voices was accompanied by clapping, while sweating bodies shook to the rhythm of war bells, driven on by drums. A single wave of raised arms and heels digging deep into the belly of the earth" (97, 101). There el rey Benkos would answer them, while a furious wind was shaking the ceiba tree's branches: "I did not die. Nor did they silence my voice! The knot around my throat gave me our Ancestors' life!" (102).

The memory and the myth of King Benkos live on in today's San Basilio. Friedemann (1998:85, 95) argues, "The strategies of escape and confrontation . . . have been vital principles of the resistance and cultural creativity of the African Diaspora, which in San Basilio is still expressed in the diverse characteristics of the contemporary community: in social organization, funeral rites, and language. . . . Total deculturation did not occur."

Not only has the cultural memory of palenques survived in San Basilio, but it has also inspired contemporary articulations of the organizing processes on the Pacific Coast. Prior to the establishment of community councils beginning in the mid-1990s, some communities named their river organizations palenques. This strategic naming has enabled PCN to articulate its contemporary political project in a grounded historical and geographical imagination. I discuss this strategy in more detail in chapter 4.

Palenques on the Pacific Coast

While palenques were quite common on the Caribbean Coast, they were much less so in the Pacific lowlands. In fact the Palenque El Castigo (1732) on the Patía River is the only officially registered palenque in the Pacific region (Friedemann 1998; Zuluaga and Bermúdez 1997:38–58; Zuluaga and Romero 2007:118–48), although there is mention of others in the oral tradition, such as the Palenque de Tadó in the Chocó and the Palenque de Zanahoria.

Colombian historians Francisco Zuluaga and Amparo Bermúdez (1997) have carefully combed through the rare existing historical documentation on El Castigo, drawing in particular on the writings of the monk Fray Juan de Santa Gertrudis, who speculated on its probable existence and referred to its inhabitants as thieves and criminals. Addressing the methodological implications of examining an often distorted local history, Zuluaga and Bermúdez explain, "During almost the entire 17th century and the beginnings of the 18th century, the Patía was an ignored territory. For that reason, when one tries to research the emergence of Palenque El Castigo, it is necessary to move between the hypothetical and legend" (38).[14]

According to these authors, Palenque El Castigo emerged at some point between 1635 and 1726. The year 1732, often given as El Castigo's date of origin (e.g., Friedemann 1998:89), most likely refers to the first written confirmation of its existence in an official document by the Jesuit priest Miguel de España, who visited El Castigo after three of its inhabitants had asked the Jesuit cleric José María Manferi in Pasto for the presence of a priest among them. On his return Miguel de España confirmed this petition: "In the name of all who were hidden in that place, slaves and freemen, a priest is required to administer them the holy sacraments so that they may live like Christians, since they were so only in name, lacking as they did a priest who would educate them" (Archivo Eclesiástico de Popayán, quoted in Zuluaga and Bermúdez 1997:41).

El Castigo—the name translates as "punishment"—emerged as an ambiguous space. While the resident population, made up not only of maroons but also mestizo bandits and other runaways from the law, actively sought out religious services from church officials, they resisted the entrance into their palenque of colonial administrative authorities. Zuluaga and Bermúdez (1997:58) argue that El Castigo is important in understanding the social formation of the Patía region because "resistance practices were generated there, which found continuity and consolidation in Patía society as a maroon society."

Could it be that this continuity is found today in the resistance practices encountered by development projects that mirror the experience of Spanish colonialism's failure to successfully penetrate the Patía region? Of course capitalist modernity's priests nowadays come disguised in the more secular robes of development aficionados, and black communities are no longer the *Homo sacer* of the erstwhile maroons. Yet if we conceive of "place" as relational, then these historical connections and relations in place—the consolidation of the Patía region as a maroon society—need to be considered in order to better understand the significance of memories of resistance from today's perspective.

Automanumisión: Self-Liberation in the Pacific Lowlands

Geographical location and the structure of the slavery system in the Pacific region account for experiences of gaining freedom quite different from those on the Caribbean Coast. While most slave labor in the latter was employed on haciendas and in household work, the dense tropical rain forest of the Pacific lowlands provided the setting for the exploitation of alluvial gold mines using relatively small and mobile *cuadrillas*, or slave gangs. The organization of large numbers of maroons in palenques was not a frequent occurrence on the Pacific Coast. It was more common for the enslaved to buy their freedom in gold, which some were able to accumulate, typically working on their "days off." This practice began around 1690 and is known as *automanumisión*, or self-liberation. According to Romero (1993:28), "This seems to have been the most recurrent form for the slaves in the Pacific to obtain their freedom. There, escapes were quite rare." From 1775 onward the enslaved began to make extensive use of this option, although it has to be said that accumulating sufficient funds to buy their freedom could take years.

The legislation regarding automanumisión should not be understood as a philanthropic gesture by the Spanish Crown. Rather an economic rationale underlies its practice, considering the specific structure of the slavery system on the Pacific Coast. Gold mines were characterized by an absent owner (typically living in a city in the Andes), who left an administrator in charge of the mines and a *capitán de cuadrilla* to supervise the slave gang.[15] This capitán was frequently of African descent himself. Such a structure, together with relatively high maintenance costs for the enslaved laborers, meant that with declining profits from gold mining, it would often make economic sense for the owner of a mine to agree to an enslaved man buying his freedom. Not only was the responsibility for maintaining the enslaved laborer taken off the mine owner, but he also received significant compensation from the former. Not surprisingly it was mainly the older and less productive enslaved workers who obtained their freedom this way.

Yet in spite of declining economic returns from the gold mines, many slave owners were bitterly opposed to the abolition of slavery. Some, anticipating its end, sold their remaining slaves to make maximum profit. Such was the case (narrated in the interlude) of Julio Arboleda from Popayán, the owner of gold mines in the Timbiquí River basin. Only a few testimonies describe his cruelty. Local historian and activist Sabás Casamán remembers one of these, exposing the slave owner's brutality. This verse also includes a witty reference to the black leader Lujuria, who set out to free the enslaved on a hacienda where they had not heard about the decree of abolition. At this hacienda Lujuria (whose name means "lechery") also came across white women from Popayán:

El sanguinario Arboleda
mataba negros con furia,
pero las popayanejas
gozáronla con "Lujuria." (Casamán 1997:70)

(The bloodthirsty Arboleda
killed blacks with fury,
but the ladies from Popayán
enjoyed themselves with "Lujuria.")

Here, as elsewhere, the oral tradition recovers the enslaved, the maroons, and the libres as historical subjects, emphasizing their agency in acts of resistance. Collective memory among the communities living along the San Francisco River on the Cauca coast, for example, recalls an uprising of the enslaved, during which they threw kitchen instruments and work tools into the river. When the owner of the mine returned and saw the destruction, he called the place Cascajero ("a mess"), which is how the community got its name (INCORA 1998c). The process of naming is important in this respect. Although given to the settlement by the owner of the mine, in the cultural memory of the community the name Cascajero stands for the uprising.

Similarly on the upper reaches of the Guapi River the settlement of Balsitas, where Doña Celia was born and spent her childhood, is named after the small rafts on which maroons escaped from the gold mines. Here too the naming of the place has kept alive collective memories of resistance (INCORA 1998a, point 2.1.1).

Anansi and Other Legends of Resistance

The history of black resistance in the Americas teems with figures-turned-legend that symbolize slave revolts. Possibly the most famous of all, Mackandal in Haiti, the "first self-liberated democratic island republic in the Americas" (Whitten and Torres 1998:19), defied French colonial rule and was ascribed supernatural powers, inspiring the black rebellion on this island.[16] In Brazil it is the mystic figure of Zumbí associated with the great Quilombo of Palmares, who was resurrected after his death in the Quilombo of Cumbe to fight Portuguese colonial rule.[17] In the Caribbean it is Nanny, the beautiful priestess of Jamaica, who reigns over thunder, lightning, sun, and winds, a "great woman of burning clay, lover of the gods, who wears no more than a necklace made of the teeth of English soldiers" (Córdoba 1994:4). This woman-goddess is said to have led the maroons in their wars for freedom. Even the mosquitoes obeyed her at the hour of combat, a natural and efficient weapon against invading armies on tropical soils.

Nanny is the same figure that Arocha (1999) associates with the spider sisterhood of Ananse (hermandad de Araña), the goddess of the Fanti-Ashanti people in the Gulf of Benin, who is also known as Bush Nansi, Compé Nansi, and Aunt Nancy in Costa Rica, Belize, Nicaragua, Panama, Surinam, and Trinidad and Tobago, as well as Miss Nancy on the Colombian archipelago of San Andrés and Providencia. In his *Cuentos de la Raza Negra*, the Afro-Colombian anthropologist Rogerio Velásquez ([1959] 2000) documents numerous stories of Anance, which show her shrewdness and capacity for survival in extreme conditions of poverty.

In the Colombian Pacific region Anansi is said to possess the ability to walk on water. An informant told Friedemann and Vanín (1991:190) that his greatest desire as a child was to walk on water like Anansi, so he studied Anansi's prayer and would recite it three times before submerging himself in the waters of the San Juan River. The best results were had during holy week:

Oh, divina Anansi,
préstame tu poder!
para andar como tú
sobre las aguas del río,
sobre las aguas del mar,
oh, divina Anansi.

(Oh, divine Anansi,
lend me your power!
to walk like you
on the waters of the river,
on the waters of the sea,
oh, divine Anansi.)

Human, animal, spiritual, and waterscapes are entangled in this prayer. To walk on the waters of the river and the sea—like a spider, like Anansi—is a wish that intimately connects the riverside dweller to the aquatic space of which he forms a part. The aquatic space emerges in this account as an assemblage of relations, where the human and nonhuman cannot easily be separated.

In her beautiful book *Swamplife*, anthropologist Laura Ogden (2011) applies what she calls "landscape ethnography" to unravel the entanglements of people, alligators, and mangroves in the Everglades of South Florida. With that she proposes to "signal an approach to writing culture that is attentive to the ways in which *our relations with non-humans produce what it means to be human*" (28). Following Deleuze and Guattari's (2007) spatial philosophy, she draws on the figure of the rhizome as a metaphor to theorize the Everglades landscapes and as a writing strategy that follows more than dissects "the complex and changing assemblages of relations that dissolve and displace the boundaries of nature and culture" (29).[18] In one of her many evocative descriptions of alligator hunting, Ogden explains that the hunter "becomes alligator" in the pursuing, catching, killing, and skinning of the animal (43–66). The alligator hunters' Everglades are also an aquatic space, which comes into being through the relations of the human and nonhuman world, just as the Pacific Coast resident in Colombia quoted earlier "becomes Anansi" in his interactions with his aquatic space.

Settlement Patterns in Fluvial Territories

Contemporary settlement patterns in the Pacific lowlands are the result of processes that began with the Spanish conquest, when colonization and gold mining activities initiated what Aprile-Gniset (1993) refers to as an Afro-American settling cycle. As West (1957:97) points out, "The Pacific lowlands of Colombia were significant to Spaniards only for the rich gold placers along the upper and middle courses of rivers."

Three main centers of gold mining were established during colonial times: the area around the upper San Juan and Atrato River drainages in the heart of the Chocó, the area around Barbacoas on the Telembí River in the southwest, and the upper and middle sections of the numerous rivers between Buenaventura and Guapi (West 1957:98). Between 1605 and 1610 tentative military excursions from Popayán and Pasto established the first mining camps around the rivers Saija, Guapi, and Micay in what is today the Cauca Coast. But the first significant Spanish settlement in the Pacific Coast region was Santa María del Puerto (today's Barbacoas) on the Telembí River, established in 1610.[19]

The second phase of extensive agrarian colonization and independent mining, related to the processes of cimarronaje and automanumisión, led to the construction of a free Afro-Colombian territoriality. Contrary to what many writers claim, however, free women and men did not necessarily search for the remote areas of the Pacific rivers. Instead, following the mobile cuadrillas, they often continued to work alluvial gold mines until at some point they settled down. According to Friedemann and Espinosa (1993:564), "Some must have stopped following the slave gangs to organize themselves in family settlements of gold panners along the rivers."

The libres continued to mine, as well as work in agriculture and fishing. This led to a potentially conflictual cohabitation, in which free Afro-descendants effectively existed side by side with the slavery system exploiting the same resources. Romero (1993:28) argues, "Maybe the most difficult thing for the group of *libres* was confronting the aggression of the white miner, who saw them as competition, not only for space, but also because they attracted his slave gangs to emulate them. Slavery had entered into a new phase; it had as its neighbor the referent of the construction of a free black territoriality."

Territoriality, or the control over territory, can be exercised only in conditions of freedom. This link has important implications today, as landownership is regarded as a manifestation of a hard-fought freedom. Casamán (1997:50) explains, "Those who suffered the rigor of slavery and the persecution of the landowners knew that freedom was the possession of land. But we had a generation that did not understand this. . . . They sold their little piece of land, because they had never seen a 1,000 Peso bill before, only to go and live in inhuman conditions in the city."

With unprecedented levels of forced displacement from their lands today, black communities are losing ever more their hard-fought territoriality in the Pacific lowlands. In fact some activists refer to the current uprooting as a second exodus, following the kidnapping of their ancestors from the African continent. A prominent Afro-Colombian activist told me in 2004, "This is the second time we are being uprooted from our lands. They uprooted us from Africa. Our ancestors had to come to the Americas to serve as slaves. Then they obtained their freedom. But now, in full twenty-first century, they are displacing us from the territories that we had obtained and appropriated all this time since the abolition of slavery. And now they send us to the large cities into slums and turn us into beggars."[20]

Toward Free Black Territorialities

It was not until the formal abolition of slavery in 1851 and the decline of the gold mining economy in the Pacific region that black settlement patterns spread significantly along the riverbanks. As West (1957:87) argues, there are very practical reasons for these "outstanding features of riverine distribution of the Pacific lowland population": "Along the lower courses of streams natural levees afford the highest land, the best soils for cultivation. Similar advantages are found on alluvial terraces along the middle and upper courses of rivers. Even for non-farmers the river banks are attractive by reason of the usual abundant supply of fish, fresh-water crustaceans and molluscs, and a variety of aquatic and amphibious mammals. Moreover, rivers are the highways in this forested land where interfluves, because of their swampy or rugged nature, are hard to traverse." Poor soils, however, initially favored quite dispersed forms of settlement. With increasing population density, these turned into sporadic village-like settlements, or *poblamientos aldeanos* (Aprile-Gniset 1993:95). Aprile-Gniset identifies seven steps in a typical evolution of settling patterns among black groups in the Pacific lowlands:

1. A settler arrives in an uninhabited area along a river bank, cuts down some trees, and plants corn, plantain, and banana trees. He also constructs a *rancho*, a rudimentary shelter, for himself and for storage use. The river functions as a communication artery, as "it is intimately integrated into the everyday life of the farmers and continually participates in their multiple domestic activities" (98).

2. The settler improves the rancho and brings his family to establish a "complete habitat" (99) with proper housing, including a patio.

3. A second settler, frequently of the same family, arrives at the invitation of the first, giving rise to an "associated bifamiliar habitat." A path parallel to the river links both houses, and both families share labor between them.

4. A multifamily neighborhood is established, a *vecindario*, and a street is built that connects the houses.

5. A spatial separation occurs between habitat and productive activities in a process known as *formar pueblo*: first state institutions are established; a school and a chapel are built. A proper street of up to three hundred meters is constructed, with houses arranged in linear fashion facing the river.

6. As time goes by, a village center emerges with shops and bars, attracting merchants from outside the region. This leads to a rupture of the previously homogeneous architecture, as these merchants tend to build their houses and shops on the other side of the street,

FIG. 3.2. House construction along the banks of the Guapi River.

FIG. 3.3. *Formar pueblo*: Calle Primera (First Street) in Guapi, with storage houses facing the river.

closer to the river, thereby obstructing the view to the river for the first houses.

7. As a final step the village reaches a linear extension of almost one kilometer. The need arises for a second street, built parallel to the first one, away from the river. The state is ever more present with its institutions.

Although Aprile-Gniset (1993) gives a fairly structural perspective on the evolution of settlements among rural black populations, the general pattern that he describes can still be observed today. The organizing axis in these processes is still very much the river, giving orientation, shape, and dynamics to the settlement patterns.

Family Territoriality: Kinship Ties and the River

When people migrate from the Pacific Coast to the cities of the interior, these rural kinship ties are reproduced, and the settlement structures often give rise to an "urban village system," or *sistema urbano-aldeano* (Mosquera 1999:51), as migrants tend to stay with relatives. It is an unwritten rule for kinfolk to receive the newcomers in their house and provide them with the necessary support to survive in the city. This includes a space to sleep, food, money for transport, and all kinds of contacts that can be of help to the newly arrived to get settled. Urban migrants remain in constant contact with relatives in the Pacific river basins, sending money whenever possible to support their families there. When they periodically return to the river basins to visit, they often act as what French geographer Odile Hoffmann (1999:89) calls "ambassadors of modernity," bringing with them the latest fashion in clothes and music. The urban and the rural are intrinsically intertwined in these ways.[21]

I am interested in examining what Romero (1998:123) calls "family territoriality" in the rural setting, how a family lays claims to a territory, over time forming extended kinship ties along and between particular river basins. During one of my first interviews in the Pacific region, in April 1996, Afro-Colombian historian and poet Alfredo Vanín explained, "The family spread out along the river in such a way that there was a piece of land, the forest backland, that belonged to a member of a family that dispersed along the rivers. The land in general belonged to the family and could be divided between the children as well. But it was in the name of the head of the family. That is to say, there was ownership of the land, although it was not titled."[22]

These kinship ties to particular river basins and surrounding lands become important in my later discussion of social movement discourse, when PCN activists frame their claims for territorial rights by invoking the notion of the "logic of the river," not merely demanding land rights but referring to an ethnic-territorial life project that has at its center this intimate relation with the riverscapes.

Troncos and the River

Friedemann has examined the complex relation between kinship ties and territoriality through the notion of tronco. Observing black miners in the Güelmambí River in Nariño, Friedemann (1985:207) states that "troncos in the Güelmambí may be described as consanguineal kinship groups whose members trace their descent to a common ancestor through a line of males or females in a series of parent-child links." While the general applicability of such a highly structured representation of family relationships has been questioned,[23] Friedemann's careful attention to territorial implications in kinship ties is useful not only to understand historical patterns of a free black territoriality in the Pacific lowlands but also to further excavate these deeply embedded, intimate relations between people, lands, and river.

Friedemann (1985) observes, for example, highly systematized links between family structures and territorial rights. A tronco's common ancestor, the antepasado fundador, is considered the original owner of the lands that have been passed on to his descent group. Individual members of this descent group have rights to live on and work these lands. However, there is a degree of flexibility in the ways a person may "activate" these rights: "An individual can choose to affiliate with one tronco in preference to another through options provided by either a maternal or a paternal link. Each nuclear family unit also has the option of activating rights in any of the troncos to which either the man or the woman can trace ancestral lines. This optional affiliation creates a flexible system that can adjust to circumstances such as personal preference for residence, better mining opportunities, and cultivation on sites belonging to the woman's or man's tronco" (211). The rights of affiliation of any one individual may thus spread across a significant section of space and between different territories and river basins. This choice widens with marriage. While a man would usually bring his wife to his dwelling, the couple retains latent rights to the mine and territory of the woman's tronco, which on occasion they may choose to activate. Each tronco then owns a territory within which its members have active rights both to construct a dwelling—a process known as *parar vivienda*—and to a small plot of land near the house, the *chagra*, which they can cultivate with subsistence crops such as plantain.

Friedemann (1974:49) considers such a highly systematized social organization based on extended family links and the construction of a family territoriality a "strategy of socio-technological adaptation" to the aquatic environment in the Pacific lowlands. To coordinate and maximize the efficiency of mining activities, agricultural tasks, and construction work, the active participation of all family members is drawn upon in communal labor: "Since working the ecological medium basically consists in gathering people's physical energy, it is important for a family unit to have the possibility to invoke this help through kinship ties. . . . They are conscious of this reciprocity, as well as of the fact that help is given because 'that guy is my uncle and it is my duty' " (42).[24]

"Family territoriality" then means that identification with a family (or tronco) is at the same time identification with a particular river basin and its surrounding lands. A local miner in the Güelmambí River basin expressed this relation to Friedemann (1974:28) in the 1970s: "In this river we are all relatives."

I have heard similar expressions over and over again throughout the Pacific lowlands. The river is part of the family, and the family is part of the river. It is not surprising, then, that certain family names dominate in particular river basins. For example, on the Cauca Coast the most common family names in the Guajuí River basin are Bazán, Cuero, Martínez, Montaño, Hurtado, and Angulo (Consejo Comunitario Río Guajuí 1998). In the Micay River basin they are Riascos and Torres. The people I talked to in the town of Guapi all considered themselves *guapireños*, "people from Guapi." Yet it was important to them to point out which river they came from and that they had family there. They felt particular responsibility toward their river, and although they lived in the town center of Guapi, they felt it was their right to participate in local organizing processes in their river of origin, as their families owned land there and therefore so did they.

Social movement scholars Charles Tilly and Sidney Tarrow (2007:117) have argued that "social networks have been shown to be the crucial building blocks of social movements." As we shall see, the social networks of a family territoriality dispersed along the river basins were to become a cornerstone of mobilization for the social movement of black communities. Chapters 4 and 5 show that it is with the appeal to such a spatial logic that community councils as newly created territorial authorities were constituted from the mid-1990s onward.

The River as Space of Social Interaction

It should be clear by now that the river is central to all economic, domestic, and social activities. Houses are constructed on stilts along riverbanks, transport is river-based, fishing and collecting of shellfish are important contributors to the local diet.

The river is also the space of social interaction per se, where people bathe, women wash clothes and fetch water, and children come to play. Figure 3.4 shows an early afternoon scene of this kind at the landing steps of Guapi. Apart from the washing and playing, a number of engine-driven canoes arrive, bringing people and merchandise to town. In the background travelers wait for an embarkation to take them upriver. Here at the landing steps in Guapi this assemblage of human activity and river flow resembles an impressionist painting by Monet more than the landscapes of Constable, as people melt into the waterscape and become part of it.

The activities by the riverbank are of an almost ritual nature, accompanied by laughter, storytelling, and gossiping. This is most evident on market days, when people from surrounding settlements arrive to sell their products and stock up on necessary food items and general merchandize and also to exchange information and stories. The market, usually held along the riverbanks, is the most important and often the only source of information and means of communication for many inhabitants of more isolated communities. In these sociospatial constellations, the river emerges as a collective space of everyday social interactions that are based on cooperation and solidarity. Silveria Rodriguez, a community leader in Guapi, told me, "I remember, as a girl, I never went alone to wash clothes in the river. We were always at least four. Or to do the dishes. We always did things together."[25]

FIG. 3.4. Landing steps in Guapi, where people bathe, women wash clothes, and children come to play: the river as a space of social interaction.

Figure 3.5 shows such a scene on the Guapi River, where two women have come together to do their family's washing. I took the photo from a small boat while traveling downstream, the women's activities by the river bank a mere snapshot of quotidian life. Snap. A quick shot, and we had passed the scene. As can be seen by the exposed riverbank, it was low tide, a good moment for washing clothes in clean water.

This doing-things-together as an expression of solidarity and a collective spirit extends into the fields of agriculture and construction in rural communities. Joint labor forces are often applied to save energy and to fulfill tasks that would prove too big for an individual or for any one family. These collective forms of labor are known as *minga* when locals come together to perform work for the benefit of the community as a whole. They are referred to as *cambio de mano* when someone helps out a neighbor or relative who later repays the favor—quite literally "exchanging hands." Again Silveria Rodriguez: "In the fields we used to work in groups a lot. For example, when I went to plant a hundred plantain trees, I can't do this alone in one day. So I went with my neighbors, and we did it and got the work done together."[26]

This practice was also common in the construction process, as Teófila Betancourt, another community leader from Guapi, explains: "When

FIG. 3.5. Women washing clothes in the Guapi River.

you built your house, all the men came together. The owner of the house prepared food that day, and all the men came together. This house, well, they built it in one day. That's how everything went."[27] Although paid labor has partly replaced these relations, the traditional practices of cambio de mano and minga can still be observed and are particularly important in more isolated river sections.

Mental Maps and the Logic of the River

I want to draw briefly here on a collective mapmaking exercise to further show the centrality of the river in people's geographical imagination. From 1995 to 1999 the Geographical Institute Agustín Codazzi (IGAC 1999) carried out a project of ecological zoning of the Colombian Pacific region. This project formed part of the wider Program of Natural Resource Management, drawn up by the Ministry of Environment in 1993 in order to promote the sustainable use of natural resources and to strengthen institutional capacity for environmental management.[28] While the use of aerial photography and radar images formed a central part of the ecological zoning project, local territorial perceptions were explored in workshops of cognitive mapping. The objective was for locals to produce mental maps of what they conceived to be their territories (Vargas 1999).[29] The results of this exercise were then translated into scientific maps and served as an important tool in the process of collective land titling.

Figure 3.6 was drawn by participants in a workshop exploring local territorial perceptions in the middle section of the Atrato River in the Chocó Department. It clearly shows the centrality of the main river in the local geographical imagination. Not only was the river the first cartographic reference drawn on the paper, but it was also given the longest possible extension, from the bottom left to the top right corner of the map. Next, participants drew the various tributaries, paying attention to river channel width and noting the individual names of the waterways. The swampy nature of this environment is noted by the numerous references to *ciénagas*. Finally the locations of settlements and crops and other productive activities are identified in reference to what can be thought of as local mental river coordinates.

Such cognitive mapping exercises reveal a spatiality in the Pacific lowlands, in which *el río* refers not only to the principal river but also to tributaries and surrounding lands, as well as to the sociocultural features that make up a particular river basin.

Moreover the various river sections are intrinsically connected in this geographical imagination. Communities in the middle section or at the headwaters, for example, depend on the productive activities of communities living near the river mouth, especially the provision of fish and mollusks. As can be seen, family territoriality extends along the entire river basin; people living upstream may own lands farther downstream or vice versa. Thus the interconnectedness along a river basin is evident in terms of exchange of foodstuffs and also in terms of land distribution and property relations. PCN activists have referred to these spatialized social relationships along the river basins as "the logic of the river." It is worth quoting the description at length:

> In the logic of the river, the characteristics of land use are determined by location: in the upper section of the river, emphasis is given to traditional gold mining, and hunting and gathering activities are exercised in the forest hills; towards the middle section, emphasis is placed on agricultural production and small-scale logging, as well as hunting and gathering activities in the forest backlands; towards the lower section, emphasis is given to fishing and the gathering of shells, mollusks and

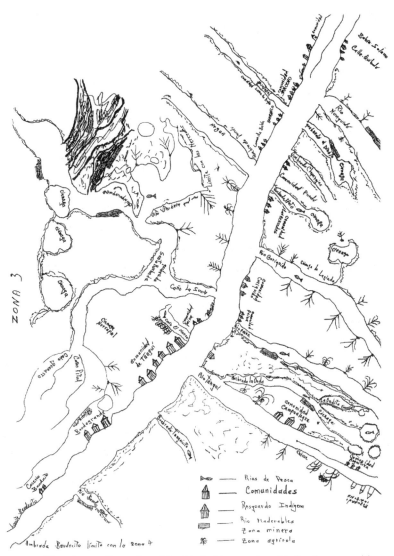

FIG. 3.6. Mental map of a section of the Atrato River produced by local communities.

crabs, together with agricultural activities. Between all sections there exists a continuous relation between the upper and the lower parts and vice versa, and of the middle section with both, characterized by a mobility that follows the natural course of the river and of nature. Its dynamics strengthen and permit kinship relations and the exchange of products, with the productive unit in these dynamics being the dispersed family along the river. (PCN 1999:1)

This context is very different from the river described in Gabriel García Márquez's ([1967] 2006) literary masterpiece *One Hundred Years of Solitude*. There José Arcadio Buendía is desperate at the backwardness of his village and enthralled by the latest magnificent scientific instruments that Melquíades and his troupe of traveling gypsies periodically bring to the people of Macondo. From false teeth and flying carpets to the secrets of alchemy, all these marvelous advances come from somewhere beyond the river; a river that separates Arcadio Buendía and his people from modernity. One day he confesses to his wife, Úrsula, in desperation, "Incredible things are happening in the world. . . . Right there across the river there are all kinds of magical instruments while we keep on living like donkeys" (8). This river separates the local and backward world from another, scientifically advanced world. The river is a border, a hindrance, an obstacle; it holds back people and their imagination.

Not so in the Pacific lowlands. There the river connects and displays a distinct spatial orientation. The river is not seen as necessary to cross (although that does of course happen as well), but to travel along, following its current. The river is not regarded as a separating but as a connecting line. One does not look beyond the river but up and down, *arriba y abajo*. The entire orientation toward the river is different from the one portrayed in Gabo's novel.

It is also quite different from other aquatic environments, such as those described in South Asia. James Novak (1993) beautifully evokes the effect of the monsoon rains in Bangladesh, for example. Referring to regular large-scale flooding during the summer months as "the time of the river," he writes:

> From mid-June to the end of October is the time of the river. Not only are the rivers full to bursting, but the rains pour down so relentlessly and the clouds are so close to village roofs that all the earth smells damp and mildewed, and green and yellow moss creeps up every wall and tree. . . . Cattle and goats become aquatic, chickens are placed in baskets on roofs, and boats are loaded with valuables and tied to houses. . . . As the floods rise, villages become tiny islands, . . . self-sustaining outposts cut off from civilization . . . for most of three months of the year. (24–25)

The time of the river refers to a temporal change in the landscape of Bangladesh as a result of seasonal monsoon rains. The landscape in the Colombian Pacific lowlands also has its own temporality, yet one that is less influenced by seasonal change than by the diurnal changes in tidal rhythms. The logic of the river is a meandering one. It goes backward and forward, upstream and downstream. And it rises and falls. Al compás de las mareas. To the rhythm of the tides.

Perhaps more than any other phenomenon, it is the tidal rhythm that has given rise to a temporality in the Pacific lowlands that resists being molded into a 24/7 clockwork of modernity. Instead the tides provide a temporal rhythm that bows to the lunar cycles, one that locals seize and run with. You go against this rhythm at your own peril. On more than one occasion did we get stuck in the mangrove swamps at low tide, when the receding waters made navigation in the shallow river channels impossible. While swarms of mosquitoes feasted on us, all we could do was wait—wait for the waters to rise to give us a helping hand. "Waiting, always waiting," as the New Model Army used to sing in bleak desperation.[30]

Convivencia acuática: Seizing the Tides

> In Guapi, a man walks the streets whose stomach inflates during high tide. With the receding waters at low tide, his stomach deflates accordingly, until it reaches its normal proportions again.
> —Story told in Guapi

The town of Guapi lies some seventeen kilometers from the Guapi River mouth at an altitude of two meters above sea level. The newcomer to the region who arrives in the morning can be forgiven if she is surprised in the afternoon by the fact that the river flow seems to have changed direction. A tidal range of 4.5 meters and a low river gradient mean that twice a day at high tide brackish water reaches far beyond Guapi. During relatively dry periods, levels of saltwater intrusion can be significant. The local activist Teófila Betancourt explains, "When it stops raining for a week, the river gets salty, because we are quite close to the sea here. Then we go upstream to Temuey, which is a fairly large stream, and the water doesn't get salty there. So we go and collect water in dugout canoes, and we use that water."[31] This also means that activities such as washing clothes in the river (figure 3.5) are performed at low tide in order to avoid the laundry's contact with salt water. Locals are very much aware of the rhythm of the tides and plan the day's activities according to the tidal clock rather than a tide-insensitive wristwatch.

Moreover at low tide the receding waters expose the coastal mangrove swamps, an important zone of ecological productivity and economic activity (West 1957:70–72). Arocha (1999:73) writes, "Only very few economic activities in the Pacific littoral are imaginable without the mangrove. During high tides, estuaries absorb the swell of the waves, thus enabling navigators to row in dugout canoes to faraway places. The great number of organisms that the mangrove areas sustain form the first link of a complex food chain in the Pacific. Its trees are used for firewood and tannin, charcoal is derived from its roots. Finally, the lives of many women depend on shells and crabs that live in the mudflats."

The women Arocha refers to are known as *concheras*, or shellfish pickers. They travel into mangrove areas, often from afar, to collect shellfish (*conchas*), which live buried in the mud. In order to extract the conchas more easily, they do so at low tide, when the mudflats are exposed. Part of the catch is sold on local markets or to middlemen. What is left provides a welcome addition to the local diet and is usually cooked at home in coconut milk. The concheras meticulously plan their travels into the mangrove areas according to the tidal rhythms, so that they may navigate more easily in their dugout canoes. The case of Doña Celia's daughter Anunciación and her daughter-in-law Luz Ofelia provides an example of how shellfish picking can be seen as an activity that draws on and coproduces the aquatic space through complex relations.

For both women the picking of shellfish is only one of their diverse economic strategies. Anunciación works mainly as *revendedora*, or reseller. She buys large bunches of *chontaduros* (the fruit of the peach palm) on the local market and then sells individual fruits for a profit in the local neighborhood. She also resells fish this way, which she buys in large quantities from fishermen at dawn. Luz Ofelia, apart from being a mother of eight children at the age of thirty-three, occasionally works in the nearby palm hearts processing plant, Alimentos Enlatados del Pacífico (Canned Products of the Pacific [ALENPAC], a case I discuss in chapter 4). When the two women arrange to travel together by *potrillo* (dugout canoe) to the mangrove estuaries downstream to pick shellfish, they calculate their departure during low tide so that the receding waters of the Guapi River speed up their journey and so that on arrival the mudflats are exposed. For their journey they take some food with them, which they prepare the day before. This is usually the traditional steamed fish and plantain dish known as *tapao*. On arrival at the mudflats, they may spend up to five hours picking shellfish. Once their task is fulfilled, they wait for the rising waters of the high tide to give them a helping hand when navigating upstream in their potrillo. This system of transport makes it possible for the concheras to travel large distances to and from the mangrove swamps with relative ease.[32]

It is not just the concheras who set their traveling schedules according to the tidal rhythm; everyone does. If that means an early departure at three or four o'clock in the morning in order to make use of high tide, so be it. Particularly longer travels upstream have to be timed carefully to make sure there is enough water in the upper parts of the river channels to allow for navigation.

On one occasion, when traveling to a youth meeting in San Antonio de Guajuí, an upstream journey of about three hours, we left Guapi at 5 a.m. As we were approaching San Antonio, the water level in the Guajuí River sank considerably, until the spinning propeller blades of our outboard motor hit the riverbed. We had no choice but to wait one hour before enough water had filled the river channel to continue our journey. As it turned out, we had set off too early from Guapi. Arriving in San Antonio before the rising waters of the high tide had made it there was clearly not an option (figure 3.7).

Such a scenario can get exacerbated during relatively dry periods, when the riverbed in the upper sections is frequently not deep enough for even a small dugout canoe to pass. As Friedemann (1974:19) observed in the 1970s, "The river is the principal street of this forest. Traveling on it in canoe is difficult in the upstream parts towards the foothills, when it is necessary to pull the embarkation or leave it behind, and keep walking along the beaches and paths that communicate one settlement with another."[33] This is exactly what Celia did in her childhood years, when she navigated the upper stretches of the Guapi River around Balsitas in her potrillo. Doña Celia remembers that, as a young girl, she often had to pull her canoe along the riverbank and around a bend before she was able to paddle again (see chapter 2).

FIG. 3.7. San Antonio de Guajuí at high tide. At low tide the river channel narrows considerably and is not deep enough for even a small dugout canoe to pass.

Lumberjacks also listen to the tides. Colombian anthropologist Eduardo Restrepo spent much time among tree cutters in the *guandal* forests of the southern Pacific region.[34] Analyzing their work patterns, he observes that the effect of the tides "not only determines the appropriate time to set off for work, but also for returning from work, so that the working days get either shorter or longer" (1996b:366). As the following section shows, logging activities are in fact dependent in many more ways on the rhythm of the tides, particularly when timber has to be transported over long distances from felling site to sawmill.

Palo bastante, coge bueno con vaciante: Logging and Tidal Rhythms

A typically overcast sky accompanied us on our way back to Guapi. Activists of the women's group Matamba y Guasá had invited me to join them on a visit to Doña Irene's marvelous *azotea*, a raised platform garden typically kept near the main lodging and planted with medicinal and alimentary herbs (figure 3.8). One of the group's main aims was to promote the use of these traditional azoteas among rural populations to increase self-sufficiency and empower women as heads of household. I was interested

FIG. 3.8. Irene Sinisterra and her impeccably kept azotea in the middle section of the Guapi River.

in this project, as it formed part of a wider recovery effort of traditional lifestyles that was framed within an emerging cultural politics in the Pacific lowlands.

A group of seven in a dugout canoe powered by a 40-horsepower outboard engine, we were returning from that visit. The wind was blowing in our faces, as spray from the river pleasantly cooled us down. The kids sitting up front were having a riot of a time and urged our captain to go faster, when all of a sudden he did the opposite, throttling the engine and slowing down to snail-like speed. What was going on?

Later in life I would get used to South Florida's "slow speed, no wake zones" in waters where manatees might be present. But on the Guapi River? Our captain had spotted a raft-like structure, still quite a bit ahead of us. As we were coming closer, I could make it out more clearly. It was indeed a raft, made of some thirty large logs tied tightly together. Four young men sat on top; one of them seemed to steer the raft with a paddle. As we approached they acknowledged our presence with a slight nodding of their heads. Our captain waved to them. A routine encounter on the Guapi River.

FIG. 3.9. Raft made of logs floating downstream, Guapi River.

Teófila, the president of Matamba y Guasá at the time, was sitting next to me. She explained that these young men had been cutting trees at the Temuey tributary upriver. They had tied the logs together to form a raft and were now on their way to the sawmill at the northern end of the town of Guapi. They had waited for low tide to make navigation easier. Our captain had slowed down so that the waves we generated would not endanger their raft. We had entered the "slow speed, rafts and potrillo zone" of the Pacific lowlands. Shortly after, we went again full throttle, the kids up front squealing their delight into the still overcast sky.

This brief raft encounter embodied the workings of the aquatic space as an assemblage of relations in which the human and the nonhuman interact in complex ways. Escobar (2008) refers to the dense networks of relations and materiality in the rivers of the Pacific lowlands as "relational ontology." Tidal rhythms, the mangrove and its microorganisms, its aquatic and amphibian life (crabs, shrimp, shellfish, fish), and even supernatural beings come together to constitute a world that is enacted minute by minute, day by day, through an infinity of practices that connect a multiplicity of human and nonhuman beings. The process of traditional logging further shows how these human (tree cutters) and nonhuman (forest, waterways) relations co-constitute the aquatic space.

Timber extraction is group work, and it depends on the aquatic infrastructure of the forest. Once felled, the tree is pulled over the forest floor to a nearby water channel or river. There, depending on the channel's width, various logs are tied together with natural fibers to form a raft, which then floats downstream until it reaches the sawmill. Restrepo's (1996c:252–53) detailed ethnography of the *tuqueros*, the tree cutters in the guandal forests of Nariño province, describes two distinct and complementary forms of transporting the logs. One way is over land and requires the temporary construction of *carreteras* (literally "roads") by placing thin logs some three meters apart and parallel to one another from the felling site to a watercourse. The felled tree (*tuco*) is then pulled over these logs until it reaches the waterway on which it can be transported downstream. A longer lasting "road" for the transport of logs is often constructed in the form of ditches of one meter in width and two meters in depth. These *cunetas* fill up with water after prolonged periods of precipitation or at high tide. When they fill with enough water, the logs are placed in them and floated to a larger and wider waterway. Both cunetas and carreteras constitute the fundamental infrastructure for timber extraction on the southern Pacific Coast.

Once the logs are tied together as a raft, the tree cutters travel on them to direct, steer, and protect them. This journey can take hours, even days, depending on the distance to be covered and the tidal impact. Again, at low tide the raft travels faster downstream than at high tide, when it would be going against the river's flow direction. The tuqueros are usually well prepared for these trips, carrying with them cooking utensils and foodstuffs such as plantains. Fish can be caught in the river, or occasionally it has already been prepared before departure. Although it is usually men who cut the trees and deliver them to sawmills, frequently their wives help in this task.

Doña Celia, for example, remembered going logging with her husband in the forests around the Temuey River. At the end of the working day they would build a raft with the felled logs and travel downstream until they reached the Guapi River. There they would wait for high tide to help them travel upstream until they reached the sawmill. So it was the double effect of the tides upon which they depended for transporting the felled logs to the sawmill. All of this was achieved without any powered engines, using only the natural rhythm of the tides, careful calculation of the precise time to travel, and one's steering ability while navigating the fluvial infrastructure in the Pacific lowlands. Doña Celia remembers:

The trees we cut went to Don Nicolás. He had the sawmill here in Guapi. When he moved the sawmill to where it is now [farther upstream], we had to take the logs up there. All the timber we cut was from Temuey. At low tide we transported the logs to the mouth of the Temuey [River]. And when the water rose, we moved it upstream from the mouth of the Temuey, on a raft. That took some two to three hours. When there were a lot of logs, we just sat on top of them. You travel like in a canoe. And with your paddle, you help the water. . . . I didn't like just sitting quietly on the raft. I preferred to help it move more quickly. And the other one [her husband] as well. The moment we climbed onto the raft, we helped the water to move us. To the sawmill of Nicolás Martán. Once we moved seventy-five logs from Temuey to the sawmill. First we came down with them during low tide to the mouth of the Temuey, which was a small tide. It gave us just about enough water to travel downstream to the mouth of the Temuey. And from there, plam, plam, plam, from here to there. You know of course that lots of logs side by side travel fast at low tide.

Palo bastante, coge bueno con vaciante—"Lots of logs side by side travel fast at low tide." This saying encapsulates the complex relations in traditional logging activities through which the aquatic space is constituted.

While I have so far emphasized the "traditional" activities in my discussion of the place-based aquatic relational ontology in the Pacific lowlands, I also want to point to the impact of an ever deeper penetration of modernity into the region, which has invariably led to a reshaping of some of the activities described. Evidence in the 1970s, for example, already suggested that dynamite was used at times in river fishing (Friedemann 1974:20; see also Restrepo 2013:222). In the Napi River on the Cauca Coast this has resulted in a significant depletion of fish stocks through indiscriminate killing (IIAP 2000:89, 135, 236).[35] Such a practice raises questions about the putative sustainability of natural resource exploitation by rural populations. Arocha (1999:156) has referred to this ambiguity as "contradictory ecosophy," while Villa (1998) warns against the construction of what he calls an "illusory sociologism," assuming that rural black populations necessarily live in harmony with the environment, when many of them are actually involved in environmentally damaging activities, such as large-scale timber extraction and gold mining using mercury.

Moreover the introduction of mechanical dredges and hydraulic equipment in the exploitation of gold mines along the rivers has contributed to an alteration, and in some cases even a sterilization, of the ecological landscape. In April 1999 fishermen on the Timbiquí River complained to me about drastically reduced catches and deformations of some fish, which they linked to the use of mercury in the gold extraction processes applied farther upstream. In spite of a court order to stop these activities, gold mining continued in Cotete in the upper reaches of the Timbiquí River. The mayor of Santa Bárbara de Timbiquí was simply too afraid to act against the miners there, as powerful interests were behind these investments.

Similarly around the same time in San Antonio de Guajuí, local communities tried in vain to expel *retroexcavadoras* from their territory; these backhoes and retro power shovel earthmovers clear rain forest and chew up river bottoms and banks. Recent years have seen a huge increase in industrial gold mining throughout the Pacific lowlands, fanned by skyrocketing global gold prices, which set off a veritable gold rush in 2010 and 2011, although there are indicators that this trend is beginning to slow down as global gold prices have declined significantly since 2014.

One may argue that the aquatic space itself is being transformed, with locals often deeply entangled as agents in these technologies and processes. This is of course precisely the point of conceptualizing the aquatic space, following Deleuze and Guattari (2007), as a temporary site of assemblage of always *changing* relations. And these changes are imbued with conflict. When PCN activists denounce these changes as an attack on the long-standing aquatic relational ontology in the Pacific lowlands, they defend a world understood through and based on "local models of nature" (Escobar 2008), or what Restrepo (2013) calls a *gramática local del entorno*, a local environmental grammar. If we consider these changing relations in Lefebvrian terms—thereby politicizing them in ways relevant for my argument about the geographies of social movements—the aquatic space emerges in activist articulations as a differential space, which gets mobilized in a cultural politics that defends these particular constructions (or local models) of nature.

The logic of the river, as I have outlined, is but one manifestation of this relational ontology, one that has found particular expression in both social movement discourse and practical application in the field. As I show in the following two chapters—thereby moving the discussion into the political field proper—the spatial and territorial ordering logic of the river has taken on concrete forms in the formation of the newly sanctioned territorial authorities of the community councils, which were set up, by and large, along the river basins on the Cauca Coast, often contrary to what government officials had in mind.

FOUR

Mobilizing the Aquatic Space
The Forming of Community Councils

Colombia's new Constitution of 1991 marked a watershed in the relations between the state and the country's Afro-descendant population. Until then "black" Colombians were not formally regarded as a differential category, as was, for example, the indigenous population, which had been subject to special legislations since colonial times. As British anthropologist Peter Wade (1993) has repeatedly argued, the indigenous was the "other" in Colombia. *Indio* was an administrative category, and Colombia's indigenous population was counted in official census data. "The 'indio' was definitely an institutionalized identity. . . . The category 'black' has historically not been defined and has often been ambiguous" (Wade 2005a:10, 11). A black Colombian was just that: a black Colombian, *un negro*. Racialized stigma was attached to this reference for sure. But no official acknowledgment of difference was made. Colombia was characterized by a racial order in which black people were both included (as ordinary citizens, participating in the overarching process of *mestizaje*) and simultaneously excluded (as inferior citizens who only marginally participated in national society and were discriminated against). This, in a nutshell, outlines the ambiguous workings of the ideology of racial democracy.[1]

All of this was to change with the new Constitution. Or would it? In the 1980s Colombia was "on the brink of chaos," as one publication put it (Leal Buitrago and Zamosc 1991). The closed bipartisan political system, tightly controlled by the Conservative and Liberal parties, had ensured the exclusion of broad sectors and movements from political participation. At the same time, powerful guerrilla movements, right-wing paramilitary groups (often supported by the armed forces), widespread corruption, and the all-pervasive influence of the illicit drug trade had reduced the legitimacy of the state in the eyes of many and brought governability nearly to a standstill in the late 1980s. Decentralization was designed to diffuse tensions within a framework of broader and more inclusive political participation. Above all it aimed at strengthening democracy at the municipal level and bringing government closer to the people. One step in this direction was the popular election of mayors from 1988 onward. Another was the passing of a new Constitution in 1991. As the country hoped to redefine itself and diffuse political tensions, it aimed at opening up channels of political participation to hitherto marginalized groups. Recognizing Colombia's cultural diversity was part of this realignment of the nation-building narrative.

When the Constituent Assembly met in 1990, charged with drawing up a new constitution, some voices called for the formal recognition of the country's black population as a differential cultural group within the nation-state. I want to stress two principal outcomes here as they pertain to the Afro-Colombian population. First, for the first time black Colombians were recognized as an ethnic minority and thus worthy of protection as a cultural group. Second, a transitory article (AT-55) was attached to the Constitution at the last minute that opened a path for later legislation to grant collective land rights to rural black communities in the Pacific Coast region. This law was passed in August 1993 and became known as Ley 70, or Law 70 (Diario Oficial 1993). The potential scope of this legislation was tremendous, as it opened up five million hectares, 50 percent of the entire Pacific Coast region, for collective land titling. Black communities would emerge as the legally recognized territorial authority in these lands, and anyone interested in exploiting natural resources on these lands would have to deal directly with the communities affected. Law 70 states that "in order to receive the awardable lands as collective property, every community will form a community council as a form of internal administration" (Chapter 3, Article 5; Diario Oficial 1993). Regulating Law 70, Decree 1745 of 1995 prescribes the steps that a rural community has to follow in the creation of a community council "as the highest authority of internal administration within the lands of black communities" (Chapter 2, Article 3).

I am not interested in critically examining the real possibility of wider social change in Colombia through these constitutional provisions. They may well turn out to be just another "rhetorical make-up" of the type that Eric Hobsbawm (1990:42) observed in the "absurd regimes typical of many parts of South America during the 19th century, characterized by a rhetorical, formal constitutional innovation, by a few social and economic changes and a chronic political instability." I also do not want to go into great detail at this stage into what may appear to be a glaring contradiction at first: the fact that a neoliberal Latin American state in the 1990s formally defers part of its territorial authority to an ethnic minority within a wider framework of multiculturalism. Suffice it to point to the work of Charles Hale (2002), who outlines the logic behind what he calls "neoliberal multiculturalism," which functions as a cultural project that partly responds to indigenous demands while containing them in a broader neoliberal order. He calls this the "paradox of simultaneous cultural affirmation and economic marginalization" (493). From this viewpoint not much seems to have changed from Wade's earlier affirmation regarding the inclusion/exclusion entanglement of official mestizaje discourse.

In chapter 5 I examine in detail the legislation pertaining to the Colombian version of neoliberal multiculturalism and return to some of these concerns. Here, however, I want to look at the ways in which the aquatic space—as relational ontology—is reflected in the context of political mobilization in the early 1990s. I want to hold back legislative speech and political theory for a moment and ask instead: What happened in the river basins where these newly sanctioned community councils were to be established? What did fishermen, concheras, gold panners, and tree cutters make of these changes? How would their world change? Would it? How would their knowledge be used to make sure these political changes writ large would be meaningful on the ground? How would the everyday geographies of the aquatic space be mobilized? Or would the logic of the river be bent to accommodate other interests in the region?

To answer these questions I first examine how the spatialized social relationships of black communities along river basins have been fundamental in the constitution of community councils. Then I show how political mobilization in the Pacific region has been mediated by capital interests and the state, both of which pursue their own, often related interests in these processes. It is precisely these entanglements between state discourse, capital's profit-seeking drive in the region, and the local organizing processes that I aim at highlighting in this chapter. These entanglements are responsible for at times very different experiences in the formation of community councils. But let's start this journey, quite literally, on the river.

Organizing along the Rivers

Along the rivers, people with their singing, dancing and their games now have other reasons to meet. It is not anymore only the ritual encounter with the saints or with their dead. Now the *decimero* arrives at the meeting to remind them of how the river organization was born; to evoke the journey that some of the community made to Bogotá in order to talk about the territory for which they fought and to tell of what life was like for the people of the Pacific. Singing and dancing are integrated in the dimension of the political meeting. The elderly tell the history of the river settling processes. They mark on maps the places where the first elders settled. They tell the histories of slaves and masters, of food and celebrations of the past, of Indians and blacks, of history, which in the meeting becomes the bearer of identity. But the journey on the river is not only the oral exercise. It is also the real journey; the one that the settlers of the San Juan River embark upon over various days in 1992 from the delta to Istmina. Hundreds of the Peasant Association of the San Juan River embark in their boats and stop in each village, getting off with their *chirimía*. And from the beach they put color into the meeting with *jotas* and *contradanzas*.[2] The journey is a geographical recognition of a territory that they now understand as theirs. (Villa 1998:444–45)

This is how Colombian anthropologist William Villa describes the sheer enthusiasm with which black communities in the Chocó Department embarked upon the historical journey of legalizing their territorialities. Law 70 set off an "hora de encuentro" (Villa 1998:443), a time of meetings, throughout the rivers of the Pacific lowlands. River organizations were formed and mobilized. Their representatives began to debate the new legislation and the possibilities that it opened up and to discuss the kind of future they wanted for the Pacific region. Shared histories of rural black populations were evoked in numerous meetings along the riverbanks and collective memories mobilized to reflect upon the past, but also to look ahead by projecting *their* vision for the region. The elderly and *decimeros* like Don Agapito (whom we met in chapter 2) had important input into the reconstruction of an Afro-Colombian collective memory that would be put to political ends. Traditional musical rhythms filled the Pacific air. Tradition was present. But (political) change was on its way.

In these meetings an "ethnic-territorial" identity was forged that defended black peasants' rights to cultural difference as intrinsically linked to their gaining and sustaining control over their territories. As one of the most influential organizations, the Process of Black Communities, would later state: "The ethnic-territorial organizations of black communities do not only plan the appropriation but also the *defense of the territory from a perspective past-present-future*, which understands, assumes and develops the tradition and the history of resistance of Afro-Colombians and their aspiration to maintain, develop and realize a *different and alternative life project* together with the indigenous peoples as ancestral inhabitants of these territories and the region" (PCN 1999:2, emphasis added). The reference to an Afro-Colombian tradition of resistance is telling here, for PCN thus establishes a link between the current mobilization of ethnic-territorial appropriation in the Pacific lowlands and the larger history and experience of resistance against slavery. Territory was and still is crucial in these struggles. Just as the *palenques* represented a free black territoriality within the colonial state, the community councils should emerge as territorial authorities within the Colombian nation-state. At least that was the hope.

Henri Lefebvre would have been excited to chart these processes, as they so clearly articulate the movement's "quest for a counter-space" ("different and alternative life project") that draws on a historically and spatially sedimented concrete space ("defense of the territory from a perspective past-present-future"). This quest is materially embedded in the locale, as it draws on the river networks as (re)sources for mobilization. Communication of the new legislation meanders from one riverine settlement to the next, and the "fluvial messengers" of the river organizations pass the word around, just as Doña Celia did in her childhood, only this time the message is of political processes.

The leaders of the river organization ACADESAN filmed such a journey and later edited it as the visual testimony of the Primera Expedición Fluvial de Autodescubrimiento Territorial y Defensa de Identidad Étnico-Cultural por el Río San Juan (Stemper 1998:170–71), the First Fluvial Expedition of

Territorial Self-Discovery and Defense of Ethnic-Cultural Identity along the San Juan River. The video tells the story of the more than six hundred members of ACADESAN who traveled by boat and canoe on the San Juan River during October 1992 from the river mouth to the town of Istmina to spread the word of the coming legislation.[3] The main river and its countless tributaries functioned in this context as the "aquatic street network" essential for the communication process.

Three years later, following Decree 1745 of 1995, black communities began to form into community councils that could apply for collective land titles.[4] Most of them decided to take their respective river basin as a spatial organizing unit (with some important exceptions that I discuss below). This is apparent, for example, in both the spatial constitution and the naming of the community councils Río Napi and Río San Francisco in the Cauca Department. In both cases the area delimiting the community council's territory comprises the lands around the entire river basin and includes the headwaters and the mouth of the particular river.

Yet more than merely in terms of its physical location, the river basin must be understood in its sociocultural meaning for local communities. In the case of the settlement of La Soledad, it becomes apparent how a particular sense of place, rather than cartographic location, has informed the spatial organizing structure of the community council. La Soledad is a village of about six hundred inhabitants at the headwaters of the Guajuí River, some twenty-five kilometers from the river mouth (map 4.1). Shallow depths and numerous rapids in the upper reaches of the river prevent navigation for the last five kilometers, even for small dugout canoes. The principal route of communication is a trail that connects La Soledad to Belén, a settlement at the headwaters of the neighboring Napi River, which can be reached on foot in around two to three hours. As a result the inhabitants of La Soledad are more connected physically, commercially, and emotionally to the Napi than to the Guajuí River. All merchandise destined for La Soledad, for example, is transported via the Napi River to Belén, and then on the trail to La Soledad. People from La Soledad who need to go to Guapi do so by traveling on the Napi River. The physical location of La Soledad at the headwaters of the Guajuí River seems topographically accidental in this context. Locals do not feel attached to this river. Instead the inhabitants of La Soledad have developed a strong sense of belonging to the Napi River.

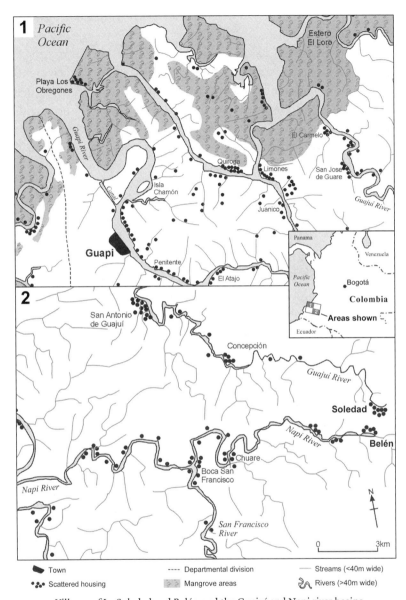

MAP 4.1. Villages of La Soledad and Belén and the Guajuí and Napi river basins.

When it came to forming community councils in the region, the inhabitants of La Soledad made it clear that they wanted to be part of the community council of the Napi River. This intention was at first rejected by leaders of the Guajuí River Association ASODERGUA,[5] who initially argued on grounds of physical location that La Soledad should belong to their community council. However, these leaders were of course attuned to the desires of the people of La Soledad and quickly gave in. Locale (or local geographical imagination) won out over cartographic location, and today the population of La Soledad forms part of the community council of the Napi River. (Moreover the first and long-standing legal representative of this community council was from La Soledad.) In other words, the aquatic sense of place was mobilized as a tool in the constitution of this community council.

Entanglements of State and Capital in Local Organizing Processes

The organizing processes of black communities take place within a field of shifting power relations. The very constitution of community councils has affected, or is perceived as affecting, a whole range of interests in the region. In the local political arena, for example, some community councils have pointed to the lack of support and even open hostility from mayors, who are powerful political figures in the region.[6] The legal representative of the Community Council, Guapi Abajo, explains:

The politicians didn't want Law 70. They feel it gets in their way. It won't let them keep pushing the people around the way they like to. We even experience this with the mayor now. He doesn't want to know that the community council is the people's highest authority in their territory. He doesn't want to understand this. Look, as the legal representative of the council, I was one of the mayor's best friends before he took office. And I thought that with this mayor in place, our community council would benefit more. But now the opposite is true. . . . Law 70 is a law for black people. And the mayors, being black, why are they not proud of Law 70? This hurts me a lot. I would like to have a space, a media, where I can make this public to the world, well, for the world to be aware of this. Because they [the mayors] will have to explain one day to the communities why they hate Law 70, why they don't want to understand that in reality Law 70 belongs to the black people.[7]

Although not all community councils have had such a negative experience with their mayor, it is clearly not necessarily a harmonious relationship. Some mayors see Law 70 and the constitution of community councils as curbing their own political influence and power. Traditional party politics and clientelism are so deeply embedded in the political and social structures in the Pacific Coast region that the emergence of community councils as political actors is bound to upset the interests of some mayors and other local politicians, many of whom fear seeing their political influence evaporate in the humidity and heat of the Pacific rivers.[8] Therefore, although "the mayors are black," "race" as a mobilizing category does not *necessarily* act as a unifying force in the struggle of black communities to attain cultural recognition and territorial rights. Issues of class, gender, and the complex power relations in the region have to be examined in more detail to account for the relation between "new" and "old" political identities, their entanglements, and the differences in organizational experiences *within* black communities.

The community councils are new political spaces, deeply entangled with local political structures and economic interests, at times challenging them, at others cooperating with them. To illustrate these aspects I examine the creation of the Community Council Unicosta in the Department of Nariño and show how the processes of community representation were mediated in this case by the interests of capital on the one hand and by government institutions on the other. I then discuss in more detail strategies by the Colombian Institute of Agrarian Reform (INCORA) to influence and shape the organizational processes of black communities.[9] As one of the social movement leaders in Nariño pointed out when reflecting on movement strategies, "If we don't have clear criteria with relation to government institutions, we can easily fall into their clientelist webs" (Cortés 1999:138).

Entanglements, Part 1: Enter Capital

The Community Council Unicosta lies in the municipality of Iscuandé in the northwestern part of the Department of Nariño with a population of about 1,500.[10] INCORA awarded an area of 16,063 hectares as collective lands to the community council in Resolution 158 of February 9, 1998 (IGAC 1999:99). Unicosta was the first community council to be awarded a collective land title in the Department of Nariño. There were good reasons for this.

For sixteen years the company ALENPAC (Alimentos Enlatados del Pacífico, Canned Products of the Pacific) had been exploiting lands in this area for the extraction of palm hearts from the *naidí* palm tree. The naidí—in Colombia often referenced as *Euterpe cuatrecasana* but more commonly as *Euterpe oleracea*—is a rock star in the palm world today.[11] A slender and elegant clustering palm species native to northern South America, it produces a small, edible black-purple fruit that contains a single large seed. Also known as açaí berry, it is all the rage among health food enthusiasts in the Global North for its high concentration of antioxidants. Consumption of açaí fruit pulp is also said to reduce levels of metabolic disease risk in overweight adults (Udani et al. 2011). It is quite simply the superfruit of the twenty-first century.

While modern health gurus have only relatively recently begun to bow to the magic of the açaí berry and spread the word, the naidí has long been appreciated by locals in the southern Pacific Coast, where its fruit is made into sweetened snacks or a thick, deep-purple-colored juice, the much beloved *pepiao*. In common parlance, the fruit is *bueno pa' la sangre*—good for the blood—giving physical strength and increasing sexual potency. In the complex classification and valuation system of rural black populations, it is considered a "cold food," its consumption forbidden, for example, to women during their menstruation cycle, when they require "hot foods" (Restrepo 1996b:355–56).[12]

The palm tree itself is considered a wild plant, as it belongs to the forest and is not cultivated. It is therefore subject to destruction, which, given its perceived abundance, is not seen as problematic. Traditionally the palm is felled in order to collect the fruits. No attempt is made to conserve the tree (Restrepo 1996b:357), although more recently the fruit is also collected by climbing up the tree, machete in mouth, an activity often performed by children (figure 4.1). Increased pressure on the *naidizales* (palm stands), however, has led to an acute awareness that this abundance is indeed only perceived. Accelerated extractive exploitation has led to a scarcity of the palm, which is felt on local markets by sharp increases in the price of the fruit.

Now, you don't mess with the naidí in Guapi and the surrounding area. During my six-month stay in the field in the late 1990s, I could feel the emotions rising as locals loudly deplored the lack of their beloved pepiao. The blame was squarely placed at the door of ALENPAC, the palm hearts can-

FIG. 4.1. Boy climbing a naidí palm tree to collect the fruit.

ning plant on the outskirts of Guapi. For not only does the naidí palm provide fruit-induced joy for locals; it also produces a premium-quality heart of palm, highly regarded on the global gourmet circuit (while shrugged off with disdain by the river's daughters and sons).

The swift journey from forest to can is roughly as follows (worth bearing in mind the next time we sink our teeth into a tender piece of palm heart). First step: a harvester cuts down a naidí palm. Second step: the almost one-meter-long palm heart at the top of the tree is cut out. Third step: the *palmiche*, as the palm heart is locally referred to, is delivered in bulk to a storage center and then to the processing plant in Guapi. Fourth step: the palm hearts are peeled, cooked in a hot steam bath, cut into pieces, and placed in cans. Final step: the finished product, referred to as *palmito*, is shipped in bulk to Buenaventura, Colombia's largest port, and from there to export markets, mainly in Europe. In the 1990s France was the only buyer for ALENPAC. Now that's one heck of a journey for a happy palm heart . . .

ALENPAC received its first permit for palm heart exploitation in 1982 (issued then by the National Institute of Renewable Natural Resources, IN-DERENA) over an area of 5,065 hectares in the municipalities of Iscuandé and El Charco (ALENPAC 1990). This permit was renewed twice, in 1990 and 1993, over the same area (Vallejo et al. 2011:197). However, following Law 70 of 1993 these proceedings have changed. Corponariño, the regional development corporation, now issues an exploitation permit to the community council, which then contracts the company (Decree 1791 of 1996).

ALENPAC's director was well aware of this change, so he promoted the formation of a community council that would encompass the lands from which the company was extracting palm hearts. The only logic of formation of this community council was to be the capitalistic logic of accumulation, not the ancestral logic of the river. To this end the director financed workshops in eight communities on issues regarding Law 70, produced handouts, and gave operational and logistic support in arranging meetings. He also provided the necessary means to complete the application for a collective land title to be made to INCORA by local communities. It should come as no surprise, then, that both the president and the coordinator of the newly formed community council were contractors of the company. In April 1999 Corponariño issued a permit for the extraction of naidí palm hearts to the Community Council Unicosta over an area of 6,850 hectares.[13] In return the community council granted an exclusive contract for exploitation to ALENPAC. Clearly in this case the co-opting and mediating power of capital managed to successfully shape community representation according to its own interests.

In order to legitimize its intervention in the organizing processes of black communities, ALENPAC frequently appealed to the supposed sustainability of the naidí palm hearts extraction process (a requirement for all production practices following Law 70). In one of my visits to the processing plant in Guapi in February 1999, the administrator took great pride in pointing out that ALENPAC had opted for "sustainable forest management" (*manejo sostenible del bosque*) as a strategy to guarantee the naidí's natural reproduction. The company rejected the alternative strategy of reforestation and plantations of naidí palm trees on the grounds that pests might be provoked in this way.[14] If one wanted to be a bit more cynical, one could argue that the latter strategy would also be far more expensive for the company to implement. In all, ALENPAC's arguments neatly reflected the wider official discourse of "sustainability" that spread through the Pacific Coast region in the 1990s (see Asher 2009; Escobar 2008; Escobar and Pedrosa 1996; Hoffmann 2004).

At first sight, ALENPAC's enterprise seemed indeed a promising venture for local sustainable development. Although it appeared irrational to cut down a whole palm tree for the extraction of a single palm heart, the company argued that with good management only the mature shoots of the palm tree cluster would be cut, leaving the younger shoots to keep growing. A typical naidí cluster consists of between twenty-five and forty-five palm shoots that can reach a height of up to sixteen meters. Thus, so the logic went, a palm cluster could be harvested for up to fifteen years. Moreover, as the administrator pointed out to me, in contrast to other extractive activities such as timber and gold mining, the palm hearts were processed locally in the canning plant, thus providing employment for up to fifty people in Guapi. Sounds good?

Alas, the complete picture looked somewhat different, and serious doubts were raised over the claimed sustainability of the extraction process. While the naidí palm does indeed reproduce fairly quickly as an invasive species if allowed to regenerate, one of the main problems was in the management of the extraction process. First, the harvesters were not employed by the company; they were simply paid for the number of palm hearts they delivered to storage centers and the processing plant. In February 1999 the company paid 130 COP (Colombian pesos) for each palm heart received, a whopping US$0.10. By March 2010 this had gone up to 200 COP, still equivalent to only US$0.10 (Vallejo et al. 2011:200). For the individual cutter, only a bulk harvest of at least 150 palm hearts made the labor worthwhile. As a result harvesters often extracted not only the mature shoots but also the younger ones to increase the number of palm hearts delivered. Moreover it is hard work to cut around the young shoots to reach the mature ones; to make the task easier and to speed it up, harvesters quite simply often prefer to cut the younger shoots as well (Restrepo 1996b:366–67).

Second, it was quite common for the processing plant in Guapi to receive palm hearts extracted not only from the sites in Nariño for which ALENPAC had an exploitation permit but also from surrounding areas. This was of course illegal. Yet on one of my visits to the processing plant I noticed a dugout canoe filled to the rim with naidí palm hearts arriving from Penitente, a settlement on the Guapi River across from the plant. Although the company's administrator assured me that ALENPAC did not receive any deliveries of palm hearts from areas other than the designated sites for which they had exploitation permits, I observed how the plant workers went straight to processing the recent delivery.[15] Taken together these factors have contributed to a significant depletion of the naidí palm in the southern Pacific Coast.

As for providing significant local employment, it should be noted that labor in the processing plant in Guapi was seasonal and that the entire process was dependent on external markets. Then, in March 1999, ALENPAC closed its doors, as the company's only clients in France had started to import the cheaper *chontaduro* palm hearts of the peach palm tree from Ecuador. Not only did the workers at the plant lose their jobs, but the harvesters no longer had a recipient to sell the palm hearts to. Local opinions of the company's director changed rapidly from seeing him as "the gentleman from Bogotá" who provided work (*el caballero de Bogotá*), to "the guy who did not keep his word" and abandoned the workers (*el tipo que no cumplió*).

In 2004 ALENPAC reopened its processing plant in Guapi, now as a cooperative employing fifty workers, the Cooperativa de Trabajadores de Palmito (COOTRAPAL), with the former owner and administrator still in charge.[16] Permits were given to the Community Council Unicosta in 2006 and 2009 for the naidí extraction of a total of 4.5 million shoots.[17] The legal representative of the community council is the same since day one, Florentino Carvajal. The problems of unchecked and overexploitation of the naidí palm also remain the same. A recent, utterly fascinating report on the matter concludes, "The history of palm heart exploitation on the Colombian Pacific Coast has been characterized by disorganization and the lack of management, research and environmental conscience" (Vallejo et al. 2011:208).

I have dwelled on this case of ALENPAC and Unicosta, as it illustrates well how the specific interests of capital in retaining control over a territory for its continued exploitation were legitimized by discourses of sustainability and how they were channeled into processes of mediation and co-optation of local organizations. The formation of the Community Council Unicosta followed less the spatial logic of the river basin as organizing structure than the specific demands of capital.

What is worrying about this scenario is the fact that naidí exploitation seems to replicate the boom-and-bust cycle of its predecessors in the Pacific lowlands: rubber, tagua (ivory nut), and tannin (see Whitten 1986). The invariably busted outcome of all these extractive economies has left a devastating legacy for local communities, as natural resources are depleted and locals find only temporary work in unstable and uncertain conditions. The implications for local organizing processes are clear. If a community council is formed around the extractive logic of naidí exploitation, and this industry falls into decline, then the community council loses its very raison d'être. Breaking with the logic of the river in favor of capital demands has potentially set off a spatial segregation of the river basin, which may express temporary economic reasoning based around naidí exploitation but which in the future, with the decline of this extractive economy, may significantly weaken local organizing structures. In other words, the quest for a counter-space, which PCN activists aim for, has been powerfully mediated by capital, which in its profit-seeking drive reproduces dominant representations of space of the Pacific as a region of natural resource extraction.

Entanglements, Part 2: Enter the State

The example of Unicosta is not an isolated case; its experience has been welcomed and further promoted by government institutions. A report of INCORA's regional office in Guapi states, "The Community Council Unicosta is the first of its kind in the municipality of Iscuandé, and it should become a model for future councils. Its communities should assume the role of leaders to support and give orientation to neighboring communities in the organizing process" (INCORA 1997, point 10).

This "orientation" was indeed given to the communities living on the lands of a second large area of naidí extraction in the middle section of the Patía River. There too ALENPAC provided financial and logistic support. As a result El Progreso became the second community council in the Department of Nariño to be awarded collective land rights.[18]

The quotation from the 1997 report reveals INCORA's functional interest in these matters. As a government institution it had to comply with the requirements of Law 70 and Decree 1745 of 1995 to establish community councils and award collective land titles. There was not necessarily a real concern for community representation in the institution, and many of INCORA's reports that I reviewed displayed a patronizing attitude toward local communities. The following was redacted after INCORA officials visited communities along the San Francisco River: "With the commitment that the process of collective land titling implies for black communities, officials of INCORA's Guapi branch visited all the settlements along the banks of the San Francisco River in order to get to know in detail the socio-economic, historical and cultural reality of *the people whose level of life we intend to raise by organizing them* in a community council administered by a central committee that will have the function to co-ordinate and pre-serve the natural resources and ethnic-territorial control of the lands that they have owned and protected since the 18th century" (INCORA 1998c:1, emphasis added). Black communities appear in this quotation as passive receivers of their organization by the grace of state intervention that "organizes them in a community council." Little trust is placed in "the people whose level of life we intend to raise."

Throughout my time spent with campesinos, fisherfolk, activists, and government officials, I encountered such patronizing attitudes. One episode was particularly revealing. In April 1999 I had joined an INCORA official on her visit to the settlements of the Community Council Guapi Abajo to conduct a basic census. At first I noted a certain tactlessness on her part, as she stormed into people's homes and began to fire questions at household members, demanding to know their names, identity card numbers, level of education, and so on. Not surprisingly the locals answered rather reluctantly. At times they refused to hand over their ID cards. After each visit we boarded again the small, 40-horsepower-engine dugout canoe, only to disembark some twenty meters farther downstream to continue the exercise. As the day wore on, the official became increasingly annoyed or tired, or both. Eventually she screamed at people from the canoe before we had even landed, "What's your ID number?"

While the whole experience was utterly surreal, the questionnaire itself bordered on the quixotic. First, it asked for the names of household members, which were often quite difficult to establish. Due to high levels of short- and long-term mobility, many family members stay only temporarily in a given household. Second, the questionnaire asked for identity card numbers. This was also problematic, since many people do not have ID cards. The third question concerned the level of education, asking, "Can you read?," which many interviewees answered shyly, "Firmo mi nombre" (I sign my name). This affirmation was judged confirmation of illiteracy. The fourth question inquired about residents' place of birth, with most people originating from the area. However, it was question five that really brought the house down: "How many of the normal household members are currently absent and where are they?" Ethnographic fieldwork can be many things: exciting, confusing, boring, dangerous, tedious, conflictual, seducing, and more. But it can also be very funny. I had to hold back tears of laughter, observing how the increasingly irritated INCORA official was trying to make sense of answers outlining who was a current household member and who was not, and where she was who was not, and why she was where she was . . .

Hilarious or not, the underlying implication was, of course, that because of the typical extended family and family territoriality (as discussed in chapter 3) there is a constant coming and going in any particular house on the riverbanks. Household members are on the move, attending to faraway plantations, gold panning, cutting trees, or fishing at sea for days or weeks. There is no point in trying to establish who is where at any one time. Yet the modern territorial state, in its agonizing attempt to put people in their place, requires statistics, no matter how meaningless they are.

As shocked as I was by the government official's insensitive approach, I used those moments to ask locals about their views on the community councils and what they thought about Law 70 and the notion of collective land titles. As it turned out, the vast majority responded negatively to my questions. Most did not know what a community council was; they had not even heard of such a thing. I would continue to make this finding throughout my fieldwork in the river basins around Guapi. It corroborated my initial suspicion that the meaning of the new legislation had not trickled down to the very people affected by it. Clearly the socialization process of the legislation had been less successful in this region than elsewhere, quite in contrast to the celebratory fluvial expedition of territorial self-discovery in the San Juan River basin, as depicted by Villa (1998:444) at the beginning of this chapter.

A report by the Institute of Environmental Research for the Pacific Coast (Instituto de Investigaciones Ambientales del Pacífico [IIAP]) comes to a similar assessment, stressing the lack of people's awareness of community councils in the municipality of Guapi (Villa 2000:26–28). And a report by IIAP's branch in Guapi that evaluated an environmental management plan for the Community Council of the Napi River comes to the damning conclusion that 90 percent of locals did not have the slightest idea of the existence of the community council, its functions, and the people's part in it. The problem is described in this report as a "lack of awareness of the concept of a community council both by the board of directors and by the community in general [caused by the] weakness in the formation of leaders, the bureaucratization of the leaders in the region and the misappropriation of public and NGO funds obtained to socialize Law 70 of 1993 and its statutory decrees" (IIAP 2000, point 4.5.2.1).

This was not the first time that a state-created organizational form was not successfully adapted by black communities. It is worthwhile reflecting at this stage on the prior experience of a state program that was introduced in the Pacific region, from the failure of which important lessons can be drawn for contemporary community councils.

The Agricultural Cooperative of the Pacific (COADEPAL)

The Agricultural Cooperative of the Pacific (Cooperativa Agrícola del Pacífico [COADEPAL]) was a state program established by INCORA in the mid-1960s to promote the commercialization of coconut. The term *cooperative* is deceptive here, since it was a strategy implemented and regulated by the state and not a peasant initiative (Grueso and Escobar 1996).[19] One of its problems lay in the fact that campesinos never really accepted it as their own organization. Many never understood what the cooperative was all about. When I met Don Ricard in Guapi in 1999, he was the legal representative of the Community Council of the Guajuí River. He frequently told me of his experience as a former member of COADEPAL's Vigilance Committee (from 1972 to 1976) and later as bookkeeper (until 1983, when COADEPAL ceased to exist). His is a privileged insight into the complex workings of such a state program:

The cooperative was created in 1965. . . . It was a program of INCORA. It was to take charge of the commercialization of products, especially coconut. . . . But the individual member did not have sufficient knowledge of what a cooperative was. So what happened? He didn't learn how to manage it. Only a few of us understood what a coopera-

tive really was. . . . The administration was between INCORA and the cooperative's employees. But not the members. . . . INCORA gave members a loan and said, "This is for you to be a member." But they didn't explain what this loan was for. . . . So people joined the cooperative without knowing what it was for. After that, INCORA sometimes organized workshops. Some folks understood something; others nothing. That's how the cooperative failed. Because the members didn't understand. The members said, "No, the cooperative belongs to INCORA."[20]

COADEPAL clearly failed as a state strategy to organize campesinos. It was always considered "INCORA's cooperative" (Grueso and Escobar 1996:95). Like many other state initiatives aimed at "developing" the Pacific region, COADEPAL was a paternalistic and bureaucratized state intervention that was implemented without creating sufficient awareness among the people it was meant to benefit.

From the Agricultural Cooperative of the Pacific to Community Council

The parallels to contemporary community councils are frightening, as the councils may also become mere bureaucratized spaces, owing more to legal requirements than to real efforts at raising awareness among local populations over their rights. Many community councils were established before locals really knew what they were all about. As INCORA pressed for the rapid establishment of community councils in the Cauca Coast region, for example, their policy of sending contractors from Bogotá opened up scenarios of political corruption and favoritism (politiquería), in which some contractors channeled their own political interests and state resources to influence local organizing processes. Activists have recognized the danger of establishing community councils without first creating conditions for popular participation. They stress the need for more training of community leaders, so that the councils become an "organizing authority of wide participation, where we discuss and gain in orientation of the social movement with the base groups" (OCN 1996:248).

When I met Don Por in January 1999, he was the legal representative of the Community Council Cortina Verde Nelson Mandela in Nariño. With a long history as a peasant leader, he was one of the most active voices in the southern Pacific Coast pushing for the implementation of AT-55. He also formed part of the regional organization Palenque de Nariño. Don Por was very much aware of the dangerous connections between personal political interests, clientelism, and the establishment of community councils:

In the creation of the community councils we encountered some difficulties. INCORA was in charge of distributing the funds for the formation of community councils. It channeled part of it through the Process [PCN], and another part through the politiqueros [corrupt politicians]. With certain people from Bogotá, they channeled funds via the politiquería to create four councils. And they are the ones that have the most problems with collective land titling now. . . . At INCORA they told a certain person who lived in Bogotá, "Why don't you work in the process of Law 70? Take these funds and go and form this community council!" So this person looked for someone else of the same political line and told him, "Here, take these funds and go and form that community council!" . . . But since they are politiqueros, the result is a badly formed council. Well, in spite of this, we do our work and try to change these things. So that people understand what a community council is, and what it is for. But this is how INCORA works.[21]

And this is how INCORA worked on several occasions. In 1997 the Institute's national director, who was from Guapi, sent a fellow guapireño, who also resided in Bogotá, to the Cauca Coast to establish community councils. However, when this person arrived in Guapi, he soon realized that locals had already organized themselves into a community council and that they resisted his intention to set up various smaller councils. The legal representative of the Community Council Guapi Abajo vividly recollected the scenario two years later:

When this person arrived here to constitute the community council, we had already formed one. He came afterwards. The people from COCOCAUCA had requested in Bogotá the constitution of the council.[22] Around one month later, this person arrived with the establishment of a small community council. He came to form a community council between Temuey and Sansón. So that the rest of the territory was somehow up in the air. But we had already formed the council from Boca de Napi to Playa de Obregones [see map 2.1]. So the community told him, "No, we already have our council constituted." And then the guy said that in Bogotá they had given him money for this, and that he had to justify his work.[23]

The communities of the Napi River had a similar experience with IN-CORA's intervention in their organizing processes, as the same contractor from Bogotá was sent. The legal representative of this community council explained to me:

We formed our community council with funds from INCORA, which I requested from the contractor of these funds. Well, he wanted to organize a community council in every village. But since we already brought a dynamic with us through Law 70—we had already attended a number of meetings—we thought that it was not worthwhile to form a community council in every village. Instead, we said that we would create a single community council along the river basin. And that's how we started.[24]

In this case the logic of the river resisted institutionalized intervention. In the case of the Micay River in the northern part of the Cauca Coast, however, things turned out differently. There local mobilization had barely started, and INCORA's representative, a native from Micay living in Bogotá, encountered little resistance when he proposed the formation of five community councils around key settlements within a short time. In April 1997 all five councils held their first General Assembly and elected a council board. Yet in January 1999 the communities themselves requested from INCORA in Bogotá that these councils be re-formed, since even board members felt uneasy about their positions, not knowing what their tasks and responsibilities were. These were precisely some of the "badly formed" community councils about which Don Por talked, wherein no or only little awareness was achieved prior to their formation.

INCORA's attitude toward the land titling process, once the community councils were formed, has also been criticized, as movement leaders accused government officials of deliberately delaying this process. In the case of three community councils on the Cauca Coast (Río Alto Guapi, Río San Francisco, and Río Napi), it took a whole year between INCORA's decision to grant collective land titles and publishing them in a local newspaper, a necessary step to validate the titles.[25] This happened only after the community councils concerned had threatened to take INCORA to court. Thus while INCORA displayed a desire to rapidly establish community councils, it considerably delayed handing over land titles.

This shows the ambiguous nature of INCORA's involvement in these processes. Rather than acting as a homogeneous unit with a consistent politics toward local organizing processes, it should be regarded as a fragmented institution in which individuals operate who may favor the organizing processes of black communities, others who impede them, and still others who do not really care. The same can be said of other state institutions, and Colombia itself can be regarded as a "fragmented state," which is constituted by institutions that hold at times quite different positions and politics toward the Pacific Coast region.[26] From this viewpoint the state must be understood as an arena in which concrete politics are constantly negotiated and redefined. It is hence also an arena in which the organizations of black communities can and do interfere, articulate their demands, and defend their aims. I want to illustrate this by briefly examining the conflict over mangrove areas.

Defending the Logic of the River

The aspirations of community councils go beyond mere administrative functions as stipulated by the state. In fact black communities continue to challenge the state on the very definition of *tierras colectivas*. This confrontation became apparent in the struggle over mangrove areas, which for years the central government refused to include in collective land titles since it considered the extensive mangroves in the southern Pacific Coast as "areas of public interest" and thus not eligible for inclusion. Yet many rural black populations insist that they effectively live in mangrove areas, a complex ecosystem and one of the world's most productive, rich in fish species, mollusks, and shellfish, upon which local populations depend in their fishing and gathering activities (Arocha 1999; Leal 1998; Von Prahl et al. 1990; West 1956). Strong social and commercial links exist between the coastal mangrove areas and the middle and upper sections of the rivers.

Black communities therefore insisted that mangrove areas be included in their collective land titles. The government's refusal meant that all of those community councils with a coastline in the southern Pacific (and therefore invariably including mangroves) were offered land titles excluding mangrove areas. This proposal was rejected by the community councils on the Cauca Coast, which demanded all or nothing. In line with the notion of the logic of the river, stressing the interconnectedness and interdependence of various river sections, locals argued that mangrove areas formed an integral part of the sociocultural system of black communities and should therefore not be regarded separately.

In one initial case a dubious agreement was reached: the Community Council Acapa in the southern coastal part of the Department of Nariño received a collective land title in March 2000 that included mangrove areas under a special concessionary status (Rivas 2001). This arrangement, however, granted the government an opt-out clause by which the mangrove areas could be excluded again in the future. Such proceedings were rejected by the community councils on the Cauca Coast. Finally, in May 2003, and after continuing pressure, the government gave in, and the Community Councils of the Guajuí River, Guapi Abajo, and Chanzará in the Department of Cauca received collective land titles *including* their respective mangrove areas.

Clearly in this conflict the locale as the physical setting of social interactions was mobilized by black communities to defend their territorial aspirations. As entangled as the quest for a counter-space may be with party politics and clientelist structures, there is a clear spatial underpinning to the ways local communities draw up the boundaries for their community councils. As I have shown in this chapter, this process has sometimes been mediated by state and capital, not always following the ideal spatial river logic. It is important to point to these differential experiences and to understand their implications for the organizing processes. It is obvious that locals in today's Community Council Unicosta, for example, at first welcomed capital intervention in the form of the naidí extraction company ALENPAC, as it offered them work opportunities and earnings. These entanglements are difficult to deal with for social movement leaders, as they face a capitalist logic of intervention that they accuse of exploiting the region and its inhabitants, but which in the more immediate present does provide locals with otherwise unavailable employment and income. On occasion this can lead to conflict between movement leaders and the base. In chapter 5 I discuss a confrontation in the Guajuí River basin that I was lucky enough to witness between campesinos and their community council representatives over a controversial job offer by timber merchants. The community council as organizational figure, I argue, provides a privileged field of inquiry into the interactions between dominant representations of space (state discourses, politics, and legislation) and representational space (the aspirations of local communities to meaningfully appropriate their territories).

FIVE

Ideals, Practices, and Leadership of the Community Councils

The Ambiguity of the Community Councils

The community council is an ambiguous organizational figure. On the one hand, it constitutes a legally recognized new territorial authority in the Pacific region that for the first time officially acknowledges claims to collective land rights by black communities. Thus it can be argued that it entails a formal recognition of local representational space, accepting the notion of collective landownership as traditional practice among these communities. From this viewpoint, and following my argument of a Lefebvrian spatial dialectics, the community council, as the administrative authority of the lands that it entails, may be seen as a step toward the kind of counter-space that social movement activists aspire to. Not only would it protect territorial rights against outside interventions (at least on paper), but it would also be the space from which the alternative life project envisaged by PCN could be put into practice. The fact that some community councils have been co-opted by capital and the state, as I argued in chapter 4, is not so much a problem or a fault of the organizing figure as such as an expression of the entanglements and struggles that surround each and every council's constitution in its particular circumstance.

On the other hand, however, the community councils form part of a wider state strategy of *ordenamiento territorial* (territorial ordering) since the late 1980s. There exists a broad consensus among scholars that the state's sovereign authority and its national territory have been fragmented throughout Colombia's history (Bushnell 1993; Pécaut 2001; Safford and Palacios 2002). State institutions have been characterized by weakness and unequal spatial reach, with alternative authority regimes thriving in the face of the state's failure to control large areas of the country (Agnew and Oslender 2013; Mason 2005; Pizarro 2004). State reforms set in motion in the 1990s saw peace negotiations with the country's most powerful guerrilla group, the Revolutionary Armed Forces of Colombia (FARC). Yet they also reached out to marginalized groups, such as Afro-Colombians. From this viewpoint one may argue that the constitution of community councils in the Pacific Coast region forms part of the state's strategy to extend its institutions, norms, juridical practices, and authority into spaces hitherto beyond its de facto control. By 2013 a total of 159 collective land titles had been issued to black communities over roughly five million hectares, or 50 percent of the entire Pacific lowlands (map 5.1).

In other words, while black communities have gained some degree of territorial autonomy, they have also become subject to the state's institutionalizing reach. Rather than providing a radical departure from the modern territorial state model, the community councils may be seen as complementing it and enhancing its legitimacy through democratic practice. As the political scientist Ann Mason (2005:50) concludes in her observation of a range of authority alternatives in Colombia, "Paradoxically, the state's legitimacy may be enhanced through challenges to, and the delegation of, its authority, to the extent that alternative social arrangements become a force for progressive reforms, norm observance, and the reconstitution of the state-society relationship."

This seeming ambiguity associated with the figure of the community council can be read in the legislative texts that created it. Particularly illuminating in this regard are the detailed directives laid out in Decree 1745 of 1995. These refer, among other things, to the formation of a general assembly that elects a board of directors and a legal representative for each community council, as well as to a range of technical committees that community councils are expected to set up. They also prescribe a conservationist function to the community councils to preserve the natural environment. These legal impositions require local communities to organize in ways acceptable to the administrative logic of the state. Can the community council, then, be considered a counter-space, or is it

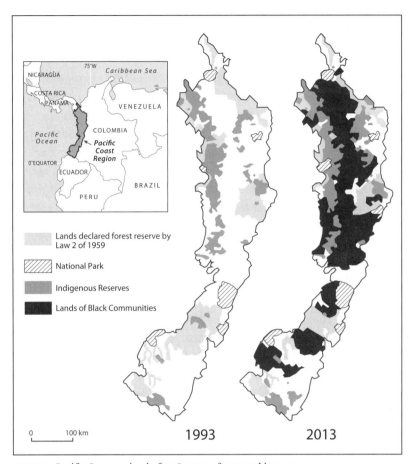

MAP 5.1. Pacific Coast region before Law 70 of 1993 and in 2013.

instead the result of a complex process of state co-optation? Or may it even be both?

From Tradition to Obligation: Conservationist Strategy and the "Discursive Fix"

The new Constitution of 1991 introduced important changes to the structures of the Colombian state. Among others, it "recognizes and protects the ethnic and cultural diversity of the Colombian Nation" (Article 7) and "enables the participation of all in the decisions that affect them and in the economic, political, administrative and cultural life of the Nation" (Article 2).

In fact the Constitution marks a watershed in the changing relationship between the Colombian state and the Afro-descendant population. With reference to the ten million hectares of tropical rain forest in the Pacific Coast region, Transitory Article AT-55 states, "Within two years of the current Constitution, Congress will issue . . . a law that grants black communities that have been living on state-owned lands [*tierras baldías*] in the rural riverside areas of the Pacific basin, in accordance with their traditional production practices, the right to collective property over the areas that the law will demarcate. . . . The same law will establish mechanisms for the protection of the cultural identity and the rights of these communities and to foster their economic and social development."

This constitutionally mandated law was passed on August 27, 1993, and became known as Law 70. In Chapter 1, Article 2, it delineates the area of the Pacific Coast basin (point 1), names the rivers included in this area (point 2), defines the rural riverside areas as "the lands adjacent to the river banks . . . that are outside the urban perimeters defined by the municipal councils" (point 3), and refers to tierras baldías as "the lands situated within the limits of the national territory that belong to the state and have no other owner" (point 4). It further defines "black community" as "the total of families of Afro-Colombian descent that have a culture of their own, share a history, and have their own traditions and customs within a countryside-town relationship, and which reveal and conserve an identity consciousness that distinguishes them from other ethnic groups" (Chapter 1, Article 2, point 5).

This legislative context marked what Colombian anthropologist Eduardo Restrepo (2004a, 2013) has referred to as the "invention of black community" or the "ethnicization of blackness in Colombia." In this understanding "black community" is a social construct that refers to the advent of a new political actor in Colombia rather than a culturally cohesive category. From the state's perspective, there was a need to define a new political interlocutor in relation to the novel legal framework that would draw the Pacific Coast region closer into the territorial state. Thus Law 70 can be regarded as a mechanism of state governance that incorporates black communities as claimants into a direct relationship with the state.[1]

In Chapter 3, "Recognition of the Right to Collective Property," Law 70 deals specifically with the areas to be titled as "lands of black communities." Article 5 outlines the creation of community councils (*consejos comunitarios*) as forms of internal administration. In particular the community council is "to watch over the conservation and protection of the rights to collective property, the preservation of cultural identity [and] the good use and conservation of natural resources" (Chapter 3, Article 5). Throughout Law 70 this conservationist function of the community council is further specified: "Forest use . . . will have to guarantee the persistence of the resources. . . . Soil use will take into account the ecological fragility of the Pacific basin. Consequently, successful applicants will develop practices of conservation and management compatible with ecological conditions. For that purpose, appropriate models of production will be developed . . . designing suitable mechanisms to stimulate them and to discourage unsustainable environmental practices" (Chapter 3, Article 6).

At first glance this may seem a somewhat bizarre statement. There really should be no need to remind rural black populations about the importance of sustainable production practices. After all, that is what these communities are said to have been doing for hundreds of years.[2] So why does Law 70 stress the *compulsory* nature of this relationship? Why are local communities now *obliged* to conserve the environment? "In the administrative act, by means of which collective land property is granted, the *obligation* will be assigned to observe the norms on conservation, protection, and on the rational use of the renewable natural resources and the environment" (Chapter 3, Article 14, my emphasis). The right to collective land property is thereby directly linked to the obligation of conservation, for which the local communities are now held responsible. The legislation is then not simply a recognition of ancestral territorial rights, customs, and traditions—as representational space—but effectively produces new representations of space that view the Pacific Coast region as a container of "megabiodiversity" that needs to be conserved for future potential exploitation. In this reading black communities are ascribed the role of "guardians" of the tropical rain forest and its biodiversity (Escobar 1996; Wade 1999a).

Biodiversity Conservation and Proyecto Biopacífico

The empowering of ethnic groups as guardians of fragile ecosystems needs to be seen as belonging to wider global strategies and politics of sustainable development and biodiversity conservation since the 1980s. Spurred by a global awareness over environmental destruction—which found its most vivid expression in the UN Brundtland Report in 1987 and consequently in the Río de Janeiro Earth Summit on Environment and Development in 1992—the Colombian government was keen on presenting the Pacific Coast region as a laboratory in which such global concerns (and accompanying finances made available by the World Bank) could be channeled into a regional development strategy based on biodiversity conservation.

A product of the Río Summit, the Global Environment Facility (GEF) was set up by the United Nations Environment Program, a multibillion-dollar fund administered by the World Bank. One of its first operations was the Project for the Conservation of Biodiversity in the Colombian Pacific Region, to be funded with US$9 billion by GEF and the Swiss government. Launched in August 1992, Proyecto Biopacífico began operations in Bogotá in March 1993.[3] Its most immediate aim was a comprehensive mapping of the region's biodiversity, with a view to establishing "the scientific, social, economic, and political elements necessary for a new strategy of biodiversity conservation and the sustainable utilization of the region's biological resources" (GEF-PNUD 1993:3). For this the support of black communities was enlisted, as these were generally acknowledged as having preserved the environment for hundreds of years. As Escobar (2008:188) fittingly states, "More than in the mainstream biodiversity approaches favored by northern NGOs, [Proyecto Biopacífico] registered from the start the correlation between biological and cultural diversity, and the importance of taking into account traditional knowledge and practices."

As a reflection of this recognition, most of Proyecto Biopacífico's regional coordinators were appointed from the ethnic-territorial organizations, including PCN. My initial contacts in the field were the coordinators Libia Grueso in Buenaventura, Alfredo Vanín in Tumaco, and Oscar Alzate in Guapi, all of whom were linked to the social movement of black communities. Proyecto Biopacífico also supported many local organizing initiatives, such as the women's network Matamba y Guasá on the Cauca Coast, which focuses on the recovery of traditional production practices and women's empowerment in the communities.[4] Proyecto Biopacífico, it may be argued, set off a new kind of discourse on the Pacific region, in which notions of development, biodiversity conservation, and traditional knowledge have become intrinsically entwined.

With the following quote from an INCORA report—awarding a collective land title to the Community Council of the San Francisco River—I want to illustrate how these discursive entanglements are expressed in specific scenarios. Here we can see how the connection is made between traditional production practices of black communities and their conservationist trends on the one hand, and the obligatory character of this relation as set out in the new legislation on the other:

> The traditional productive systems used by the Black Community of the San Francisco River have been the most appropriate forms of conserving the natural ecosystem up to today. . . . They have accumulated knowledge of hundreds of years of experience . . . based on living with nature and on respect of the collective, cooperation, solidarity, and interdependence. The region where the community that is interested in the collective title is situated is considered within the National Environmental Policy as a *strategic ecosystem* that has to be conserved, since the *valuable genetic resources* and the biodiversity that exist today in this great ecosystem constitute a public good, property of the Nation. The Colombian State recognizes the ancestral knowledge of the communities . . . with a view to guaranteeing the protection of these ecosystems, *considered vital for the future of humanity*. That is why Law 70 of 1993 imposes a *set of obligations* onto the beneficiaries of the collective titles in environmental terms. . . . The collective title includes property over the areas of forests delimited in it with the *clear obligation* for the community to make a persistent and sustainable use of the same. (my emphasis)[5]

The tropical rain forests, which have been heavily cut down by commercial logging, are now discursively produced as a "strategic ecosystem" containing "valuable genetic resources" that are "considered vital for the future of humanity." This quote reveals a crucial strategy underlying capitalist restructuring in the face of crisis. I call this strategy the "discursive fix."

Nature Conservation and the Discursive Fix

The contemporary ecological crisis has triggered a shift in discourse from "nature" to "environment," from timber-rich resource base to "strategic ecosystem," and from rural black riverside dwellers to guardians of "this great ecosystem." This discursive realignment is a crucial precursor for turning idle capital into profitable investment. By terming this process the "discursive fix," I draw on David Harvey's (1982:415) original identification of a "spatial fix" as capitalism's capacity for responding to the crisis of overaccumulation in the space economy (idle productive capacity plus unemployed labor power).[6]

The discursive fix sets the context for a new phase of capitalist restructuring. It prepares the ground for new ways of thinking about nature—in terms of "environment"—and mobilizes universal feelings of concern for a global environment under threat. From the UN Brundtland Report's notion of "our common future" (UNCED 1987; Visvanathan 1991), via the Kyoto Protocol, to recent suggestions about "earth stewardship" in the Anthropocene (Ogden et al. 2013), references to a global ecological crisis have become commonplace parlance. In these observations "nature" has been substituted by "environment."[7] This substitution is part of a global discursive response to the accelerated deterioration of nature as production condition. The latter has been theorized in historical materialist terms as capitalism's "second contradiction," in that capitalism's expansionist drive on nature, exploiting its resources, has eroded nature's very possibility of survival, reaching dimensions that threaten the reproduction of capitalism itself (O'Connor 1988, 1989).[8] The internal contradictions of capitalism therefore produce constantly changing geographical landscapes that must adapt to self-imposed crises. Harvey (1985b:150) writes, "Capitalism perpetually strives, therefore, to create a social and physical landscape in its own image and requisite to its own needs at a particular point in time, only just as certainly to undermine, disrupt and even destroy that landscape at a later point in time. The inner contradictions of capitalism are expressed through the restless formation and re-formation of geographical landscapes. This is the tune to which the historical geography of capitalism must dance without cease."

This tune is now played in the global arena, where debates on sustainable development, biodiversity conservation, and, more recently, climate change mitigation provide the discursive ground for capitalist intervention and restructuring. Just as concessions to workers were used as a tool to diffuse class conflict and prevent further deterioration of the production condition labor (capitalism's first contradiction), capitalism's current restructuring takes the form of conceding certain "benefits" to nature by gradually shifting from exploitation and destruction toward management and conservation. Reflecting on these "misadventures of capitalist nature," Martin O'Connor (1993:8) states, "The primary dynamic of capitalism changes form, from accumulation and growth feeding on an external domain, to ostensible self-management and conservation of the *system of capitalized nature* closed back upon itself."

I argue that the discursive fix sets in motion this restructuring of capital as a way of dealing with the second contradiction of capitalism (its ambiguous relation to nature as production condition). This restructuring may benefit both capital and nature, the former through new investment possibilities—for example, in biotechnology or energy conservation industries (solar panels, wind turbines, etc.)—the latter through a globally mobilized awareness of nature's finite resources and the implementation of conservation projects. Whether this newly forged capital-nature/environment alliance "works" or is able to stave off an imminent apocalypse is another question. What it has no doubt achieved, however, is a successful restructuring of capitalism with new outlets for capital investment and continued high rates of profitability.

In this context Arturo Escobar (1996:48) adds an interesting distinction between "two logics of ecological capital." On the one hand, he sees modern forms of nature's exploitation, such as the continued and often unsustainable extraction of natural resources; on the other, "postmodern forms of capitalization of nature" have ushered in an ecological phase of conservation and sustainable development. In the case of tropical rain forests, for example, the ecological phase often takes place with a view to the pharmaceutical potential that these ecosystems are considered to have in terms of high levels of biodiversity.

Such a "biologic" is expressed in Colombia in the Proyecto Biopacífico. According to the project's national coordinator, it was conceived within a "national biodiversity strategy that considers the defense of the biological and cultural diversity [of the Pacific Coast] as a vital factor for the development of the region" (Casas 1993:11). It was inscribed in the search for a new development strategy for the region that at the same time was to strengthen the option of Colombia's geopolitical future as a "bio-power in the concert of international relations" (10). These claims express a discursive trend toward an ecological phase of conservation centered on biodiversity, even though, at the same time, modern forms of capitalization of nature, such as large-scale and largely uncontrolled timber extraction and alluvial gold mining employing heavy machinery and mercury, still wreak havoc in the region. While the two logics of ecological capital coexist on Colombia's Pacific Coast, the impact of the globally induced new round of development discourse can clearly be felt with the discursive focus on "postmodern forms of capitalization of nature."

These processes are far from clear-cut. In fact they are shot through with ambiguity, discontinuity, and plain contradiction. Let's take this quote from Chapter 4 of Law 70, entitled Land Use and Protection of Natural Resources and Environment:

> The members of the black communities, holders of collective land rights, will continue to conserve, maintain or cause the regeneration of the protective vegetation of the waters and guarantee, by an adequate use, the persistence of particularly fragile ecosystems, such as mangroves and wetlands, and protect and conserve the species of fauna and wild flora that are threatened or in danger of extinction (Article 21).

For state legislators to remind black communities to protect mangrove areas, but then refuse to include them in collective land titles (as explained in chapter 4), may appear just a bit ironic. Stressing the obligation to "protect and conserve the species of fauna and wild flora that are threatened or in danger of extinction" turns frankly cynical, however, in light of more recent interventions. Truth is often stranger than fiction, and the following story might not be out of place in one of Gabriel García Márquez's short story collections. As I have scribbled in my field notes more than once, Guapi was my personal Macondo, where magical realism infused everyday life, which is, of course, precisely the point of Gabo's fictionalized accounts of Colombian reality.[9] So here we go:

Coca Crops, Aerial Fumigation, and the Fucked-Up State

In September 2000 the national antinarcotics police began extensive aerial fumigation in the Departments of Nariño and Cauca of what were thought to be illegal coca plantations. These areas served as "testing grounds" shortly before massive U.S. aid was to be channeled into the large-scale drug eradication campaign known as Plan Colombia. Hours before fumigation started in the area south of Guapi, small police aircraft dropped thousands of glossy leaflets over the town that announced in brightly colored letters, "In Colombia the days of illicit crops are numbered."[10] On the other side of the leaflet farmers were advised, "If you continue to sow illicit crops, we will continue to eradicate them. Look for an alternative legal crop to sow." In other words: We told you so. Shortly after, fumigation planes were covering the forests with clouds of glyphosate, making no distinction between what might be a coca plantation and what were local food crops. Among immediate reactions, people reported skin rash from exposure to the toxic clouds and after bathing in the rivers, of particular concern among children. The elderly suffered from asthma attacks, as they were caught outdoors while the area was being fumigated. Long-term consequences of contaminated rivers, affected fauna and flora, and damaged food crops are difficult to estimate.[11]

Colombia is the only country in the world to use aerial fumigation. The strategy is outlined in the Programa de Erradicación de Cultivos Ilícitos mediante Aspersión Aérea con Glifosato, or Program of Illicit Crop Eradication with Glyphosate, which began in 2000. The impact of aerial fumigation on the health of local populations and legal crops is intensely debated in Colombia. While the government argues that the pesticides used are harmless to people and the environment, Afro-Colombian communities have denounced the displacement of populations as a consequence of water contamination, land degradation, and loss of food security caused by fumigations.

After hearing repeated condemnations from local organizations in Guapi in 2010, I organized a campaign demanding an immediate stop to fumigations in the Cauca area. Letters signed by fifty-seven academics and other professionals, most with direct work experience in the Pacific region, were sent between April and August 2010 to the Colombian embassies in the United Kingdom, France, and Spain; to Colombia's outgoing president Alvaro Uribe, and to incoming president Juan Manuel Santos on the day of his inauguration; and to the U.K. Foreign Office. (My focus was on the United Kingdom, as I was working at the University of Glasgow at the time.) The Guardian newspaper in the United Kingdom and El Espectador in Colombia published open letters in their editions.[12] Colombian authorities generally respond well to these kinds of campaigns. They are keen players in a public relations crusade to change the nation's image as a drug-producing powerhouse (instead touting Shakira, Juanés, vallenato, cumbia, and el fútbol). President Santos in particular has spent considerable effort denouncing the demand for cocaine in Europe and the United States as the principal driving force behind illegal drug production in Colombia, thereby stressing the responsibility of countries in the Global North to curb consumption at home. (He's quite right on that point of course.)

In line with these attempts at whitewashing the nation's identity, we received answers from the Colombian Embassy in London as well as the antidrug unit of the national police in Colombia. The Colombian ambassador to the United Kingdom invited me to London on July 5, 2010, to personally explain the position of his government on aerial fumigation, which, unsurprisingly, condemns coca cultivation as the real culprit of environmental destruction. Since manual eradication is considered too dangerous in the Pacific lowlands due to the presence of armed groups (including guerrillas, paramilitary groups, and ordinary criminal gangs known as *bacrims* or *bandas criminales*), the government is left with the only option of aerial fumigation. So it goes . . .

I can't go into detail here to dispute these affirmations. Suffice it to say that overwhelming evidence exists as to the uselessness of aerial fumigation. Peasant farmers who openly admitted to cultivating coca in the Napi River basin shrugged off my question of what they would do when antidrug units were spraying their crops. They didn't seem too concerned. They told me that they would simply "prepare" their coca crops by spraying the leaves prior to fumigation with a sugary syrup mix of *panela* and water. This would cover and protect the leaves from the glyphosate, which would thus be isolated and not able to interact with the leaf. With the next rains the whole mixture would get washed off and most of the coca crops would be saved.

While this may be only anecdotal evidence (although pretty powerful if indeed it works as smoothly as suggested by my interviewees), aerial fumigation has also been declared a useless strategy by scientific studies that see coca cultivation simply shift from an area under fumigation to another, fumigation-free area. A study that examined data for all 1,125 municipalities of Colombia—the first of its kind—concludes that "fumigation policy is failing in Colombia, because it does not eradicate, but diffuses coca production, shifting it to forests of ecological importance and to areas inhabited by low-income, especially Afro-Colombian and indigenous communities, which as a result are increasingly displaced" (Rincón-Ruiz and Kallis 2013:61). Locals deploy a cheeky spatial metaphor to refer to this process of diffusion: *la coca anda*, or "the coca leaf walks."

This Macondoan side trip into the magical realism of state bureaucracy and aerial fumigation logic shows up not only the limitations of official biodiversity conservation discourse but the contradictory nature of state discourse as such. How pathetic the state that issues legislation obliging black communities to "protect and conserve the species of fauna and wild flora threatened or in danger of extinction" (Law 70, Chapter 4, Article 21) and then goes and fumigates forests, lands, and rivers, pushing these species closer to extinction. This is no longer just a "fragmented state," as I argued in chapter 4. This is a contradictory, cynical, and fucked-up state . . .

In the meantime, however, let us return to the beautiful letter of the law. Ah, Gabo, those magnificent laws!

Regulating Community Representation: Decree 1745 and Its Stipulations

> I believe that we are acting, thinking, conceiving and trying to go on making not a real country, but one of paper. The Constitution, the laws . . . everything in Colombia is magnificent, everything on paper. It has no connection with reality.
>
> —García Márquez, quoted in Jenny Pearce, *Colombia*

On October 12, 1995, Decree 1745 was passed. It would regulate Chapter 3 of Law 70 with regard to the constitution of community councils and the process of collective land titling. In Chapter 2 it stipulates that the community council consist of a general assembly and a board of directors:

> The General Assembly is the maximum authority of the community council. It will meet each year to take decisions, to pursue and evaluate the work of the community council's Board of Directors, and to discuss topics of general interest. . . . The Assembly in which the first Board of Directors is elected will be called by the existing community organizations that are recognized by the community. From then onwards, it will be called by the Board of Directors. If the latter does not do this appropriately, one third of the members of the General Assembly can do so. . . . The notice of meeting has to be given at least thirty days in advance. (Article 4)

Article 6 defines in detail the functions of the general assembly to elect the members of the board of directors; to approve the plans of economic, social, and cultural development that the board designs; to watch over the use and conservation of natural resources in agreement with environmental legislation and traditional production practices; and to elect a legal representative for the community council.

Clearly the legal language used owes more to liberal democracy discourse than to traditional organizing forms among rural black populations in the Pacific lowlands. Indeed, one may argue, there is a risk that to insist on the universality of liberal democracy is to impose on other cultures systems of government unrelated to their skills and talents, potentially reducing them to "mimics, unable and unwilling to be true either to their tradition or . . . imported alien norms" (Parekh, quoted in Slater 1997:269).

This is a difficult issue to resolve. As shown in chapter 4, there have been real problems with rural populations not appropriating the legislation and not participating in full in the organizing processes. The imposition of an outside logic of governance has not always found widespread acceptance among black communities. The legislation itself is the result of complex interactions between the inside/outside and the local/global in the processes of restructuring territorializations at the national level. Political geographer David Slater (1997:259–60) calls attention to these entanglements in the geopolitical arena:

> In the context of social movements, struggles for a decentralization of political power within a given national territory, and for a radical restructuring of the territorial power of the state can be identified as exemplifying the more inner-oriented form of the geopolitical. . . . In a parallel way, it is possible to argue that in the analysis of democracy and processes of democratization there is also an inside—the territorialization of democracy within a given nation-state, and an outside—the struggle for a democratization of institutions that operate at the global level, but which have multiple effects within the territorial politics of the countries of the South. Clearly in the cases of social movements and democracy, the inside and outside of the geopolitical are not to be realistically seen as separate, but as overlapping and intertwined in a complex of relations.

This "complex of relations," characteristic of the inside/outside and local/ global couplets, nevertheless has to find a *common* form of expression and a *common* language in which the "overlapping and intertwining" take place and the (dis)agreements, concessions, and results are expressed. Whereas leaders of black communities in Colombia act on both the inside (locally, place-based) and the outside (globally, discourse-based), their negotiations with government representatives and the resulting legislation are expressed in the hegemonic logic and grammar of liberal democracy. Black leaders assume this logic as a tool in order to press for the "radical re-structuring of the territorial power of the state," about which Slater writes. The problem, then, lies not so much in the use of a *grammar from the outside* being applied by black community leaders in their discourse as in the implementation of *structures from the outside* in local communities. If we consider these structures as tools that provide black communities with new legal means of territorial appropriation, then more emphasis should be placed on how to make these structures more "culture-friendly," by, for example, articulating them in local languages and logics. This seems to me one of the great challenges for black community leaders: how to translate an *outside structural logic* into an *inside mode of appropriation*.

Mobilizing along the Rivers: From *Palenques* to Community Councils

Relatively few community organizations existed in the Cauca river basins prior to the new Constitution of 1991. The scenario there was different from the experience in the Departments of Chocó and Nariño, where a number of campesino associations were active that would bring a significant dynamic to ethnic-territorial mobilization.[13] On the Cauca Coast, in contrast, the discourse of social mobilization prior to Law 70 was less peasant-oriented and more influenced by state-driven initiatives. As Humberto Villa, legal representative of the Community Council of the Napi River, explained to me, "We had a Committee of Communal Action, an Ecclesiastical Committee that dealt with the management of the church, a Parents Association, and later, when the Family Welfare System was created, we also had a Welfare Committee."[14]

These committees formed part of the wider paternalistic logic of a state aiming to exercise control over rural populations by organizing them. From this viewpoint these committees may be considered precursors to the territorially bounded community councils envisaged by Law 70 that testify to the continuous role of state mediation in social mobilization. These previously existing committees also formed part of nationwide initiatives that failed to implement a more culturally specific logic according to the region. They were much the same in the Pacific lowlands as they were in the Andean region.

One of the few organizations that differed from this state-sponsored approach in Guapi was the Association of Fishermen, ASOPEZ (Asociación de Pescadores), which aimed at improving living and working conditions for fishermen in the lower part of the Guapi River. Walberto Banguera, legal representative of the Community Council Guapi Abajo, remembered this short-lived organizational experience of the early 1990s: "In this river here, there was no organization before Law 70. The only one that existed was an association of fishermen that we founded, ASOPEZ Guapi Abajo. We fought for legal recognition, but we didn't get it. So when the community council was formed, we decided that the organization should be part of the community council."[15]

As a special case on the Cauca Coast, I should briefly mention the Saija River basin, which had an important river organization prior to the Constitution of 1991. Similar to experiences in the Chocó, where the Catholic Church played a significant role in mobilizing peasants, the Asociación Prodesarrollo del Río Saija (ASOPRODESA) was actively supported by a priest. Mirna Rosa Herrera, a leading community activist from Timbiquí, explained the significance of this organization to me: "The Saija is a different case. Here we've had an older organization. It was better formed, a different process. With ASOPRODESA . . . it was supported by a priest, Father Epifanio Sotelo. With all respect and initiative of the people, but well, external people had a lot to do with this. The Father was the founder of ASOPRODESA."[16]

Besides these two exceptions, however, the Cauca Coast was pretty much a clean slate when it came to community-initiated political mobilization prior to the new Constitution. Law 70 of 1993 forced these communities to take a more active stand. For social movement scholars this is a classic case of an emerging "political opportunity structure" shaping mobilization. Unlike in previous state-driven development initiatives, however, local populations had to define the extent of their territorial administration. A historical reference point that linked blackness to territorial empowerment was found in the figure of the palenques, the fortified maroon settlements that I examined in chapter 3. As Walberto Banguera explained, in order to discuss the stipulations of the new legislation, black communities created temporary spaces they called palenques: "The palenque organized the people, while the community council was being constituted. When the community council was put in place, the palenque disappeared. The palenque existed since 1993, with Law 70. The people from JUNPRO supported the palenque in those days. They helped us establish it."[17]

Relating the experience in the Napi River basin, Humberto Villa stresses the historical link that communities were making to maroon resistance during times of slavery: "*Palenque* is the name of the process of struggle. You have heard of the Palenque de San Basilio. Well, we call ours Palenque de Napi, because there slavery lived its historical process too, you see. One of the oldest villages in the area was the village of San Agustín. Slavery existed there. A lot of things happened there. So we decided to call ours Palenque de Napi."

There is no doubt that "a lot of things happened" in the Napi River. As far as we know, however, what did not happen was the formation of a maroon settlement in colonial times in this particular river basin. In fact most riverine dwellers would not have heard of a palenque prior to the political mobilization of the early 1990s. The collective amnesia among rural Afro-Colombians regarding the history of slavery is well documented (Losonczy 1999; Restrepo 2001). So why call the community organization in Napi a palenque now? Clearly the act of naming evokes a powerful historical imagination of resistance, as the legendary Palenque de San Basilio on the Caribbean Coast gets transplanted as a reference point for contemporary territorialization struggle on the Cauca Coast.

PCN's organizational strategy also drew on this rich symbolism of resistance, as the movement created a set of regional palenques as umbrella organizations, which were then represented in the National Coordinating Committee.[18] These regional palenques were considered spaces for discussion, decision making, and policy orientation within the movement. One of the most important was the Palenque de Nariño, based in Tumaco. However, owing to systematic pressure and threats to their lives made by paramilitary groups, many of the leading activists were forced to leave the region, and the Palenque de Nariño finally dissolved in 2004. Today the Palenque El Congal, based in Buenaventura, is PCN's most important regional association.

For the river-based organizations the palenques were only temporary spaces. The ultimate aim was the creation of community councils. Humberto Villa describes this process in the Napi River:

First, we conducted a census. After that, we looked at the history of all the villages: how they began, who were their first inhabitants, and so on. Then we formed the Board of Directors and called the Assembly. We appointed members according to the number of families of each village. This Assembly took place in May 1997. From that we got the Board of Directors, of which I am the president, the legal representative. We then registered with the mayor's office and began to prepare the application for the collective land title with INCORA.

In his narrative Humberto Villa describes the typical process of the constitution of a community council, as required by Decree 1745. Article 9 states that board members must be registered with the mayor's office, which then advises the Office of Affairs for Black Communities at the Interior Ministry in Bogotá. Article 20 expands on the report that a community council has to present to INCORA as part of the application for a collective land title. Information required includes a physical description of the lands to be titled (point 1); *antecedentes etnohistóricos* (ethnic-historical records, point 2); a demographic description of the community (point 4); and a description of traditional productive practices (point 7).

There is a justified concern that these heavily bureaucratized procedures alienated many rural dwellers who could not be motivated to participate in these meetings. However, for those who did attend, the requirements of forming a general assembly and of preparing a report containing detailed information on local history, landownership, and conflict situations opened channels of participation and discussion that they felt to be new and exciting. It is to this awakening sense of conscientization that I turn next.

The General Assembly as an Arena of Conscientization

The territory has been, is and will continue to be the space that makes possible the development of life throughout the ages.
—Consejo Comunitario Guapi Abajo, "Solicitud de título colectivo del Consejo Comunitario Guapi Abajo"

The Cauca Coast did not see a mobilization en masse comparable to what happened in the Chocó. There were no antecedents like the boat journey along the San Juan River that members of the river organization ACADESAN embarked upon (described in chapter 4). For many people on the Cauca Coast, it was the General Assembly that constituted their first *hora de encuentro* (hour of meeting) and that would mark the beginning of their personal involvement in the political mobilization in the river basins. These assemblies were often vivacious affairs shot through with cheerful singing and clapping. *Decimeros* were called upon to perform oral poetry that reflected on the old days, remembering the history of settlements along riverbanks and collective work forms such as *minga* and *cambio de mano*. The assemblies became performative spaces of the people's collective memories, with the oral tradition as the vehicle of articulation.

There was seemingly no end to the remembering, often interspersed with complaints that certain practices were being "forgotten" as new spatialities and temporalities associated with modernity were transforming life patterns. Fisherfolk still practiced *posear*, when the catch is shared equally among all participants, and campesinos *la cogienda*, a way of sharing the harvest or the loan of land and seed with those who lack it, a favor to be repaid at a later point. Yet the elderly cautioned that these practices were being replaced by monetary relations, effectively losing their collective character. They also recalled that patron saint festivities used to last two whole weeks and that trees in the forest needed to be felled by axe and only in times of *menguante*, the period of the waning moon, which only then would guarantee the timber's good quality. They admonished that these traditional practices were not respected any longer, as sawmills, indifferent to the moon cycle, demanded a continuous timber supply. The insensitivity of modernity's instruments was effectively breaking with traditional temporalities and spatialities and their relation to nature. In these enunciations the assemblies began to turn into a space of critique. Much of the criticism was not really new to anyone; it was voiced countless times in bars, on market days, or during fleeting encounters. But now this critique had a formal platform.

The elderly, for example, talked about the time when Guapi still produced rice and eggs in excess and exported these goods, together with fruits and other products, to the port of Buenaventura. (Don Agapito hints at this relation in chapter 2.) This was before INCORA promoted coconut monoculture in the region in the 1960s, while at the same time discouraging the local production of rice, which it argued was not profitable compared to the large-scale rice plantations in Tolima and Huila in the interior of the country. This discussion in the General Assembly quickly turned into a critique of the state, which local populations felt had abandoned them. *Los ancianos* (the elderly) remembered the beetle pest known as *anillo rojo* that decimated coconut palms in the region in the 1980s. As a result campesinos lost their source of income and no longer had subsistence crops such as rice to fall back upon.

This traumatic experience engendered a profound distrust toward agricultural intervention by the state. In my travels up and down the rivers of the Cauca Coast in 1998 and 1999, I visited a number of initiatives by local farmers who had resumed small-scale rice cultivation along the river banks. This was in sharp contrast to recommendations made by officials from the regional development program Plan Pacífico and the Municipal Unit of Agrarian Assistance (Unidad Municipal de Asistencia Técnica Agraria [UMATA]). When I interviewed the director of Plan Pacífico's regional office in Guapi, he still supported the official argument that small-scale rice cultivation in the Pacific lowlands should be discouraged for not being *eficaz* (efficient).[19] Yet his recommendations had fallen on deaf ears, as I observed countless small rice paddies being tended to along riverbanks. What locals did demand from UMATA was the provision of mechanic rice hulling mills, known as *piladoras* or *molinos*, which they wanted to see installed in various strategic locations along a particular river. This would significantly facilitate rice hulling, which otherwise was done manually with a pestle in a *pilón*, the traditional wooden mortar, a strenuous task mostly performed by women.

The interventions of INCORA in the 1960s (promoting coconut monoculture and discouraging local production of rice in the Pacific lowlands) and UMATA in the late 1990s (discouraging small-scale rice cultivation in the region for not being "efficient" enough) are classic examples of what geographer Bruce Braun (2002) calls "technologies of displacement": mechanisms that state actors employ to exercise control over resources of indigenous and peasant peoples and to promote new capital relations, often at the expense of vulnerable populations living under a different set of sociocultural relations.[20] The state's vision of development has enabled new actors and "experts," such as the director of the regional office of Plan Pacífico in Guapi, to speak for and control the livelihoods of *guapireños*, leading to a displacement of local cultural geographies. The condemnation of these state initiatives by locals now gathering in the space of the General Assembly should be seen as a wider critique of these technologies of displacement.

Two more examples show how the General Assembly, beyond being the bureaucratic space for electing a board of directors, became for many rural populations their first experience of political engagement. First, the communities that later were to form the Community Council Guapi Abajo composed a formal, written complaint during their initial assembly, specifying that there was no running water supply, no sewage system, no telecommunications, and no health center in any of their villages. Only two of sixteen communities (Chamón and Sabana) enjoyed an electricity supply, and this only for four hours daily (Consejo Comunitario Guapi Abajo 1998).

Second, the communities that came together on September 28, 1997, for the General Assembly of the Community Council of the Guajuí River went beyond filing a formal complaint. They used the meeting to agree on a common strategy to confront a group of illegal loggers active in the middle section of the river near Guare. They referred to Chapter 6 of Decree 1745 (in particular Article 37), according to which permits for the exploitation of natural renewable resources on lands that were likely to be titled collectively to black communities could be issued only to benefit the communities affected. Clearly, therefore, the thirty-five men who had come from Buenaventura to log the forests around the Guajuí River were acting illegally.[21]

As these examples show, the General Assembly was much more than a simple fulfillment of legal requirements. Beyond its bureaucratic function of electing a board of directors, for many communities it was a first awakening to the various dimensions of the new territorialization processes. It was in the General Assembly where they voiced their critique of the state and where they analyzed existing territorial conflicts and other problems. Although these issues had always been discussed on an everyday basis, the General Assembly turned them into an organized form and a collective articulation through the medium of the report that accompanied the application for a collective land title.

It is important to point out that the events just described were a general trend, the intensity of which differed from river to river. As I documented in chapter 4, many people I interviewed along the lower Guapi River were not even aware of the political mobilization along their river basin. (I discuss another case of this sort below.) Yet precisely because these local processes may at times appear to be slow, ambiguous, or disjointed, both spatially and temporally, there is a danger of rendering them invisible or of underestimating their potential for social change, a danger to which academic passers-by may easily succumb. Only by spending a prolonged period in the field can we hope to witness the often interrupted nature of local organizing processes, when nothing much seems to happen for months at a time, and then all of a sudden an intense mobilizing dynamic arises. It is only through a serious engagement with ethnography, deep ethnography, that we can hope to uncover and render visible these mobilizing dynamics in all their complexity.

Social Cartography as a Tool of Territorialization

> In the local definitions of territory, use and meaning prevail over the establishment of boundaries and their defense. These definitions are ample and cover all necessary spaces for the physical, social and cultural reproduction.
> —Patricia Vargas, "Propuesta metodológica para la investigación participativa de la percepción territorial en el Pacífico"

The General Assembly was one important mobilizing dynamic. Workshops on social cartography were another. In these workshops riverine dwellers produced a sketch of the land area for which they wanted a collective title deed (Decree 1745, Article 20, point 1). Technical assistance was mostly provided by NGOs and Colombia's Geographical Institute, IGAC. The communities in the lower section of the Guapi River, for example, were supported by a Cali-based NGO, Fundación La Minga. To the foundation's managing director the project of social cartography implied the development of maps with and for local communities on their own terms.[22] La Minga provided paper and pencils in these workshops, and their cartographic "expert" accompanied and encouraged discussions that locals held about their territory and advised on how best to draw a map of it. (In chapter 3 I showed how such a process of cognitive mapping allowed the exploration of local territorial perceptions among the communities in the Atrato River basin; figure 3.6.) Next, workshop participants were instructed in the use and reading of "official" maps, to then produce a new map that

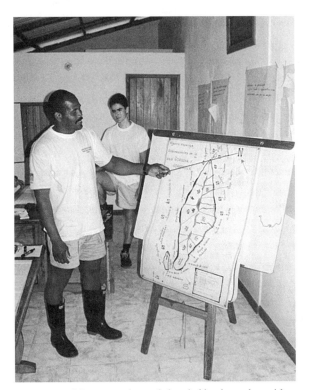

FIG. 5.1. Social cartography workshop led by the author with
the resident population on the island of Gorgona, July 8, 1999.

considered scale and technical details such as coordinates, topographical
features, and a legend. This new map would accompany the respective
community's application for a collective land title presented to INCORA.
The objective of social cartography for participants was hence twofold:
first, to know their territory, an *internal* process of conscious territorialization; and second, to make their territory known, an *external* process of
communicating their territorialities.

Although some community leaders claim that they "have their cartography clear in their heads,"[23] the exercise itself raised important questions on
the very act of drawing boundaries. First, whereas private property among
rural black populations, even in the absence of individual title deeds, is
clearly delimited in space—mainly by referring to natural boundaries such

as certain streams, rocks, and trees—the mountain backland, the *monte de respaldo*, which is used in activities such as hunting and gathering, is perceived as open, collective space without clearly marked boundaries. The newly introduced requirement to delimit these areas on maps may be seen as running against traditional spatialities and territorial understandings.

Second, this act of marking boundaries of inclusion and exclusion has at times led to tensions in interethnic relations between indigenous and black communities. Traditionally cohabiting in the Pacific lowlands, both groups have mostly peacefully interacted for hundreds of years and established what I have termed "overlapping territorialities" (Agnew and Oslender 2013). Afro-Colombians may usually enter and use what is indigenous collective territory and vice versa, always if their respective activities do not infringe upon the other ethnic group's territorial rights. The Western logocentric project of exclusionary boundaries runs into a wall in the Pacific lowlands, where we find "fluid boundaries" instead. Colombian geographer Patricia Vargas (1999:149) examined these interethnic relations more closely and found that "between neighboring groups there exist fluid territorial and social boundaries crossed by relations of co-operation and commerce. Resources or land that belong to one group can be used by others if the social relations are sufficiently close in order to turn strangers into practical members—yet without them acquiring rights."

Law 70, however, solidifies these fluid boundaries in space and on maps, rendering them stable and unmoving. It disrupts local epistemologies, forcing black communities to translate their territorial aspirations onto maps that state institutions will accept as legitimate documentation for their land right claims. This "epistemological tweaking" is a little-discussed but important side effect of the legislation. It has at times increased tensions between black and indigenous communities, as pens on paper were rewriting interethnic territorial relations. On the other hand, given the increasing penetration of capital in the region, the drawing of clearly established boundaries does protect the land rights of both indigenous and black communities (at least on paper). Potential territorial conflicts between the two groups may therefore be considered the lesser evil. As a way of avoiding conflict from breaking out, interethnic committees for discussion and negotiation between indigenous and black communities have been set up, charged with taking the final decision over the delimitation of territories involving claims from both groups (Decree 1745,

Article 22, point 5). Overall they have been a successful mechanism to keep interethnic tensions at bay.

Making the Legislation Their Own: Resisting Outside Intervention

As I hinted, black communities have applied the new legislation in a number of cases to protect their territorial claims against outsiders keen on exploiting the region's natural resources. I want to narrate two experiences from the Cauca Coast in more detail, as they reveal the practical implementation of such legal empowerment, while at the same time showing its limitations. The first experience, from the Napi River, I was told about by the community council representative. The second one I experienced myself as I accompanied members of the Guajuí River Community Council to a conflict situation upstream that had arisen with timber merchants. I was privileged to partake in a heated debate that testified to the difficulties of turning the political opportunity structure afforded by Law 70 into a working reality on the ground.

One of the most eloquent activists I worked with over a period of six months on the Cauca Coast was Humberto Villa, legal representative of the Napi River Community Council. In one of our many hour-long conversations he told me about the community's decision to confront a company that intended to exploit alluvial gold deposits in their river:

A company wanted to enter the Napi River, and we had to stop them. First of all, their procedure was not the most adequate, because they dealt with people who did not have credibility in the community. Second, they made clear to us that they would go ahead at any price, because they had the money. That was the fear we had in the region. . . . We are afraid of this because we have already lived an experience like this. We knew that where these people arrive, there is already the guerrilla, there are paramilitaries, and there are common criminals. So we are not friends of these kinds of people, because they maybe walk around with criminals to defend their interests. . . . So the community spoke out, people organized themselves, and in each village we began to have meetings. We managed to repeal a concession given by CRC [the regional development corporation of the Cauca Department]. We had to go to the Ministry of Environment, the Ministry of Mining, and the Ministry of Defense. Well, we protested in front of all these state institutions. That was in 1996. We began to look at the destruction that the retro power shovel had caused in the Timbiquí River, because there was a serious problem. . . . In the case of mining and the forest, the companies should also leave *something behind, not just take what is there and then disappear. We have to prepare the future for those who come after. So we should not finish what is there, as if we were the owner, no. We have preserved this for such a long time. So we denounced them, first in the mayor's office, then with CRC, and then we went to the Institute of the Environment. They eventually issued a resolution over the issue, and we have a copy, that no company can come in without the consent of the community council. That Decree 1745 existed, which gives autonomy to the community councils, for them, together with the regional corporations, to give permits for the exploitation of resources. . . . We declared that we were not enemies of the companies that come to exploit our resources, but that they have to leave a contribution with the community. But the ones who think they can simply come here to grab the resources and then leave, no, there we have to resist.*

It is important to stress (with Humberto Villa) that neither campesinos nor community leaders are opposed per se to the extraction of natural resources from their lands. Rather a consciousness is being generated and articulated around the fact that these extractive processes have to be sustainable. Whatever this means exactly in technical terms, in practice the consensus seems to be, as Villa suggests, that one has "to prepare the future of those who come after."

For the most part the exploitation of natural resources on the Pacific Coast has followed a boom-and-bust pattern that leaves locals and the environment abandoned and often degraded once profit margins look more promising in other areas. Black activists challenge this extractivist logic, both in environmental and in human terms with regard to quality of life. As Villa relates, the new legislation provides an important tool for local communities to defend their rights against outsider interventions in their rivers. At least in theory. It is of course another question altogether when one is faced with armed groups such as guerrillas and paramilitaries—a point to which I shall return.

In the second scenario, I was fortunate to witness an act of local resistance firsthand during a trip to the Guajuí River, where I held an informal meeting in the settlement of El Carmelo with members of the river organization ASODERGUA on Sunday, February 7, 1999. One hour into our conversation, the meeting was interrupted as rumors spread that two sawmill owners had assembled the people of San José de Guare, a settlement farther upstream, to come to an arrangement regarding the establishment of a sawmill opposite their village. Alarmed by this news, we immediately set off in two speedboats to arrive half an hour later in San José. With us were the community council's legal representative, Ricardo Castro (Don Ricard), and a young anthropologist, a member of ASODERGUA's directive committee. When we arrived a group of around forty people had assembled at the local school building. Tension was in the air and clearly discernible in the murmurs echoing around the building.

The young anthropologist took charge of the situation and politely asked the two sawmill owners to leave for about half an hour so that the community could discuss their proposal. During this time members of the directive committee explained to locals the parts of the new legislation that referred to timber extraction and to the rights of local communities. A heated debate ensued, in which locals made it clear that they were in favor of working with the two sawmill owners, since they promised at least some sort of income in a region without any real employment opportunities. The tension had now shifted. A confrontation seemed to emerge between locals—mostly campesinos, miners, and fisherfolk with little formal education—and community council representatives, who were mostly educated and with work experience outside the Pacific region. It seemed at times as if two different languages were spoken, one of ethnic and territorial rights anchored in constitutional discourse, and another one of poverty, lack of employment opportunities, and the desire to gain some income. As the half-hour mark approached, the shouting became louder. I stood on the sidelines, keenly observing the spectacle.

When the two sawmill owners returned to the meeting, they sensed the internal discord. "Are there people here willing to work with us?" they shouted in provocation. Clever move, I thought: divide and conquer. Big fellows they were too, brandishing huge clunky gold rings on their fingers, as they pointed at people in the crowd. "Are you willing to work with us?" they kept bellowing. I wondered if they were actually aware of the new legislation that required them to get an exploitation permit from the community council. Somehow I doubted it. Yet even if they did, they didn't seem to care, notwithstanding the community council's representatives doing their best to explain the situation.

As the deadlocked debate continued, the two sawmill owners suddenly demanded that the locals take a decision that same day, threatening to go elsewhere in the event that their offer was turned down. According to them, there were more than enough trees in other river basins. By that time I had become quite upset myself by the aggressive behavior of these *paisas*.[24] Ignoring the ethnographic etiquette of restraint, I got involved in the conversation and asked why it was that they had come to the Guajuí River in the first place, instead of harvesting all those trees in the other river basins. It was a rhetorical question, so I needed to oomph it up with some likely suggestions. Was it because the Guajuí was still one of the more peaceful river basins, where no guerrilla activities had been recorded until then? Was it not that the Saija basin, to which they had suggested going, was much more affected by a strong presence of the FARC guerrilla? And was it not also symptomatic for them to have come from Nariño, where the forests around the Iscuandé and Patía Rivers had been so intensely exploited that not much was left to be logged there? I really should have shut up by then, but I was mightily pissed off. So much for full disclosure.

After the sawmill owners left, threatening never to return, a loud discussion ensued among locals. Some accused the community council's representatives of only talking nonsense ("Ustedes sólo hablan carreta"), while they were suffering hunger and hardship. What alternative proposals would they make to provide income opportunities? ("Dedónde viene la plata ahora?"). It was a perfectly predictable conflict. Yet it was also a necessary conflict, because only there and then, discussing these issues, did it become clear what might be the practical implications of the new legislation. Beyond official discourses of managing biodiversity conservation, it was in this meeting where popular power, even if somewhat confused and inchoate, was articulated against external capital interests. Many locals were unhappy with the sawmill owners leaving, as they felt that urgently needed cash opportunities were evaporating in the moist air of their river. Nevertheless even the more aggressive ones admitted that the sawmill owners' attitude had been disgraceful, that they should not have demanded an immediate decision but taken their time, that further information should have been gathered over possible logging rates in the area, and that the regional development corporation should have been consulted over an exploitation permit. It was in this meeting that resistance to the extractivist project, to business as usual, began to take shape.

When I returned to San José one week later, people were still intensely debating this episode. The conflict had set off a conscientization process that might never have taken place in countless workshops on the scope of

Law 70. Leaders had been keen in pointing out that they were not generally opposed to timber extraction in the region but that it had to be done in ways guaranteeing the future exploitation of the resource. In San José de Guare the discourses on sustainability and conservation had found a practical application of popular resistance where, no matter the different attitudes internally, locals used the legislation to claim their rights.

These processes are internally contested, and there are and will always be different interests at stake, even within the same community. Yet it is precisely in these conflicts generated by the penetration of external capital that consciousness is constructed. Crucial in this scenario was the intervention and guidance of local leaders. Without them the plan of installing a sawmill in San José de Guare would probably have gone ahead, even though it would have been illegal. In the remainder of this chapter I examine more closely issues of leadership in the organizing experiences.

Leadership as Human Resource

Political process models in social movement theory emphasize the role of leaders in mobilizing constituencies. In this section I want to read these issues in particular through the lens of resource-mobilization theory (RMT). In other words, I focus on leadership as a human resource to be mobilized in social movements. This approach is of particular interest in the mobilizing dynamics on the Pacific Coast. While the organizational structure of the community council has been prescribed in legislation, it is not immediately clear who is meant to take on a leading role at the local level. Who are the leaders of the community councils, for example? Where do they come from? What previous organizational experience, if any, do they bring to the new political mobilization? What motivates them to engage as leaders in these processes?

To start with, a general trend can be observed when comparing black leadership in the river-based community councils with urban-based social movements. Whereas black activists in the cities are often young, educated former students or professionals, the majority of leaders in the river basins are older campesinos with more organizing experience in popular or state-driven initiatives. This distinction often translates into differences in discourse and vision between younger and older leaders. Although it would be too simple to talk of a generation gap, it is clear that the older peasant leaders often have a more materially based discourse rooted in on-the-ground experiences prior to Law 70, whereas the discourse of younger urban activists has predominantly been formed around Law 70 and its ethnic-territorial aspects.

One of the more senior campesino leaders with a long-standing tradition of working in peasant associations is Porfirio Becerra, or Don Por, as he is affectionately called. While spending time with the regional organization Palenque de Nariño in Tumaco in January 1999 I had ample opportunities to observe the interactions between this energetic crowd of young leaders and Don Por. They got on very well together and respected each other, sharing the common goal of meaningful territorial empowerment for black communities, yet certain differences in interpretation could be observed. Following Robert Benford (1993), these differences within a movement regarding leadership styles, strategies, and analysis can be seen as "frame disputes." More than just a pervasive aspect of movement dynamics, these frame disputes are actually crucial features of the everyday life of social movements. A sensitivity to these disputes helps us to refrain from treating a particular social movement as a monolith. In fact movements "do not develop a single collective identity, but, rather, within any movement several collective identities are typically constructed and may vie for legitimacy" (698). To illustrate the diverse movement framing strategies at play in Nariño, I quote at length from my interviews with Don Por:

I am sixty-two years old, and I come from the minga experience, from rice production, from plantain cultivation, from canoe construction. I know all these things. I know how to till; I know a lot of things. But the Process [PCN] is not led by people who know these things. It is led by people who were born here [in Tumaco], who only know of the city. This is a critique that we have made for some time now, that intellectually one can do certain things, but that this position makes other people wonder, "This one is not a farmer, that one does not know how to row a canoe. So why is he leading the Process?" . . . You see, people believe a veteran more than the young ones; they believe more in their experience. It is not the same as saying things like, "I am from the Process of Black Communities." All that is important, but it does not reach people the same way as when it is said by a skillful person with a lived experience. That is to say, it is not the same "doing" as "being." To be is one thing, and to do is another. The directives that come from above, they do not sink in here.[25]

Don Por's critique may sound a bit harsh, which might have something to do with the fact that he had just come out of a meeting with some of the younger leaders and was, shall we say, a bit annoyed, when I interviewed him. We should refrain from essentializing the differences he remarks upon in binaries of young/old, rural/urban, and so on. After all, social movements are constituted by and through their internal differences. It is important, however, for the movement to work on these differences, to make sure they don't become divisive.

One aspect stands out in Don Por's critique. To him the differences in age and in "lived experience" have resulted in different approaches to economic development and conservation. In his words:

Regarding the process of economic development, there are two tendencies. One that we, the older campesino leaders, put forward, that any institution, state, international or other, support environmentally sustainable programs and projects of agricultural activities. This is one position, which I support. And the community council supports this one. There is another tendency, of the younger leaders, supporting management plans and territorial ordering. But people begin to ask themselves why we need a management plan, because what we have managed well until now, within the communities we do know that. We know when to hunt, we know that. We know when to hunt rabbit, for example. And we can impose a closed season during their gestation period. We know that. We know that this area is suitable for the production of chontaduro [peach palm], we know that through practical experience. We know that we have to look after this land. We know that. This is fundamental. Because people have always done that. It is not necessary to order it, to systemize it. But now people are talking of management plans and territorial ordering. This is the discourse right now.

Don Por's critique of the management plans as being somewhat superfluous and not serving local people's interests resonates with similar concerns about the obligation to draw fixed boundaries for land right claims in the context of local fluid boundaries and overlapping territorialities. The management plans form part of the state's strategy to extend its institutions, norms, and juridical practices over preexisting practices of territorial management in the Pacific lowlands. Like the formalization of boundaries, they are one of the technologies of state power to bring the region and its inhabitants into closer alignment with the rationalities of the modern territorial state.

Black communities are forced to "play the game" if they want to achieve legal recognition of their collective territorial aspirations. This necessity has been recognized by the younger social movement leaders, maybe more so than by the older campesino leaders, who are more concerned with practical hands-on support for local communities in the rivers whose life they have shared for decades. I return to this difference at the end of this chapter.

The Formation of Leaders: Personal Experience as Driving Force

Ricardo Castro was twenty-six years old when he left his native village of El Carmelo on the Guajuí River to work on the sugar plantations in Palmira in the Valle del Cauca Department in 1960. There he also studied commerce and accounting in the evenings. He was actively involved in union activity, and in 1966 he was elected general secretary of a sugarcane workers' union. Then, in 1967, Don Ricard returned to the Cauca Coast to work as a teacher in Coteje on the Timbiquí River. There he also became secretary of the Communal Action Committee (Junta de Acción Comunal [JAC]). The JACs are a nationwide state-driven initiative that organize in local committees to watch over everyday community affairs. Their structures and hierarchies do not necessarily encourage active popular participation, and in many cases they exist only on paper without any real impact on community welfare. As Don Ricard explains:

In 1967 I came to Timbiquí. I was around thirty years old. They appointed me to the JAC, because the teacher, as the most able person, always occupied the post of secretary of the JAC. Then I went to Belén on the Napi River, as a teacher as well. And there too I was secretary of the Communal Action Committee. They said the same thing there: the teacher had to be the secretary of the JAC.

In 1972 Don Ricard retired from teaching and dedicated himself to agriculture in his native village of El Carmelo. There he was a member of the Agricultural Cooperative of the Pacific, COADEPAL, the rural agricultural program set up by INCORA that I discussed in chapter 4. He remembers:

After I retired from teaching, I dedicated myself to agriculture. I had a loan from INCORA, since we had land in El Carmelo to cultivate coconut. There I became a member of the Agricultural Cooperative of the Pacific. This was a program of INCORA. So, as a member *of the cooperative in El Carmelo, they chose me as delegate to the Assembly in 1972. And in the Assembly they elected me member of the cooperative's Supervising Committee, which watched over the management of the cooperative. During four consecutive periods, I was a member of the cooperative's Supervising Committee.*

Around the same time Don Ricard was elected secretary of the Municipal Board of Directors of the Peasant Association ANUC (Asociación Nacional de Usuarios Campesinos) from 1974 to 1975. He also held the post of treasurer of the Parents Association (Asociación de Padres de Familia) from 1992 to 1993 and acted as president of the same association from 1994 to 1995. Furthermore in 1994 he was town councilor of the Conservative Party in Guapi for one year. This was his only experience in formal party politics. He didn't enjoy it very much. Following Law 70, the river organization ASODERGUA formed in the Guajuí River in 1994. Don Ricard became treasurer of this organization, and on September 26, 1997, he was elected legal representative of the Community Council of the Guajuí River.

In many ways Don Ricard personifies the organic leader in the Pacific Coast river basins, rising to his current position by way of long-standing and diverse experiences of social activism. Like him, many of today's campesino leaders on the Pacific Coast left the region in their youth to find employment as agricultural workers on the sugar plantations in the Valle del Cauca region. Like him, they gained their first activist experience in trade unions there. And like him, many others eventually returned to their rivers and applied their organizational skills in social mobilization there.

Humberto Villa from the Napi River has a similar story to tell. As a young man he too left his native river to seek employment on the sugarcane plantations of the Valle del Cauca region. There he worked for thirteen years and became a union leader. He got into trouble for his militant activities defending workers' rights for a minimum wage, so he eventually left the union and quit his job, disappointed at not having achieved unity among the workers:

So I retired and went home, where I had land to work. I came here, and here I am, well, with the vision to keep working with the people. First I lived in Guapi, where I had a fiasco. I had set up a little business, but the boat sank, and I lost everything. So what else was left for me to do? I moved upstream. There were the mines. I had to make a living for my family somehow. That was in 1989. . . . So I returned to my lands, and I dedicated myself to organizing a cooperative group. We formed a mining cooperative. Of that cooperative I was vice president.

Both Ricardo Castro and Humberto Villa lived through the process of circular migration so typical for Afro-Colombians on the Pacific Coast (Arboleda 1998; Wade 1993). As young men they left their rivers in search of salaried work, which in the 1960s and 1970s was frequently found on the sugarcane plantations of the Valle del Cauca region. There they acquired organizational experience engaging in trade union work, which, on their return to their respective rivers on the Cauca Coast, would be a valuable resource for their leadership positions. Although they may judge some of their previous organizing experiences as failures, the spirit of wanting to organize remained and still nurtures their hopes today. Both of them invest feelings and emotions in their community work. As Don Ricard explains, "Some of us have lived this experience of belonging, of wanting to be involved in the organizing processes. This thing, well, it fascinates me. Yes, I like it, I like it. Maybe there were failures in the organizing question at times, maybe not all of us managed to assimilate these things. But at least for some of us the experience remains for the future."

Beyond rational choice theory à la Olson (1965), personal feelings, desires, and emotions play an important part in an individual's decision to get involved in collective action. Don Ricard's enthusiastic exclamation "Yes, I like it, I like it" comes from the bowels of his conviction. Given the dangers and threats to their lives that many community leaders in the Pacific region are exposed to, this choice is anything but rational. It is a choice that comes from the heart; it is an embodied desire to get involved in what one loves doing: organizing people along the Pacific rivers to better their collective lives.

Such desire spurred on Mirna Herrera too. A teacher in Santa Bárbara de Timbiquí, Mirna was also a leader of the local women's movement Apoyo a la Mujer (Support for Women) and a member of the National Advisory Committee of Black Communities. Referring to her personal reasons for getting involved in the organizing processes, she enthusiastically affirmed, "These are things we are born with":

I think that the organizing process, as well as other decisions that one takes, is like an ambition, a compromise, a vocation that one has as a person. When I was young, I formed part of a missionary childhood group. We sang in mass, read the holy words. It was something special that had to do with popular religiosity of the community here. Later I formed part of a dance group that made claims of ethnic values through song, music, and dance. That allowed me to share and each day long for other, more important things, always in community. The work as a teacher as well, you see. And then all of that was linked up with the Process of Black Communities that had been taking place since the Constitution, with Transitory Article 55, that somehow concerned the organized black communities, and which would later turn into Law 70. . . . The first grassroots organization that was formed here in Santa Bárbara de Timbiquí was the association Apoyo a la Mujer. We are five years old now. I was its president up to last year, up to August 7 [1998]. And now I am an advisor. But I tell you that I have been participating in all grassroots organizations that have existed in Timbiquí. I mean, the interest was that people sort of really began to participate in their things through the organizations. Really, these are things we are born with.

As the interviews with Mirna, Don Por, Don Ricard, Walberto, Humberto, and others have shown, for many of today's leaders, there exists a "logic of continuity" to their participation in the organizing processes. Drawing on previous activist experiences—in trade unions, agricultural cooperatives, religious groups, or community organizations—they channel them into political leadership roles they have now taken on in the Pacific Coast river basins. In other words, they mobilize their leadership as a resource for the movement.

Mirna Herrera also suggested that the ethnic component was already central to her dance group, expressed through music, songs, and dance moves. Present-day black ethnic-territorial organizations draw on these cultural expressions and articulate them in their political dimension. In this sense rural black identities are also mobilized as a resource in the cultural politics of black communities. Insights from both RMT and more identity-oriented perspectives to social movement theory can usefully be brought together to analyze this movement. Rather than treating them as incompatible models, as is often suggested in social movement literature, letting both approaches work together allows for a fuller picture to emerge of the social movement of black communities in Colombia.

"They Don't Want to Understand": The Discontinuities of Conscientization

After three months in the field in 1999 it had become clear to me that there had not been a massive black mobilization of campesinos on the Cauca Coast. The organizing processes at the local and regional levels had been slow, with only a few people getting actively involved. This was not just my own impression; most black leaders shared this interpretation. But why was that? What could possibly explain the widespread lack of awareness regarding community councils, collective land rights, and legislation concerning the Pacific Coast? I had talked at length to many movement leaders who were enthusiastic, committed, and constantly traveling up and down the rivers to hold meetings and workshops on these issues. I had accompanied them many times on these trips and witnessed firsthand their engagement with local communities, who seemed interested and thankful for those visits.

Yet most people I talked to—in the town of Guapi itself and in the various river basins—who were not directly involved in the organizing processes had little knowledge of them. I decided to conduct an in-depth survey in one population to try to understand what appeared to me an increasingly troubling lack of conscientization. The social movement scholar in me *wanted* to see people mobilize on a grand scale. I *wanted* to tell this wonderful story of black resistance in Colombia. This lack of massive mobilization began to worry me. It didn't fit my expectations . . .

On February 18, 1999, I crossed the Timbiquí River at Santa Bárbara, accompanied by a local schoolteacher with whom I had previously shared my concerns and who was also keen on finding out what local folks knew of Law 70. I was glad I didn't go on my own. Even though I had spent some time in Santa Bárbara and was known to many people there, a lone white man strolling along the riverbanks would have been regarded as suspicious, no matter how you looked at it. Our plan was to walk upstream along the opposite riverbank and ask locals in each house that we passed about their ideas on community councils, collective land rights, and Law 70.

The first settlement we came to was known as Calle del Pueblo. The schoolteacher knew some of the inhabitants, and we were invited into one of their houses. As I climbed the outdoor steps leading to the main door I felt good. Answers were awaiting . . . In the main room we sat down on intricately carved wooden chairs, and our host offered us *agua de panela*, after which she disappeared behind a curtain that led to the kitchen. Before she returned, however, another woman climbed the steps to the house and entered the main room. Legs firmly planted, she stood in a challenging posture in front of me. "Y usted, quién es?" . . . At that moment I couldn't help but think back to my "initiation" to ethnographic fieldwork in the Pacific, where my presence was similarly challenged in Don Agapito's house (see the interlude).

I glanced at the schoolteacher but did not get much support there. So I explained to the woman who I was, what I was doing in the area, and that I wanted to talk to people about Law 70. My attempt at explanation wasn't good enough, though. In fact she was quite suspicious of my "mission." Given the involvement of foreigners, especially Russians, in the commercial gold-mining activities in the Timbiquí River, this was an easily understood concern, I thought.[26] It turned out that the woman was an active member of the local Communal Action Committee (JAC). She made it clear that they were no longer willing to let foreigners onto their lands. My heart sank. I saw my meticulously planned in-depth survey float downstream. No answers. More questions.

At that moment—and with what seemed like the wave of a magic wand—our host emerged from behind the curtain with more cups of agua de panela. With her bubbly, good-natured attitude she calmed down my suspicious tormenter and survey destroyer. Shortly after, we were discussing Law 70. It turned out that the woman of the JAC had no idea about the legislation. And she became quite upset when we told her that a community council was to be established in the river basin. She hadn't heard about any of that. Nor had our host.

Eventually the schoolteacher and I continued our quest. In a few houses we had spontaneous meetings with neighbors turning up, curious about my presence. I talked with them about the legislation, the possibilities it offered black communities, the need to organize themselves, and the intention to create a community council in their area with their active participation. Everyone seemed interested in these issues yet appeared not to have heard of them before. Without offering a statistical analysis here, I can state that the overwhelming majority of people were not even aware of such a thing as a community council. Some locals had heard about Law 70 but were not able to give me an idea of what it meant or stood for.

Great was my surprise, therefore, to find out one week later that in fact a community council *had already* been formed in the area, including the village of Calle del Pueblo whose people I had talked to. So how should I understand this situation? Did they really not know about these issues? Did they know but didn't want to talk with me about them? Had they never been informed about the community council being formed? Did they not understand when community leaders explained issues regarding the legislation? Or maybe no one ever came to talk to them?

Addressing these questions with community leaders shed some light on this quixotic situation. Walberto Banguera, legal representative of the Community Council Guapi Abajo, was particularly adamant about what was going on:

There are people who really don't know what a community council is. These are people who don't even know how to elect someone to represent them. This annoys me a lot, it annoys me. People have to know what their position is. In our council, we have met with the council's committees. Where we met, we invited local folks and began to talk with them. About what a community council is, what it is for, what we are going to do, and what we can do with the community council.

So why did so many people claim never to have heard of the concept? According to Banguera, some people would deny knowing about these issues simply because they weren't interested, or because they perceived collective land rights as going against their own interests. When I queried him further about a particular visit to Playa de Obregones, a coastal settlement at the mouth of the Guapi River, where virtually everybody had denied knowing about the already constituted Community Council Guapi Abajo, Banguera became agitated:

That they don't want to understand is something else. They are all Obregones there, you see. They think they have their lands titled. So they say that they are not interested in Law 70, because they don't want to get involved collectively with anyone else. That's why they aren't bothered about these things. But I have been there. We have been there with Dionisio from COCOCAUCA, *yes. And we explained to them what collective land titles were. We told them what the community council was for. That they don't want to understand, that's another issue. Because they don't like to be told what to do.*

I was sympathetic to Banguera's exasperation. Underlying this "not wanting to be told what to do" attitude was the widespread myth that collective land rights would make already existing individual land titles invalid and abolish private landownership. Of course this wasn't the case. Legislation covered only tierras baldías, the "empty" public lands in the Pacific, being subject to communal land titling. Yet it was common to find opposition arising to collective processes due to a lack of clarity over these issues. As a coffee shop owner told me in Santa Bárbara de Timbiquí, "I don't want them to tell me what to do on my lands."

Throughout the southern Pacific coastal lands this was an issue, as illustrated by Don Por's experience in the river basins around Tumaco: "It was very difficult for us, this job of conscientization, of motivation, of making our people aware, in order to get them to truly assume collective land titling. Because people began to think, 'Well, if we are not able to do what we want . . .' This was difficult."

This difficulty in successfully reaching and convincing the entire rural population of the Pacific lowlands with the message of mobilization should alert us to the fact that local subjectivities are multiple and cannot be molded easily into a homogeneous whole as a single "black community." Restrepo (2013:175) calls this the "multi-accentuality of ethnicization" and warns us against overestimating the power of mediation: "After countless workshops and meetings, the subjectivities of local people have been impacted more or less strongly. But the continued complaint about the lack of 'conscientization,' or the necessity of better 'training' and 'diffusion' of the rights of black communities . . . constitute only the tip of the iceberg in that the mediations, technologies of invention and forms of visualization are by no means a guarantee for a homogenous and absolute transformation of local subjectivities." This is, of course, precisely the challenge for social movements: to work toward the transformation of multiple local subjectivities into what Manuel Castells (1997) calls "resistance identities."

This task is further exacerbated in contexts where the local political imagination has been held hostage by corruption. The confusion over the extent of collective land titling, for example, was exploited by corrupt party politicians, who, as discussed in chapter 4, often worked against the creation of community councils. Walberto Banguera feels strongly about this "betrayal": "I think that people have their hands tied by traditional politics. They are dominated by the politician here, because it is the politician who arrives and buys their votes, and the one who buys the votes is the one who takes people's consciousness."

It has become common political practice in Guapi, for example, to openly buy votes during election campaigns. The candidates for mayor do not waste much time on making empty promises (Agudelo 2005). As Banguera explains, facing these clientelist practices of "buying consciousness," one equally needs resources and finances to counter them:

The work of conscientization with people, it seems very hard to me. For this work we need resources. Without resources there is nothing you can do. In order to raise people's awareness, you have to arrange meetings. During these meetings you need to provide lunch. To pick up the participants from their homes you need gasoline. And if you don't have a single peso . . .

As RMT stresses, the availability of financial resources is of great importance to social movements. While I can't examine this issue in great depth here, I want to briefly focus on some "curious" aspects that the (non)availability of resources generates. With this I want to illustrate the difference that space makes in this respect, in particular the difference that mobilizing the aquatic space makes compared to other environments. The aquatic space as a resource for black communities not only concerns the spatial underpinning and geographical reach of their land right claims; it is also the material resource and physical setting within and through which they organize political meetings. As we shall see, this setting brings special challenges with it.

"No Cash, No Food, No Transport, No Meeting": The Thorny Issue of Resources

It is frequently expected of organizers of meetings in the Pacific to offer lunch to participants, and it is not uncommon to hear locals comment on meetings that they have attended in terms of the quality of food served rather than the issues under discussion. A telling instance occurred during a workshop organized by the research project Proyecto Naidí that examined possibilities for the sustainable exploitation of the naidí palm in Nariño. On May 8, 1999, I accompanied the project's coordinators to a meeting arranged with representatives of the Community Council Unicosta in the village of Madrid on the Iscuandé River. At 8 a.m. we set off in a speedboat from a hamlet where we had spent the previous night. Meandering along the coastal mangrove-lined creeks, we picked up various community leaders at their homes. At each stop residents came out to greet us, with kids excitedly jumping into the river. There was a bit of small talk here and there; promises to convey messages were made; packages were received to be delivered to relatives and friends in Madrid. The journey was a jolly if somewhat drawn-out affair.

When we finally arrived at the meeting place at around 10 a.m., and I thought the meeting was about to start, the assembled participants demanded breakfast. *Queremos desayuno.* I was flabbergasted. How was that possible? We had spent over two hours picking up people along the way. Surely they had had breakfast before they left their homes? Important issues were to be discussed at the meeting. Why waste any more time? Particularly since we had to leave the village by 2 p.m. at the latest, before the low tide's falling water levels would dry up the river channels and leave us stranded.

Don B, the project's coordinator, just smiled at my expression of disbelief and began to unload bags of bread, eggs, and two-liter bottles of Colombiana, the orange-colored national *gaseosa*, or soda, that always reminded me of the Scottish version of hangover cures, Irn Bru. I had noticed these bags in the boat before but did not know what they contained. With the mystery solved, eggs were prepared and breakfast was had.

The meeting started at 12 p.m. It was all quite rushed in the end. At 2 p.m. we hurriedly packed up the workshop materials and left. On the way back we again dropped off the various community leaders at their homes. The mood on the boat was less jolly than in the morning. The meeting had been a disaster. No agreement had been reached between Don B and the community leaders as to their involvement in Proyecto Naidí. It was felt that not enough time had been set aside for the meeting. All the way back I couldn't get over this surreal experience. Later I was to find out that this was not an isolated incidence. At a meeting on June 20, 1999, during a workshop on environmental education plans in the village of Vuelta Larga of the same community council, one local leader remarked to me over lunch, "If there wasn't *almuerzo* [lunch], we wouldn't be here anymore."

As funny as the situation might look retrospectively, this "no food—no meeting" attitude can be exasperating for anyone trying to organize a gathering. It is a particularly serious issue if leaders do not have many resources at their disposal. It is therefore not a trivial issue at all, but can develop into a serious obstacle for successful mobilization.

Things have not always been that way. Don Ricard remembered that locals used to provide food themselves to those who came to give workshops on collective land titling:

I'll tell you one thing. In those days with Article 55 [in 1991], people mobilized. You got to a meeting and it was packed, in any community. In the Guajuí River we mobilized. And when we arrived, it was "Ah, okay, this community lives from fishing; they can bring fish. This community grows papa china [a tuber typical of the region], let them bring papa china." That's how we arranged meals. Or we went to a community, and when we got there, they said, "Well, we will make guava juice." And they made the juice. "Well," said others, "since these people already make the juice, we will prepare some food." And that's how it went. So that whenever you got to a community, they prepared lunch. After that, when Law 70 came, people were not ready any more to contribute, and all of this was lost.

One of the results of these customs being "lost" is that any kind of meeting becomes very expensive, more so if we take the characteristics of the Pacific's aquatic environment into account. First, transport on the rivers needs to be adjusted to tidal changes. As a result meeting schedules are difficult to plan, especially when participants come from different river parts or from various river basins. Second, travel by dugout canoe can take a long time, which may discourage people from attending a meeting, particularly when more urgent household activities require attending to. Third, transport in speedboats is very expensive due to high gasoline prices in the area. Normally people would not have access to funds for paying these transport costs. The meeting in Madrid was possible because of funding from Proyecto Naidí. If we hadn't picked up the community leaders on the way, they would not have come to the meeting. As Mirna Herrera reflects on these difficulties for popular mobilization, "It so happens that it is not the same calling a meeting in the North of Cauca, or in any other place in the interior of the country, because the transport conditions are simply different, completely different from here. The very geographical location. So we haven't had the space of coordination, the space of dialogue."

This "space of dialogue" is important, however, in raising levels of awareness among local populations. Real spaces of dialogue and conscientization were created, for example, in the case of ACADESAN's journey along the San Juan River (see chapter 4) or with the general assemblies. Yet while the latter were funded by the central government as prescribed in Decree 1745, local communities increasingly depend on themselves to finance meetings. In particular community leaders often hold the high transport costs responsible for exploding budgets for meetings or in the implementation of small-scale community-oriented development initiatives funded by NGOs. Using the region's typical rhyming style in their informative bulletin, Fundación Chiyangua (1998:20), a women's organization on the Cauca Coast, explained the following to the funding agencies of their project Strengthening of Women Groups Dedicated to the Cultivation of Food and Medicinal Plants on Azoteas:

Sabe lo que nos pasó
doctor, con este proyecto?
eran veinte azoteas
y cuatro grupos en esto

Pero por sus objetivos
más el evento primero
resultaron azoteas
para tirarle al hilero

Doce en la zona urbana
treinta y dos en la rural,
cómo la plata de transporte,
no se iba a disparar?

Porque a Naciones Unidas
hoy les queremos contar
no es lo mismo andar en carro
que en lancha subir y bajar.

(Do you know what happened
with this project?
Twenty platform gardens
and four groups it was going to be

But because of its objectives
and the first event
many more azoteas sprang up
all over the place

Twelve in the urban area
thirty-two in the countryside;
how were the transport costs
not going to explode?

To the United Nations
we want to say today
it is not the same to travel by car
than up- and downstream by boat.)

While high expenses alone cannot explain the difficulties of mobilization in the river basins, it is clear that the particularities of the aquatic space have a considerable impact on the forms of organization. The availability of financial resources for transport, scheduling, and other needs occasioned by the riverine environment has become of prime importance to understand the limitations of the organizing processes in the river basins today. In its crudest sense, RMT applied on the Cauca Coast can indeed mean "no cash, no transport, no food, no meeting."

Final Reflections

The community councils, as one cornerstone of the social movement of black communities, illustrate the complex processes of black ethnic-territorial mobilization in the Colombian Pacific. While they are conceived as an organizational space of community representation and as the territorial authority of the collective lands of black communities, they are also exposed to the interests and interventions of other actors, such as capital, the state, and local political elites. Through the creation of community councils the state has certainly extended its administrative reach into the Pacific lowlands in ways it had not been able to do before, and one may indeed argue that the state's legitimacy has been enhanced in this way. The community councils should therefore be studied in the context of these multiple entanglements and shifting power relations.

Such an approach also accounts for the differential experiences in the formation of community councils, whereby some simply work better than others as an "organizing body of ample participation, where people discuss and progress is made in the orientation of the social movement with the grass-roots" (OCN 1996:248). Florentino Carvajal of the Community Council Unicosta put it this way: "As far as the community councils are concerned, we are still in the early stages. This is not a process which happens overnight. This will be in the long run. But we have to carry on working towards it."[27]

I have focused in this book on the community councils as privileged spaces to observe these diverse entanglements at play. It is at this local level where the discourse over ethnic-territorial rights generated at the national level is played out on the ground, where it is absorbed, transformed, and deployed by a range of actors. Only through a serious ethnographic engagement with these processes can we hope to flesh out the discourse of resistance, detect discontinuities, and attend to real-life problems of political mobilization in particular settings. This fleshing-out is central to the critical place perspective on social movements that I propose in this book. Place is understood as relational place. It is not essentialized, unchanging, traditional, set in stone. Rather place is constituted through relations and connections at multiple scales. That is why I find Agnew's (1987) three-part concept of place so useful as a frame when thinking through the geographies of social movements.[28]

EPILOGUE

It was the best of times, it was the worst of times, it was the age of wisdom,
it was the age of foolishness, it was the epoch of belief, it was the epoch of
incredulity, it was the season of Light, it was the season of Darkness, it was
the spring of hope, it was the winter of despair, we had everything before us,
we had nothing before us, we were all going direct to heaven, we were all going
direct the other way.
—CHARLES DICKENS, *A TALE OF TWO CITIES*

A Tale of Two Pacifics

Five o'clock in the morning of a day that seemed quiet as usual. Nobody
expected at that time the terror that suddenly woke us up. We were
stunned by the screams of those who tried to flee. We heard bursts of
gunfire. With their butt rifles they knocked down the doors that we
didn't open out of fear. It was madness. Confused we screamed and
ran because we saw men armed to the teeth. . . . "The paras have arrived," one of the armed men shouted. That was when we realized who
it was. . . . We were all surprised by this tragedy. The victims were
paraded through the village in underwear; they were brutally beaten,
hands tied behind their backs, and then they were taken away and disappeared. Those of us who could see what was happening, we managed
to jump into the river and hide among the reeds. We stayed for two
days submerged with the water up to our necks, without food, desperate. . . . At 8 am helicopters of the Army's Boltígero Batallion arrived.
They circled over the village and then dropped off troops. We were still

submerged in the water among the reeds and thought that things had changed at last. But to our great surprise the helicopters began to bomb the area where we were hiding. The paramilitaries gave orders by radio to those in the helicopters and these sprayed us with machinegun fire, bombs and grenades. We couldn't believe what was happening. This was not a game; this was death that was very close. Many of my friends were killed by the gunfire; it was horrible to see them die without being able to do anything. (Córdoba 2001:249–50)

These are the words in which Marino Córdoba recalls the "night of terror" of December 20, 1996, when heavily armed paramilitaries entered the town of Riosucio on the Atrato River at dawn. Breaking down doors, tearing people out of their beds, with lists in their hands, they started to kill. A coordinated offensive by the Colombian Army and paramilitary forces, the attack was launched under the pretext of combating FARC guerrillas in the area. In the coming months this (para)military campaign, dubbed "Operation Genesis," was extended to the surrounding river basins in the northern Chocó Department.[1] Harrowing eyewitness accounts provide visceral narratives of how people lived through this time—in terror and constant anxiety. The ways in which rural Afro-Colombians perceived their homeplace would forever change. One community leader from the Salaquí River described his experience of the air bombardment to me:

One morning, on January 14, 1997, a Monday, we felt the most terrible thing. Such a horrible experience, some people even died of a nervous breakdown. We were having breakfast. I was at home in Playa Aguirre, when we felt the earth trembling. First we felt a thunder, boom, a terrible noise. Shortly after, the houses started to shake, and then it was boom, boom, boom. We went to see what was going on, and there were planes above us. The bombing began in Riosucio, on January 14. . . . Afterward they bombed all the surrounding rivers; the Salaquí, the Truandó, and the Cacarica; they bombed all these areas. . . . In Cañoseco they destroyed a school, because they bombed indiscriminately. The only zone they didn't bomb in the Salaquí River was our community of Playa Aguirre. . . . We were further upstream, and seeing this degree of destruction we thought that no one would survive downstream. Because they were bombing the whole day long. . . . And when the bombs fell over there, the houses here shook as if it was an earthquake. A horrible thing! After the bombing no one wanted to go downriver to see what had happened, out of fear. . . . Some five days later, when someone went down, *there was not a single soul along the banks of the Salaquí River. Because what had happened? After the bombing that night, everyone fled, like in an exodus.*[2]

In this narrative the river is still a central figure. Yet different from the poetic evocations of the aquatic space in the accounts of Doña Celia and Don Agapito (see chapter 2), here fear and terror dominate the structure of feeling. The aquatic sense of place becomes infused with a new and hitherto unknown quality. Overnight it was transformed into a terrorized sense of place. The season of Light was giving way to the season of Darkness. The spring of hope to the winter of despair.[3]

A Counter-space under Fire

From today's perspective the campaign around Riosucio in 1996–97 marked the beginning of a trend that would radically reshape social life in the entire Pacific region. The "arrival of the paras" would see hundreds of thousands of Afro-Colombian campesinos driven off their lands by force in the coming decades. It would see thousands of them killed and campaigns of fear and terror systematically launched against their leaders.

The Colombian Army has been deeply implicated in this terror campaign. It is common for the military to justify its operations with the argument of pursuing left-wing FARC rebels. It is easy to do so, particularly in such remote areas as the Pacific lowlands. Who would go and check, after all? Whereas images of rebel attacks, paramilitary massacres, and army operations from many other parts of the country reach the national television networks almost immediately, images from the Pacific Coast are much harder to get hold of. It took three days, for example, for images of the aftermath of the Bellavista massacre on the Atrato River banks in May 2002 to reach national television networks. One hundred and nineteen people were killed in this small hamlet when a gas cylinder bomb launched by FARC rebels went astray and exploded in the local church, where people had sought refuge during heavy fighting between FARC and paramilitaries (ONU 2002; Oslender 2008a).[4] In many other instances no images ever reached the outside world.

Whereas international NGOs and the UN Refugee Agency focus their attention on human rights violations in the Chocó Department, other parts of the Pacific, such as the Cauca Coast region, where I conduct most of my fieldwork, go completely unnoticed. So much so that on arriving in Guapi in November 2004, I collected data and testimonies of displaced people from the surrounding river basins that had appeared in no register, neither state nor NGO. There are uneven geographies of mourning and reporting too.

In such a context of invisibility it is easy for armed actors to operate under the cloak of anonymity, since they need not fear their actions will be revealed. For the Colombian Army to declare that they were chasing and fighting FARC rebels in the area around Riosucio in 1996–97 seemed a reasonable argument. Yet no reports ever surfaced of direct combat between the army and FARC guerrillas in the area (Bejarano et al. 2003:34). In hindsight it seems clear that the indiscriminate air bombing was aimed principally at terrorizing the local population and emptying the terrains. As a result, during the months of January and February 1997 alone, some twenty thousand Afro-Colombians fled their settlements in great panic. This was the first of a number of massive exoduses that have begun to transform the entire Pacific Coast region. Through threats, massacres, and the spreading of terror among local populations, armed groups dispute territorial control, with local peasants caught up in the cross-fire and often stigmatized as supporters of one group and hence eliminated by the other. As a result hundreds of thousands of rural Afro-Colombians have been forcefully displaced from their homes. They arrive with little left in the cities, where an inefficient social security system is unable to provide support. Many of them have few options but to beg at traffic lights, where they look painfully out of place, having had to swap their lands, rivers, and forests for the unknown and chaotic space of the city's concrete jungle (Oslender 2016).

It has become increasingly clear that a changing rationale for developing the Pacific Coast region lies at the heart of the unprecedented paramilitary aggression, a shift from the experiment of the early 1990s, when it looked—for a tantalizingly short while—as if common ground was found between the economic-territorial logic of the state and the needs and desires of local communities. This period seemed to promise a coalescence of interests around the notions of sustainable development and biodiversity conservation. Law 70 would set the legislative framework for such a project based on the territorial empowering of rural black communities through the creation of community councils as new territorial authorities administering communal landownership. Yet it was precisely at the moment when these communities began to receive their title deeds that they were pushed off their lands. In fact the very first collective land title in the Chocó Department had to be officially handed over in absentia since its communities had been forcefully displaced from their lands.

The trend of uprooting that spread through other parts of the Pacific region was accompanied by an aggressive return to the economic logic of exploitation and extraction, now forcefully pushed through by state and parastate actors, often cynically undermining the state's own legislation. In other words, the state and paramilitary forces act at the service of national and transnational capital in the Pacific lowlands. As a prominent black leader explained to me in an interview in Bogotá in November 2004, "The displacement in the Pacific Coast region is not a consequence of the armed conflict, the way in which the government wants to portray it to international public opinion. No. The displacement is a strategy of the conflict. The armed conflict uses the strategy of displacement to empty those lands that are needed to develop their megaprojects."

Once considered a "peace haven" (Arocha 1999:116), the region has now become fully integrated into the country's cartography of violence. The counter-space on the Pacific Coast, as envisaged by PCN, is under fire.[5] In a firsthand account a former district attorney, Gaby Márquez (2007:157), narrates life in the town of Barbacoas (Nariño) under paramilitary rule, where "the law of silence and fear had impregnated the local population." Writing under a pseudonym and now living in exile in Canada, Márquez describes the moment she and her son were stopped at an illegal paramilitary road block: "My little son thought they were real soldiers, because they dressed the same. It seems that they have the same tailors and fashion designers. How to distinguish between the real ones and the impostors?. . . . At that moment, the criminals were patting down the state's district attorney" (94).

Oil Palm and "Forced Displacement"

The link between violence and development can best be seen in the rapid expansion of oil palm plantations in the region since the late 1990s. These are often established by large conglomerates with national and transnational capital on lands collectively owned by rural black communities. These communities have increasingly resisted the appropriation of their lands in this way, drawing on the legal framework of Law 70 in their support. In order to implement their projects, oil palm entrepreneurs require the collaboration of local populations to provide land and labor for the cultivation process. Or, in cases of noncooperation, the cleansing of the territories. In this way entire communities are subjected to threats, targeted killings, massacres, and individual and collective forced displacement.

The case of Orlando Valencia, an Afro-Colombian leader from the Curvaradó region in Chocó and an outspoken opponent of oil palm cultivation, serves as an example of this common practice of repression and murder. He was disappeared on October 15, 2005, while traveling with a group of nine other people near the village of Belén de Bajirá in the Chocó Department. The car the group was traveling in was stopped by police, who took Orlando and two others to a local police station for interrogation. After he was released, a group of locally well-known paramilitaries approached Orlando, forced him onto a motorbike, and drove off. Ten days later his body was found in a nearby river.

What makes Orlando's fate particularly tragic is the fact that he had been invited by the U.S.-based religious charity Lutheran World Relief to speak at a Partnering for Peace conference in Chicago but was denied his visa by the U.S. Embassy in Bogotá. There is no doubt that his disappearance and execution must be seen in relation to his outspoken opposition to oil palm plantations in the Curvaradó River basin. Since 1996 this region has seen over twenty incidents of massive displacement and more than one hundred community members assassinated or disappeared. On September 28, 2006, a group of families from the Curvaradó region, supported by the national human rights organization Justicia y Paz, announced in a website communiqué their decision to return and reoccupy the lands from which they had been displaced ten years earlier. In their communiqué they made particular reference to the devastating impact that the forceful introduction of oil palm cultivation had on their lands, in that it "destroyed biodiversity, turned rivers of life into blood channels, and sowed seeds of death over those who were displaced, assassinated and disappeared."[6]

In July 2010 the National Association of Displaced Afro-Colombians, AFRODES, issued a report on the precarious human rights situation of black communities in the context of the "celebration" of two hundred years of republican life in Colombia.[7] In this report they denounced the assassinations of several community leaders. Felipe Landazury, of the Bajo Mira Community Council in the Department of Nariño, was one of them:

On June 24, 2008, suspected paramilitaries entered the village of Candelilla del Mar, seized Felipe, and kept the community captive. After two hours, the armed group freed the community with the exception of Felipe Landazury. The members of the community were freed, but then heard gunshots. The persons who later returned to the place learned that Felipe Landazury had been assassinated. Felipe Landazury was a distinguished Afro-Colombian leader named by his community to be the next President of the Community Council. Felipe was known as a great ethnic-territorial rights defender and a strong opponent of monocultures—the cultivation of oil palm on collective territories. (AFRODES 2010:61)

These are not isolated denunciations. Rather there exists a systematic link between the economic strategy of oil palm cultivation and land dispossession in the Pacific lowlands. A report by the Spanish NGO Human Rights Everywhere (2006:22) puts it rather bluntly, identifying a four-step "chain model" by which hitherto collectively owned lands are put under the control of oil palm companies as an "integral part of a production model or system." These steps are as follows:

1. Armed incursion with its associated crimes and human rights violations.
2. Illegal and violent expropriation of land.
3. Forced displacement of the owners of expropriated lands.
4. Planting of oil palm on "conquered" land.[8]

The entanglements of violence and development become clearer when we look at the increasing importance that the Colombian government has placed on oil palm cultivation in its national development policies.

The Push for Oil Palm

Colombia is the leading palm oil producer in Latin America today and the fifth largest in the world, after Malaysia, Indonesia, Nigeria, and Thailand (although it should be said that the lion's share of production comes from the first two). Oil palm (Elaeis guineensis) was first introduced to Colombia in 1932, but it was not until the late 1950s that it became of commercial value, mainly for the use of palm oil in the production of soaps, vegetable oils, and animal feeds (Ospina Bozzi and Ochoa Jaramillo 2001). In the mid-1960s some 18,000 hectares were in production. By 2001 this had increased almost tenfold to 170,000 hectares. Production that year reached 545,571 metric tons of palm oil, of which 459,101 were used for internal consumption and the surplus was exported for a value of more than US$20 million. The production area grew to around 330,000 hectares in 2007, almost doubling the area under cultivation since 2001.

Though domestic consumption of palm oil has also risen, the increase in production is mostly geared at an expanding export market. While 7 percent of palm oil was exported in 1995, this increased to 25 percent in 2000, to 33 percent in 2006, and was almost 40 percent in 2007 (FEDEPALMA 2007:29). Recent estimates put a growth potential of area under cultivation at a staggering 3,273,282 hectares, a projected tenfold increase (Rangel et al. 2009:29). Given the current worldwide hype over biofuels (into which palm oil can be converted), these numbers may be exaggerated, but they clearly identify the production of palm oil as one of the principal national export strategies (Human Rights Everywhere 2006; Roa Avendaño 2007). A brief look at public policies regarding oil palm cultivation helps to shed light on this development.

In 1994, under President César Gaviria (1990–94), Law 138 was passed, establishing a fund for the cultivation of oil palm (Fondo del Fomento Palmero). It was created to finance research into increasing the productivity of oil palm, support palm planting companies in the commercialization of the product, regulate markets, promote the export of products derived from oil palm, and support price stabilization mechanisms. As part of the consolidating Apertura Económica (Economic Opening) policy framework, a "strategic development alliance" was established between the National Federation of Oil Palm Growers, FEDEPALMA (created in 1962), and Colombia's government (Ospina Bozzi and Ochoa Jaramillo 2001).

During the administration of Andrés Pastrana (1998–2002) oil palm plantations were promoted as an alternative to illegal coca crops with funding under Plan Colombia, the largely U.S.-sponsored multibillion-dollar drug eradication campaign. This strategy was followed under President Álvaro Uribe's (2002–10) policy of Democratic Security. In a 2004 statement by Minister of Agriculture and Rural Development Carlos Gustavo Cano it is apparent that supporting agricultural production, including oil palm, was considered a counterterrorism measure: "President Uribe affirmed that weak agriculture leads to strong terrorism. . . . Thus our fight against terrorism can be seen as the defense of rural work. . . . Therefore agriculture acquires a strategic geopolitical value. . . . We are placing special emphasis on oil palm, where Colombia has reached the highest levels of productivity in the world" (quoted in Vélez Torres 2010:20).

In line with this policy the National Development Plan (Plan Nacional de Desarrollo) for the period 2002–6 included a section on Social Management of Rural Areas that aimed at "recuperating" 496,000 hectares of land for agro-industrial development, including sixty-two thousand hectares for oil palm cultivation. Such an approach to large tracts of (bio)-diverse rural regions required, according to the Plan, the "conditioning of lands" (*adecuación de tierras*) to prepare them for extensive plantations of monocultures.

One aspect of such a "conditioning" was the establishment of "strategic alliances" between Afro-Colombian communities in the Pacific Coast region on the one hand and multinational companies and the Colombian state on the other (Rangel et al. 2009:55). These strategic alliances were envisioned by Colombia's National Institute of Rural Development, INCODER (formerly known as the Institute of Agrarian Reform, INCORA), in Resolution 1516 of August 2005. They are only one example of how the Colombian state is trying to turn back previous legislation regarding the Pacific Coast. Law 70 of 1993 called for the protection of biodiversity and Afro-Colombian culture and communities in this region. The establishment of monocultures of any type is a clear violation of this legislation. Therefore—so the dominant logic goes—legislation has to be changed or undermined. And this is precisely what we are witnessing today. The so-called strategic alliances form part of this strategy of the state to undermine politically organized rural black communities by co-opting individual members or entire communities into participating in agro-industrial schemes that have not only proved detrimental to the environment but that ultimately lead to the deterritorialization of local populations.[9]

In short, what is at stake is the transformation of a region away from biodiversity conservation toward increasing cultivation of monoculture. Since this dominant developmental logic has met with growing resistance from organized communities, it is pushed through by a mix of co-optation (strategic alliances) and coercion (massacres, forced displacement).

Even FEDEPALMA (2007:15) had to admit that serious human rights violations had been committed in the establishment of oil palm plantations:

Several plantations were set up from the mid-1990s onwards in Urabá, part of the Chocó Department, and bordering with Antioquia. The development of these plantations has raised serious concerns, as they were founded on land (including areas of primary forest) belonging to Afro-Colombian communities who have collective rights to the land and because it has been associated with serious human rights violations. These issues have been investigated and documented by the Colombian authorities and by the Inter-American Commission on Human Rights of the Organization of the American States (OAS), which in early 2006 urged the Colombian government to protect the affected communities.

It is highly ironic that in the same self-promotional material FEDEPALMA (2007:5) claims that "the oil palm represents life itself to thousands of Colombians: it provides them with daily sustenance, stability and well-being. It is a source of opportunities for them and their families, and the pillar on which they build their dreams for the future."

The irony does not stop there. FEDEPALMA has put considerable effort into projecting its image—and that of palm oil production in Colombia in general—as environmentally friendly and at the ecological cutting edge of reducing greenhouse gas emissions. The flagship program, in Colombia known as Proyecto Sombrilla, is a Clean Development Mechanism (CDM) Umbrella Project for Methane Capture, Fossil Fuel Displacement and Co-generation of Renewable Energy.[10] FEDEPALMA hopes that this will lead to Colombia's gaining more than 500,000 Certificates of Emission Reductions per year.[11] It is therefore not surprising to hear FEDEPALMA's director of the environment program, Miguel Angel Mazorra, state that "The CDM Umbrella Project demonstrates that the oil palm growing sector in Colombia is making progress in consolidating its position in respect of the environment, that its activities are environmentally friendly, and that it is making significant contributions to sustainable development in the country" (FEDEPALMA 2007:70).

A similar environmental tone is struck by Hector Daniel Ramos, an agricultural technician at Aceites Manuelita in the Meta Department: "Oil palm plantations are ecological by definition. They are efficient photosynthesizers, extracting carbon from the atmosphere and transferring it to the soil in large quantities through the production of biomass. In this way, as in any other forested area, they have the ability to effectively contribute to the control of gases which cause global climate change" (FEDEPALMA 2007: 68).

In these enunciations oil palm cultivation in Colombia emerges as what Ogden et al. (2013) refer to as a "global assemblage": powerful mechanisms of socioecological change that often create new forms of environmental governance, in which the "local" is articulated with and transformed by global processes such as economic globalization and climate change in complex ways. As its statements show, FEDEPALMA mobilizes environmental language and sentiment that present palm oil production in Colombia as transcending the mere national interest and as playing an important role in global climate-change mitigation. (This strategy is part of the wider logic of capitalist restructuring that I call "the discursive fix" in chapter 5.)

What is striking in these declarations, as well as in the ecological logic projected in Proyecto Sombrilla, is the fact that these supposedly environmentally friendly initiatives are applied to what is a very varied physical geography in Colombia. They fail to acknowledge that it may be one thing to implement oil palm plantations in the interior of Colombia, such as the Magdalena Medio region, but a completely different thing to do so in a tropical rain forest environment that has been declared a biodiversity hot spot and where monocultures of the oil palm type have been outlawed by state legislation (Law 70). Once we critically challenge the environmentally friendly discourse on those grounds of geographical differentiation, a very different picture emerges. In fact, when combing carefully through FEDEPALMA's statements, we find enunciations that admit to problems in expanding oil palm cultivation into the biodiverse Pacific lowlands. Quoting Jens Mesa Dishington, the executive president of FEDEPALMA:

> In the case of Colombia, the expansion of the crop does not affect primary or even secondary tropical forests, because of the large amount of land available for agricultural use. Perhaps the only exception, and this is an initiative which is not supported by FEDEPALMA, is that of those investors who have recently started to get involved in oleaginous crops in the Urabá Gulf zone, in Chocó, in the northwest of the country, and whose undertakings are being investigated by the authorities to ensure that they are acting within the law. (FEDEPALMA 2007:67)

Here, then, is FEDEPALMA's template position. While they are ready to admit to problems in relation to human rights abuses and even seem to question the environmental logic of oil palm cultivation in the Pacific region, they distance themselves as a federation from these failed attempts. While they reject palm companies' activities in the Northwest (the Chocó), they continue with their operations in the Southwest (Nariño). While pointing to the "troubles" in the Chocó, they place a mantle of silence over very similar allegations in Nariño. However, it is the underlying logic of oil palm cultivation as such that is the problem. You cannot—and should not—have oil palm monocultures in a tropical rain forest environment that is renowned for its biodiversity. You cannot—and should not—do so against the will of organized local communities who have lived in and with this environment for centuries and have played a crucial part in protecting it.

Place and Social Movements

The push for oil palm in the Pacific region is clearly a reversal for the territorialization campaign of rural black communities, and the implications for the Afro-Colombian social movement have been immense. Many of its activists have been targeted and killed. Some were forced to leave the country. Others had to go into hiding. One of PCN's strong regional organizations, the Palenque de Nariño, based in Tumaco, had to be dissolved after continuing death threats to its leaders by paramilitaries. Faced with this pressure to their lives and their organization over the past two decades, the movement was forced to shift its attention from the struggle over land rights to human rights and survival. It is hard to exaggerate the toll that this shift has had on individual activists and on the collective as a whole. At the local level many community councils have ceased to function. Others have been co-opted by external actors.

What good, then, one may ask, has come of Law 70, when hundreds of thousands of Afro-Colombians have been forcefully uprooted and evicted from the very lands that the legislation granted them? True, the phenomenon of what is referred to as "forced displacement"—as if it were just about moving from one place to another, and not about a violent uprooting of one's life, the sudden end of one's life as known, a brutal push into the enforced uncertainty of life as a refugee—has haunted the Pacific lowlands for two decades now. Many communities could not even receive their land titles because they had already been pushed off their lands by armed gangs. Yet a cornerstone of the fight against "displacement" has been the legislation that was meant to protect rural black populations. Law 70 put in place a mechanism for the defense of place that black communities appeal to over and over again in demanding their rights.

Among all the chaos that reigns in the Pacific Coast today—the brutal implementation of large-scale oil palm plantations, the spreading of illegal coca crops and the accompanying aerial fumigation courtesy of Colombia's antinarcotics police, an explosion of commercial gold mining since 2005 owing to the skyrocketing gold price on the global market, the continued presence of guerrillas and paramilitary and criminal gangs—among all this chaos one constant remains: the impeccable beauty of Law 70. As García Márquez said, "The Constitution, the laws . . . everything in Colombia is magnificent." But maybe he was not 100 percent right after all when adding, "It has no connection with reality." Really? Quite on the contrary, I'd say. It has *everything* to do with reality, a reality that social movement leaders have died and continue to die for. The current war scenario in the Pacific Coast will not be the end of it. The wars will pass, the *orishas* will regain control, the *muntu* will reign once again. In order to rethink the Pacific Coast—*re-pensar el Pacífico*, as our campaign puts it—the legal framework of Law 70 is crucial.[12]

Like other boom-and-bust economies before (*tagua*, timber, rubber), one day oil palm monocultures will also fall prey to the cutthroat capitalist logic of supply and demand and will disappear from the Pacific lowlands. Global gold prices will collapse, and it will be once again economically infeasible to mine for gold with massive hydraulic equipment. And yes, one day even the coca leaves will search for other geographies to keep flourishing; after all, as campesinos know, *la coca anda*. The aquatic space, however, will remain. Not the same as today. Its assemblage of constantly changing relations will produce new expressions. Yet I dare say that *concheras* will still travel in their dugout canoes to the mangrove swamps to pick shellfish; lumberjacks will still navigate on rafts to the sawmills, as the tidal changes will still affect the region's temporality. And somewhere along the Guapi River, Doña Celia will observe her grandmother as she applies medicinal herbs and prayer to cure the evil eye, while Don Agapito is still chasing and shooting rabbits in the Guajuí basin.

I don't think that this is a nostalgic vision of things lost. I am not simply projecting my own sentimental gaze to atone for the current dehumanizing condition and relentless environmental destruction under way. Quite on the contrary, the logic of the river is at the heart of the political project of sectors of the social movement of black communities like PCN. It captures the progressive spirit and the winds of hope that blew across the Pacific lowlands in the early 1990s and that still orient the movement's thinking and acting today. No doubt some will contemptuously sneer and call this utopian thinking. Let us answer them with Henri Lefebvre (1976:35) that "today more than ever, there are no ideas without a utopia." Or with Pierre Bourdieu's (2003) appeal for collective intellectuals to work toward the production of "realistic utopias" to fire back against the tyranny of the market and to make common cause with others to resist the entrenched dogmas of domination. In sum, let us celebrate the "desire of the critical utopian imagination . . . operating in the cracks of modernity/coloniality" (Escobar 2008:196).

To continue imagining an alternative future for the Pacific Coast region and its people we need to turn back our gaze and reengage the seeds of hope that were sown in the early 1990s. For this we need to fully understand the logic of political and economic processes in the region, but also the diverse knowledge practices of place-based cultures and their "environmental imaginaries" as primary sites of contestation (Peet and Watts 1996:263).[13] This conviction lies at the heart of the critical place perspective proposed in this book. And it has shaped my narrative approach to the social movement of black communities in Colombia, not mainly through its organizational structures, strategies, and political discourse (although I have considered these too) but starting from the situated physical, social, and cultural contexts of everyday life as framing the subjectivities of ordinary people, which subsequently become articulated as social movement agency.

I am aware that this analytical and narrative strategy differs from established social movement theorizing in that I hardly engage classic concepts such as brokerage, diffusion, or scale shift. Yet, as other geographers have pointed out, the routine deployment of these concepts often results in a lack of attention to the wider complexity of social movements (Castree et al. 2008; Nicholls et al. 2013). As Davies and Featherstone (2013:241) argue, authors such as Tarrow "have adopted a mode of theorizing that seeks to develop a core set of concepts to explain common processes between radically different social movements . . . [producing] accounts of social movement activity where such activity is reduced to identification with such concepts. . . . Rather than allowing an engagement with the dynamic processual constitution of political activity, their approach reduces social movement activity to a set of generic processes and mechanisms."

I have tried to stay clear of such a generic process approach to the social movement of black communities in Colombia and have instead examined what Davies and Featherstone (2013:241) call "the generative character of social movement/political activity." In particular I have examined in ethnographic depth the ways in which this movement's activities were generated in specific places in the Pacific Coast region. Rather than merely nodding to "place" in convoluted sociospatial frameworks, I have opted to center my empirical inquiries on place-making in the Pacific lowlands as providing the soil out of which articulated social movement activity arises. Such an approach might not work for everyone. Certainly scholars interested in the transnational sphere of social movement organizing may find little of interest in such an ethnographically grounded approach to a particular social movement. But the critical place perspective proposed here has helped me to trace Lefebvre's "differential space" in the movement's articulation for an alternative life project. Given the current onslaught against people and nature in the Pacific region, it remains to be seen if and how far black communities can turn the transformative potential of their environmental imaginaries into a meaningful counter-space. The critical place perspective proposed in this book hopes to ensure those attempts are not forgotten.

Prologue

1. The Constituent Assembly was a national public body that included independent representatives from ethnic, political, and religious minorities, as well as reincorporated guerrilla fighters of the M-19, the People's Liberation Army EPL, and the indigenous guerrilla group Quintin Lamé. Conspicuously absent from the Constituent Assembly was the country's most powerful guerrilla group, the Revolutionary Armed Forces of Colombia (FARC). Under previous negotiations with the government of President Belisario Betancur, they had signed a peace treaty that led to the foundation of the Unión Patriótica (UP) as a new political party in 1984. Yet in the following months and years many of their leaders were killed by right-wing paramilitary groups linked to state institutions. Given this experience, the FARC chose not to join the Constituent Assembly process of 1990.

2. Due to weak politicization and internal division within the Afro-Colombian movement, no black representatives were elected to the Constituent Assembly. It was up to a sympathetic indigenous Constituent member, who had campaigned from a platform that addressed both indigenous and black interests in the Pacific region, and other like-minded representatives, to push for the inclusion of AT-55 (Agudelo 2004a; Arocha 1992; Fals Borda 1993; Paschel 2010; Wade 1995).

3. Other organizations include the Peasant Association of the San Juan River ACADESAN (Asociación Campesina del Río San Juan), formed in 1990, and the Peasant Associations of the Baudó River ACABA (Asociación Campesina

del Río Baudó) and of the lower Atrato OCABA (Organización Campesina del Bajo Atrato).

4. The Comisión Especial Para Comunidades Negras was created by Decree 1332 of August 11, 1992. It was made up of government officials, academics, and black representatives. The role of black leaders in these negotiations must be emphasized, for although the state had committed itself to granting collective land rights to black communities on the Pacific Coast, the extent to which this legislation was to be applied was in large part due to the tenacity of black activists in their demands. The latter had intensely prepared for the negotiations with the state. At the First National Assembly of Black Communities, held in Tumaco (Nariño) in July 1992, they developed an internal framework for the regulation of AT-55. At the Second National Assembly, in Bogotá in May 1993, delegates revised and approved the text that was to become Law 70, which had previously been negotiated between the government and black community representatives (see Agudelo 2004a; Arocha 1992, 1998; Friedemann and Arocha 1995; Grueso et al. 1998; Paschel 2010; Wade 1995; see also the special edition of the *Journal of Latin American Anthropology* 7.2 [2002]).

5. The Office for Black Community Affairs was created through Law 70 (Chapter VIII, Article 67) under jurisdiction of the Ministry of the Interior. One of its tasks was the establishment of a register of black organizations (as dictated in Decree 2313 of October 13, 1994, Article 2).

Introduction

1. His impressions soaked in a similar fashion, anthropologist Michael Taussig (2004:56) remembers his own fieldwork experience in "the riverside town of Guapi surrounded by water especially from the gray skies above." In *My Cocaine Museum*, his Benjaminesque *oeuvre maximus*, collage, and "strange apotropaic text made of thousands of spells" (315), he recalls, "Often torrential, the rain makes you raise your voice on account of the noise made clattering on the iron roof. Your clothes are soon damp and smelly. Fungus appears on my leather wallet within two days. As soon as you get inside out of the rain, it's uncomfortably hot again. The distinction between air and water evaporates; sweat and rain are one. We have changed from air-breathing creatures into something else. Like amphibians we peer through a foggy humidity to draw apart curtains of water" (52).

2. "Lluvia con Tambores" (Rain with Drums) is the title of a short, bilingual poem that I composed in this courtyard in February 1999:

> Prap, prap, prap—pra prap.
> Der Regen prallt im Salsa-Rhythmus auf die Dächer.
> Descarga aus clave, bongo und conga,

sin tregua—ohne Reue.
Wenig interessiert es
dass nebenan Vallenato spielt.
Dieser Regen ist Salsa,
reine Salsa.

Prap, prap, prap—pra prap.
La lluvia pega sobre los techos,
con tumbao y sabor de salsa.
Descarga de clave, bongo y conga,
sin tregua.
Poco importa que al lado suena vallenato.
Esta lluvia es Salsa,
pura Salsa.

GUAPI, FEBRUARY 1999

3. The term *new social movements* is often used to highlight the plurality of contemporary forms of resistance, such as those found in the feminist movement, human rights groups, popular education groups, gay rights groups, and ecology movements. There have been ongoing debates over the supposed "newness" of these movements (see, e.g., Foweraker 1995; Hellman 1992, 1995). Colombian sociologist Orlando Fals Borda (1992:303) already stressed in the early 1990s that "more than two decades have passed since a new surge of social and popular movements began to arise [and] today, these movements are no longer 'new.'" Moreover Calhoun (1995) presents an intriguing argument that many movements of the early nineteenth century already showed characteristics of what many consider "new" social movements today. And Castells (1983) points out that women had been at the forefront of many struggles over consumption long before we started talking about the newness of social movements. (Among others, he relates the example of the Glasgow rent strike of 1915, in which women protested against the increase in their rents while their men were away fighting in the war.) For these reasons I do not find the term *new social movements* very useful any longer—even if some still hang on to it (e.g., Miller 2000).

4. On scale shift, see Tarrow and McAdam (2005) and Tilly and Tarrow (2007:94–95). On a critical engagement with the notion of "jumping scale" and "the pitfalls of scaling up," see Wolford (2010:103).

5. While feminist political geography scholars have made similar calls, pushing for the embodying and grounding of politics (Dowler and Sharp 2001; Hyndman 2003; Pain and Smith 2008—thanks to Caroline Faria for pointing this out to me), my purpose here is to stress that they have not been integrated much in social movement theory.

6. Paradoxically, if it was geographers who began to point out the lack of spatial considerations in social movement theory in the 1990s (Miller 2000; Pile and Keith 1997; Routledge 1993), it is geographers working in social movement research today who frequently brush over the complexity of place, favoring instead the transnational as their "master spatiality." As Leitner et al. (2008:158) contend, "In Anglophone geography, there is a tendency not only to swerve from one fashionable spatiality to the next, but also to construct ontological rationales for the choice of one or the other as the master spatiality. The practice of contentious politics is quite different, however." Yet see Bosco (2008) for a convincing account of the importance of place in the Madres de Plaza de Mayo movement in Argentina.

7. This term comes with a playful nod to Agnew's (1994) notion of "the territorial trap," with which he attempts to challenge dominant geographical assumptions regarding state territoriality prevalent in international relations theory.

8. I am grateful to John Agnew for pointing to the need for more "middle-range theorizing."

9. See, for example, Kiran Asher's (2009:25) critique, in which she misrepresents postdevelopment theory to then discard it as merely romanticizing social movements: "But these communities and the social movements that emerge from them are not simple manifestations of radical, non-Western culture, as post-developmentalist discourses of difference imply." See Oslender (2010) for a more detailed refutation of this critique.

10. Juli Hazlewood (2012) similarly engages the notion of "geographies of hope" in her examination of resistance to spreading oil palm cultivation in the northwest of Ecuador's Pacific Coast region.

1. Toward a Critical Place Perspective

1. More recently Wainwright and Barnes (2009) have painstakingly reviewed much of the place-space literature. They write, "The larger point is that none of these metaphysical concepts are separate and independent, but are entwined in complex and changing forms, producing effects that demand critical scrutiny" (966).

2. What has attracted geographers in particular to Lefebvre's work is his constant concern with everyday life (le quotidien) and its implications for a politics of space. Furthermore he extensively deals with issues of representation in very engaged ways, which has led Gregory (1994:358) to celebrate Lefebvre's "sometimes poetic figurations." Throughout Lefebvre's work shines his political commitment to resistance practices, reflecting his own lived experiences in the French Resistance against Nazi occupation during the Second World War, as well as in the student unrests of 1968 (Harvey 1991).

3. See also Gregory (1994:354), who sees in Lefebvre's spatial history a teleo-logical tendency standing "in the shadows of the totalizing drive of Hegelian Marxism."

4. Escobar's (1995) call for an "anthropology of modernity" may be seen as ad-dressing this oversight, in that he proposes to investigate some of the inter-sections that Lefebvre lays out in his spatial triad. Applying this concept of an anthropology of modernity to the Colombian Pacific Coast, Escobar and Pedrosa (1996:10) write, "From this perspective, we are interested in analyz-ing the concrete mechanisms used to integrate the region of the Pacific to the country's modernity. Thus, we endeavor an ethnography of the practices of those social actors that represent the advancement of modernity in the Lit-toral: development planners, capitalists, biologists and ecologists, experts of all sorts, and finally, activists of the social movements, as agents of possible alternative modernities" (my translation).

5. Referring to the sometimes confusing use of the concepts of "place" and "lo-cale" in Giddens (1979), the geographer Allen Pred (1984:279) explains, "Place is not only what is fleetingly observed on the landscape, a locale, or setting for activity and social interaction. It also is what takes place ceaselessly, what contributes to history in a specific context through the creation and utilization of a physical setting."

6. I am referring here mostly to work on place by geographers. For a wide-ranging philosophical history of place, see Casey (1997). Anthropological ap-proaches to place can be found in Escobar 2008; Feld and Basso 1996; and Low and Lawrence-Zúñiga 2003.

7. In social movement research the relationality approach has been taken up by, among others, Featherstone (2008), a student of Massey's. He proposes "rela-tional geographies of contention" in examining "counter-global networks" of resistance.

Interlude. Meeting Don Agapito

This interlude draws on Oslender (2015).

1. *Agua de panela* is a commonly found drink on the Pacific Coast, an infusion made from hardened sugarcane pulp.

2. For example, geographer Rachel Pain (2003, 2004, 2006) does not once men-tion Fals Borda in her three-part "review of action-oriented research" in the prestigious journal *Progress in Human Geography*. In her only reference to PAR she somewhat surprisingly states that "participatory action research [is] more common in high-income countries" (Pain 2004:653). Equally startling is Ger-aldine Pratt's (2000:574) assessment in the *Dictionary of Human Geography* that "participatory action research is a research process that emerged out of femi-nist and humanistic geography." PAR has certainly been applied in feminist

and humanistic geographical investigations, but it emerged "as an original input from the world periphery" (Fals Borda 1987:336). I do not intend to single out Pain or Pratt for their omissions, but rather to illustrate the more general amnesia that has befallen much of the debate about action-research. For a welcome exception, see Breitbart (2010), who discusses PAR in some detail. See also Kindon et al. (2007), and Reiter and Oslender (2015).

3. Rahman and Fals Borda (1991:39) recall that PAR was initially conceived in the 1970s as a response to "the miserable situations of our societies, to the excessive specialization and the void of academic life, and to the sectarian practices of a great part of the revolutionary left. We felt that transformations of society as well as of scientific knowledge, which had generally remained in the Newtonian era with its reductionist and instrumental orientation, were necessary and urgent. To begin with, we decided to embark on the search for adequate answers to the dilemmas of those who had been victims of the oligarchies and their politics of development: the poor rural communities."

4. Similarly in the late 1960s, with the emergence of radical geographies, William Bunge (1977) argued against the "tyranny of professionalization" in the academy and took geography into the streets of Detroit to apply the discipline practically in attempts at solving real and tangible social problems.

5. Freire (1971) was mostly concerned with a new "pedagogy for the oppressed." He rejected the traditional "banking concept of education," which feeds students with information in a teacher/subject–student/object relation without encouraging critical thinking, thereby serving the interests of oppression (64). Instead he advocated a "problem-posing education," which would respond to the essence of consciousness in the student as intentional historical subject.

6. Again a comparison can be drawn between PAR and debates in geography in the late 1960s, when calls for a *people's geography* were made by early radical geographers who lamented the disjuncture between an established academic geography and real-world socioeconomic problems and struggles. To them a people's geography would study these problems with an eye to devising viable solutions. Reminiscent of earlier debates on geographical activism that can be traced back to the Russian anarchist geographer Peter Kropotkin ([1899] 1995), radical geographers wanted research to focus on politically charged questions, in which geographers themselves became involved with the communities under study to work together on solution-finding processes (Harvey 1972, 1973; Peet 1977). One of the most original attempts at such a people's geography can be found in Bunge's (1977) "The First Years of the Detroit Geographical Expedition."

7. Some may worry about this suggestion of a "truer" or "more authentic" account of history. However, I believe that there is in fact a more authentic his-

tory to be recovered from "other voices" and that it is a postmodern conceit to think that this is not the case and that we should not think in these terms. The notion of a "corrector of official history" stresses the need to take seriously those "other voices" and to uncover those previously unheard, ignored, or silenced histories that shed a new light on and thus "correct" official versions of History with a capital H.

8. Fals Borda has practiced an interesting form that this systematic return of knowledge could take. In his well-known *Historia Doble de la Costa*, published in four volumes between 1979 and 1986, the presentation of research findings constitutes a "double history" that applies two different narrative styles parallel to one another, one for academic purposes and one for local consumption. In the publication the left page narrates, analyzes, and explains the research and its results in an academic vocabulary, whereas the right page uses a more colloquial language, explaining to the academically uninitiated reader the content, context, and analysis of the problematic. This form of presentation has been criticized by some as exposing a patronizing attitude, the differentiation in tone and language chosen supposedly revealing the researchers' perceived intellectual superiority.

9. PAR has often been criticized as "nonscientific" and subjective, mainly by reactionary elements in the academy who hide behind claims of objective scientific research with little interest in engaging constructively with the subjects of their studies. Knowingly or unknowingly they promote the "continuation of a hierarchical idea of knowledge that falsifies and maintains structures of domination," as the African American feminist critic bell hooks (1991:128) would say.

10. The Free Womb Law of 1821 states in Article 6 that "it is rigorously forbidden to sell slaves outside of Colombian territory," and Article 7 prohibits all kinds of negotiations with slaves (Pastoral de Etnias 1999).

2. Mapping Meandering Poetics

All quotes from the original Spanish have been translated by me.

1. There are many versions of this story; see, for example, Wilches-Chaux (1993).

2. With "geographical imagination" I refer to Derek Gregory's (1994) work on understanding how social life is variously embedded in space, place, and landscape and on the spatialized cultural and historical knowledge that characterizes social groups.

3. As one Afro-Colombian intellectual explained to me on the dawn of New Year's Day 1999—admittedly in a haze of alcohol-fueled lucidity—"Los negros somos una curiosidad para el capitalismo [We blacks are a curiosity for capitalism]."

4. Throughout his book Arocha (1999) talks of Afro-Colombians as *ombliga-dos de Ananse*, referring to the traditional practice of *ombligada*, during which pulverized substances, in some cases spider parts (Ananse), are applied to the belly button (*ombligo*) of the newborn. This practice is believed to endow the newborn with the qualities of the respective substances—in the case of the spider, with shrewdness. The newborn is thus initiated into the sisterhood of Ananse, a goddess of the Fanti-Ashanti people originating in the Gulf of Benin in Africa (13). Arocha uses this symbolism to sustain his arguments about an existing historical and cultural "bridge" between Africa and the Americas that is said to have originated with the transatlantic slave trade. This wider set of arguments is known as *huellas de Africanía*, or "traces of African-ism" (Friedemann 1989). However, it is important to point out that relatively few Afro-Colombians are actually initiated with Ananse. Far more newborns are "belly-buttoned" with other powdered substances, such as gold dust (to bring wealth to the child), and herbs such as *paico*, *ruda*, and *centavitos*. Some argue that Arocha's attempts to link almost any sociocultural manifestation among Afro-Colombians to the sisterhood of the spider represent his zeal to promote the huellas de Africanía approach more than a well-documented ob-servation in the field (Restrepo 1996a, 1998).

5. *Viche* is a popular alcoholic drink in the Pacific lowlands, a rurally distilled unrefined sugarcane spirit (sometimes also spelled *biche*). It is drunk on its own as a "shot," or mixed with forest herbs, leaves, and roots in cured bottles known as *botellas curadas*. These bottles are usually prepared by women tradi-tional healers, the *curanderas*. They are often highly sought after and can be quite expensive.

6. The quotes from Doña Celia Lucumí Caicedo in this section stem from over fifty hours of transcribed interviews with Doña Celia that were recorded in Guapi between March and July 1999 and subsequently translated by me. Doña Celia passed away on December 21, 2013.

7. A *batea* is a round, shallow bowl carved out of wood, the diameter of which varies between fifty and ninety centimeters. It is used in traditional placer gold mining on the Colombian Pacific Coast to wash the auriferous sands and gravel, and the *jagua*, a black concentrate consisting of a mixture of tiny flakes of heavy magnetic iron oxide, ilmenite, and gold dust. This activity is usu-ally performed by women and small girls, the *bateadoras*. West (1952:72) sug-gests the word *batea* is of Carib origin, which indicates that it is an indigenous instrument. See the monograph by West (1952) for a detailed description of colonial placer mining in Colombia.

8. No data on precipitation exist for the area around Balsitas, but in accordance with similar areas in the coastal zone of the Cauca Department at a similar

distance from the sea, we can assume that rainfall in Balsitas averages some 5,000 to 6,000 millimeters per year.

9. It is common among Afro-Colombians, also in urban areas, to greet older relatives such as parents, uncles, and grandparents by "giving them a greeting in the name of God" (*dar en nombre de Dios*) as an expression of respect.

10. Dionisio Rodríguez, an activist with the regional association of black communities COCOCAUCA in Guapi, explained the evil eye to me in these terms: "The magic-religious relation in the life of our communities is central. . . . My grandmother was a healer. Once they brought a little boy to her. He had the evil eye. And she cured him. That's when I understood that there are things that they don't understand in hospital. . . . The issue of the evil eye, I regard that as a kind of magic power that mankind possesses and that we still have not learned to use properly, neither for the good nor the bad. The evil eye is a kind of magic power. And you cure it with herbs. In the hospital, they don't know about that. If you ask a doctor about it, he doesn't know what to think about it. He has no idea. That's when I understood the good and the important of our [traditional] medicine compared to the other [Western]" (interview held July 21, 1999).

11. *Compadre* and *comadre* literally mean "godfather" and "godmother." Among Afro-Colombians there are strong links and responsibilities attached to their functions with regard to their godson or goddaughter. Yet people are also addressed as *compadre* or *comadre* if they are a relative in the extended family, which is the case in Celia's account. The expression can also be used to establish a strong mutual relationship of trust and friendship, which inevitably carries with it responsibilities to each other. This was the case between Doña Celia and me, when we came to address each other as *compadre* and *comadre*.

12. This observation by Malian writer and ethnologist Amadou Hampâté Bâ at a UNESCO meeting in 1962 has become an often-cited metaphor. The late Senegalese poet and former president Leopold Senghor has also been credited with saying, "The death of one of those old men is what the conflagration of a library of thinkers and poets would be to you" (quoted in Sábato 1998:23).

13. The quotes from Don Agapito Montaño and all poems in this section stem from transcribed interviews with Don Agapito that were recorded in Guapi in April 1996 and subsequently translated by me. I would like to thank María Eugenia Arboleda for help with the transcriptions.

14. Anchicayá is a river south of Buenaventura.

15. Interview with Raquel Portocarrera, Guapi, April 27, 1996.

16. Interview with Teófila Betancourt, Guapi, April 23, 1996.

17. The *décima* or *espinela* is a poetic form that originated in Spain at the end of the fifteenth century, created by Vicente Espinel (Pedrosa and Vanín 1994:12). It consists of ten octosyllabic verses that have an obligatory rhyme structure: the first with the fourth and fifth verse; the second with the third verse; the sixth with the seventh and tenth verse; and the eighth with the ninth verse (1,4,5 // 2,3 // 6,7,10 // 8,9). In the Colombian Pacific among black communities the décima is converted into forty-four verses with an initial stanza of four verses, which carries the essence of the décima in that each of the following four stanzas of ten lines has to end in the corresponding line of the initial stanza. This highly structured form is known as *décima glosada*. Nevertheless many décimas have a less determined rhyme structure, and most décimas that I recorded with Don Agapito belong to this second group.

18. This section elaborates on arguments previously advanced in Oslender (2007a).

19. But see Limón (1994) for a groundbreaking ethnographic study employing critical poetics in his exploration of the interethnic dynamics and politics of social life in Mexican American southern Texas.

20. This is certainly not the space to review the vast literature of responses to Scott's conceptual thinking (see Sivaramakrishnan 2005). These range from critical perspectives on hegemony and state power (Mitchell 1990; Tilly 1991), to ethnographic (Ortner 1995) and linguistic (Gal 1995) critiques, to creative new readings of Scott "from an inverted standpoint" by, for example, employing the notion of the hidden transcript to the Bush administration's military order of November 2001 that established military tribunals for the prosecution of U.S.-held detainees in the war on terror (Greenhouse 2005). It is worth noting that Latin Americanists have widely drawn on Scott's work (Colburn 1989; Eckstein 1989; Joseph 1990), often extending it into new directions (Levi 1999; Lyons 2005), while others have at times vigorously opposed Scott's ideas (Gutmann 1993).

21. Sayd Bahodine Majrouh is a celebrated Afghan poet who resisted the Soviet occupation of his country, living in exile in Pakistan. He was assassinated in Peshawar in 1988.

22. I borrow for this section's heading the title of Vanín's (1998) article "Mitopoética de la orilla florida."

23. The Golden Age in Spain (Siglo de Oro) is approximately the period between 1492 and 1650.

24. There might be a mistake here in the original transcription. On several occasions I heard this décima in Guapi from various people. They all agreed that this line should read "cargando en popa una niña [carrying a lassie in stern]" and not "a mine." Although one of the décima's characteristics is precisely the fact that it can be adapted and told in slightly different ways depending on

the presenter, in this case it could possibly be a transcription error. This interpretation is also supported by two transcriptions of the same décima that Hidalgo (1995:281–83) recorded in Esmeraldas on Ecuador's Pacific Coast, where this word is transcribed as niña.

25. "La Concha de Almeja" is a "versed décima" (décima glosada) in that it begins with a stanza of four verses, each of which is repeated in the last line of the following four ten-verse stanzas with the rhyme structure ABABBCCDDC.

26. See Wade (1993) for an analysis of migrations between the Northern Pacific Coast Department of Chocó and the city of Medellín. See Arboleda (1998), Barbary and Urrea (2004), Taussig (1979), and Urrea et al. (1999) for migrations between the Southern Pacific region and Cali. See Agier et al. (1999) on Tumaco.

27. Mesmo is a commonly found local dialect for the Castilian mismo.

28. The prison was eventually closed down, and the island was declared a national park and natural history museum in July 1984. Today it is a popular holiday spot for ecotourists and serves as a marine life research station. It was also on Gorgona that I held a two-day workshop on social cartography with the resident population in April 1999.

29. The riviel is said to be a poor devil condemned to sail the open sea at night in a wrecked canoe with a light in the stern. As revenge for his fate, he rams into solitary fishermen and sinks travelers on the sea. The story of the maravelí conjures up the image of one's soul infinitely navigating on the open sea without ever finding rest and peace. Another popular visión is the tunda. A female forest spirit, she appears especially to young children as a woman they know well and who lures them into the forest to possess them. This story is often told to children to deter them from venturing alone into the forest, and mothers are warned not to leave their children alone at home. The tunda may also appear to men who walk alone in the forest at night. There she seduces them and inflicts psychological damage. In this scenario the tunda is a warning that punishes male infidelity. For the wider regional significance of these visiones, see Rahier (2013:75) on the role of forest spirits such as the tunda in the performance of the Afro-Ecuadorean Festival of the Kings.

30. Quoted in "El Pacífico vela a su virgen," Gaceta (Cali), December 6, 1998, 10–12.

31. Tsunamis are giant waves caused by earthquake shocks. Their epicenters are usually located along faults in the sea bottom a few miles offshore. Four tsunamis have been registered as seriously affecting the Colombian Pacific coastline over the past 150 years: one in 1836, with its epicenter just off Guapi; another in 1868; and another on January 31, 1906, which destroyed several coastal villages and coconut plantations and eroded large sections of beaches and mangrove swamps for a stretch of sixty miles along the coast near Tumaco (West 1957:57–60). The most recent devastating tsunami hit the southern

Pacific Coast on December 12, 1979, at 2:59 a.m. local time, affecting an area from Las Esmeraldas in Ecuador to Guapi. An estimated five hundred to six hundred people died, and around four thousand were injured, while over ten thousand homes were destroyed (Pararas-Carayannis 1982). The settlements of San Juan and El Charco in Nariño were completely wiped out by waves that reached five meters above sea level. In some areas, such as Amarales, these waves washed away large parts of cultivated fields and deposited salt that sterilized many lands for years thereafter. This effect can still be felt today, although some lands have begun to recover, with the first palm trees establishing themselves once again.

32. "I have deliberately chosen the term *spatiality* to refer specifically to socially-produced space, the created forms and relations of a broadly-defined human geography. All *space* is not socially produced but all spatiality (as it is used here) is" (Soja 1985:123).

33. "As socially produced space, spatiality can be distinguished from the physical space of material nature and the mental space of cognition and representation, each of which is used and incorporated into the social construction of spatiality but cannot be conceptualized as its equivalent" (Soja 1989:120).

34. The theme of a clash between the dogmatic attitudes of religious institutions and a determined populace is, of course, not restricted to the Pacific lowlands. In his novel *A Saint Is Born in Chimá* (*En Chimá nace un santo*), published in 1964, Afro-Colombian writer Manuel Zapata Olivella tells the story of Domingo Vidal, a paralyzed cripple who is rescued unharmed from a burning house in the village of Chimá in the Caribbean Coast region of Colombia. The people believe they have witnessed a miracle and turn Domingo into their patron saint. Tales of his miracles multiply, as he makes the rains come, cures the blind, and swells barren wombs with new life. The local priest is furious at the excess of religious fanaticism. He denounces Domingo as a pagan idol and calls the people heretics. They, however, continue to fervently worship Domingo. Through this struggle over Domingo, Zapata Olivella reflects on the inflexibility of established institutions and the potential power for change that lies within the hands of a determined people.

3. Historical Geographies of Resistance

Epigraph: Eusebio Andrade Bazán, a resident of Guapi, composed this song in 1976. According to him, it is the first bolero paying homage to Guapi. The bolero, a romantic ballad, is a popular musical genre in Latin America. Some of its composers, such as the Mexican Agustín Lara, have acquired legendary status.

1. According to IIAP (1997), 5,474 plant species belonging to 271 different families have been identified in the Pacific lowlands. In an ethnobotanic study

examining plant species and their uses among indigenous and black communities in the delta of the Patía River, Caballero (1996) identified 110 medicinal plants, 81 food plants, 30 different plant species used in construction and housing, and 22 others used in rituals and magic. That study also shows patterns of cultural exchange between black and indigenous communities who share a common environment and the common usage of "biodiversity."

2. According to West (1957:213–14), tidal ranges tend to increase northward along the Pacific Coast from Peru (around 2.1 feet) to Panama (around 16.4 feet). For Tumaco and Buenaventura on the Colombian Pacific Coast he gives the following data: Tumaco, mean range 8.7 feet, spring range 10.9 feet; Buenaventura, mean range 10.4 feet, spring range 12.9 feet. On the Baudó River, West found tidal effects some fifty kilometers upstream at the confluence of the Dubasa River. Farther south, on the San Juan River, he noted tidal effects some thirty-five kilometers upstream from the river mouth. The average of twenty kilometers that I have given here is for the Cauca Coast, the region where most of my fieldwork was situated. The measure is a rough estimate observed in the rivers Guapi, Guajuí, and Timbiquí.

3. *Litoral Recóndito* (The Hidden Littoral) is the title of a book by Guapi-born politician Sofonías Yacup (1934). He deplored the economic and cultural backwardness of the Pacific Coast and argued that the physical isolation of the region was one of the factors that had to be overcome in order to develop the region and tie it into the national economy and political life.

4. One road in the southern Department of Nariño leads from the Andean towns of Pasto and Ipiales to Tumaco on the Pacific Coast near the border with Ecuador. A second road in the central Department of Valle del Cauca connects Cali with Buenaventura. A third road links Medellín in the Department of Antioquia to Quibdó in the northern Chocó Department. Since the 1930s there have also been plans to build a road from Popayán to Guapi on the Cauca Coast. However, engineering difficulties, the lack of political will, anticipated costs, and an incalculable environmental impact have so far worked against such road construction. Furthermore unforeseen social and cultural costs have to be taken into account. Raquel Portocarrera, a teacher and specialist in folklore and local history in Guapi, points out, "Thinking about this road, some people that come here say, 'Well, without a road you really suffer.' Some local people also claim that we need the road. But a lot of us say, 'No, we don't need a road.' Because with a road come the bad habits from the interior, come the thieves, come this, come that" (interview held in Guapi, April 27, 1996). Nearly twenty years after this interview, plans to construct this road have been all but abandoned.

5. Indigenous groups in the Pacific lowlands include the following ethnicities: Embera, Embera Catío, Embera Chamí, Wounaan, Awa, Eperara-Siapidara, and

Tule. Population ratio figures quoted are generally accepted estimates, as Colombia's census data are far from reliable. For example, for the 1993 national census the National Statistical Institute DANE tried to count the country's black population for the first time. However, due to the ambiguous census question "Do you belong to an ethnic group, indigenous group or black community?," only 502,343 people affirmed belonging to a "black community" (Ruiz Salgero and Bodnar 1995). This would be the equivalent of 1.5 percent of Colombia's national population. However, a report by the Minority Rights Group (1995:xiii) around the same time showed oscillations in estimates of Colombia's Afro-descendant population ranging from 4.9 to 15 million (the equivalent of 14 to 43 percent). These considerable differences can partly be explained by the problematic definition of the term black community (Grueso et al. 1998; Restrepo 1998) and by issues of black self-identification in a dominant context of whitening (Wade 1993, 2000). The latest census of 2005 estimates that Afro-Colombians constitute 10.5 percent of the national population, a considerable jump in recognition compared to the 1.5 percent twelve years earlier. However, most observers today believe this figure should be closer to 26 percent (Agudelo 2005; Ng'weno 2007b:102; Wade 2002:6).

6. Reales de minas are mining camps and administrative centers founded in the sixteenth century.

7. The fact that it was the Liberal Party that decreed the abolition of slavery partly explains why the vast majority of Afro-Colombians today are still politically closer to the Liberal Party than to the Conservative Party (Agudelo 2005; Casamán 1997).

8. This quote is from the English translation of the novel by literary scholar Jonathan Tittler. I had numerous conversations with Tittler and Zapata Olivella over how best to translate the title of the novel into English. Zapata Olivella felt that Tittler's original suggestion, Changó, the Baddest Dude, did not express the ambiguous characteristics of the Yoruba Orisha Changó in all his complexities. He preferred Changó, That Great Motherfucker. Alas, publishing etiquette got the better of literature's irreverent freedom. Manuel Zapata Olivella joined his ancestors in November 2004, before the translation went to press, with Tittler's final title choice as Changó, the Biggest Badass nevertheless coming close to the ekobio's wish. Tittler also translated Zapata Olivella's sociorealist novel Chambacú: Corral de Negros (Chambacú: Black Slum; 1985 [1967]).

9. On palenques in the Americas, see Price (1979). For Colombia, see Escalante (1954), Friedemann (1979, 1998), Friedemann and Patiño Rosselli (1983), Maya (1998), Navarrete (2008), Zuluaga and Bermúdez (1997:38–58). For an autobiographical account of maroon life in Cuba, see the dialogue of Esteban Montejo with Cuban ethnologist and writer Miguel Barnet ([1968] 2003).

10. In the 1980s an Afro-descendant guerrilla organization emerged in the area of the Baudó and San Juan Rivers in the Chocó with the name of Benko Bioho, thus mobilizing the historical imagination of rebellion embodied by Bioho for their own political project. Not much is known about this guerrilla group, and virtually nothing on them has been documented. They seem to have dissolved in the mid-1990s (various personal communications from Colombian historians and social movement leaders).

11. On the palenquero language, see also Friedemann and Patiño Rosselli (1983). Examining the African influences in the language spoken in Palenque, Schwegler (2012) asserts that Kikongo is the sole substrate of palenquero. His argument is strengthened by suggestions that speakers of Kikongo were a dominant force in the formative phase of Palenque in the late seventeenth and early eighteenth centuries.

12. This inscription is photographically documented in Schwegler (2012:116). However, it has since been removed from the column.

13. Even Zapata Olivella (2010:449) conflates Bioho and San Basilio in his novel *Changó, el Gran Putas*, when he states in the appendix that Benkos "organized the armed struggle of the runaway slaves of the Palenque of San Basilio."

14. The identical quote appears in Zuluaga and Romero (2007:118–19).

15. Aprile-Gniset (1993) observes that at the end of the eighteenth century there were five owners of gold mines in the Timbiquí River basin and four in the Micay. They all lived in Popayán on the western Andean range. He also registers four owners of mines in Iscuandé, all of whom lived in the Andean city of Pasto. Only in Barbacoas did he find two to three owners actually living there.

16. Cuban author Alejo Carpentier ([1946] 1995) resurrects the figure of Mackandal in his extraordinary novel *El Reino de Este Mundo* (The Kingdom of This World). He makes use of this legendary and inspiring figure to illustrate Latin America's reality as what he terms *realismo maravilloso* (marvelous realism). This novel initiated the literary genre of magical realism that gave rise to the so-called boom in Latin American literature in the 1970s and 1980s.

17. The *quilombo* is the Brazilian equivalent of the palenque in the Spanish-speaking Americas, a fortified maroon settlement.

18. For an intriguing Deleuzian application of the rhizome metaphor to the social and river networks among the indigenous Wounaan people of Colombia, see Velásquez Runk (2009).

19. Between 1640 and 1683 a stabilization of mining camps can be observed around the rivers Timbiquí, Iscuandé, and Patía. Toward the end of the eighteenth century the settlements around Iscuandé and Timbiquí in particular began to show urban characteristics, with half of their populations enslaved (Aprile-Gniset 1993:50). These settlements were known as *reales de minas*.

20. Interview held in Bogotá, December 2, 2004.
21. The notion of "ambassador of modernity" can also be applied to the organizing processes of black communities. One of the founding members of the organization Matamba y Guasá in Guapi, for example, resided in Bogotá and Cali, where she worked with national NGOs. This woman functioned as an important contact person for the local organization in the national and international circuit of NGOs and governmental institutions. In that way she may be seen as the organization's ambassador, negotiating its various demands with the agents of modernity.
22. Interview held in Tumaco, April 19, 1996.
23. Restrepo (1995:65) regards Friedemann's elaborations on troncos as "comfortable and 'stereotypical' affirmations of the kinship systems of 'black groups' in the Pacific" that have not been observed elsewhere in the region. He finds no references to common ancestors in kinship relations in the Satinga and Sanquianga River basins in the southern part of Nariño. Hoffmann (1999:78) also refuses to use the concept of tronco for the case of the Mejicano River in Nariño, "although the idea exists in the discourse," because she wishes to stress the flexibility of the concept itself. Even so she acknowledges that the figure of a founder is central to kinship relations there as well.
24. For similar kinship-organized networks of solidarity among rural black populations in Ecuador's Pacific Coast region, see Rahier (2013:40–41).
25. Interview held in Guapi, April 29, 1996.
26. Interview held in Guapi, April 29, 1996.
27. Interview held in Guapi, April 23, 1996.
28. The Program of Natural Resource Management was adopted by the national government at the meeting of the National Economic and Social Policy Council on August 22, 1993. It received financial support from the World Bank to support, inter alia, the collective land titling for black communities in the Pacific region.
29. Mental maps have been widely used in behavioral geography as a tool to examine the representation of places as revealed in exercises of cognitive mapping (Gould and White 1974). More recently they have been of interest within cultural and social geography that regard these representations as constructed through social discourse and practice. Mental maps have become a key tool in the preparation of land rights claims for minority ethnic groups, such as Aborigines in Australia (Jacobs 1988), First Nations in Canada (Sparke 1998), and black communities on Colombia's Pacific Coast (Offen 2003).
30. New Model Army, "Waiting," on *Vengeance: The Independent Story*, 1987, track 5. West (1957:70) describes similar problems in his navigations around the southern Pacific Coast in the 1950s: "Travel *por adentro* along the inland channels, however, must be closely timed to correspond with periods of high tide. More

than once the writer has been stranded for several hours in a canoe stuck on the muddy bottom of an *estero* at low tide, being pestered to distraction by black flies and mosquitoes until the water slowly rose with the incoming tide."

31. Interview held in Guapi, April 23, 1996.

32. For a short illustrated account of concheras at work in the mangrove swamps around Tumaco, see the beautiful photo essay "Swamp People" by Jan Sochor: http://www.jansochor.com/photo-essay/swamp-people.html.

33. Beaches, or *playas*, in the Pacific riverine context are point bars of gravel and boulders that are exposed at low tide or during drier periods along the riverbanks or in the middle of a river.

34. The guandal is a backswamp of palm thickets of largely inundated lands found mainly in the southern part of the Department of Nariño. A similar ecosystem in the Chocó Department is referred to as *palmar*.

35. Incorrect handling of dynamite has also led to maimed arms and other mutilated extremities (Arocha 1999:104).

4. Mobilizing the Aquatic Space

1. Wade (1993) has done a great job exposing the myth of racial democracy in Colombia. On his evolving interpretation of the notion of *mestizaje*, see particularly Wade (2005b). Others have examined the complex racial politics of multicultural citizenship in Latin America. On Colombia, see Agudelo (2005), Arboleda (2007), Asher (2009), Bocarejo (2009), Cárdenas (2012), Hoffmann (2004), Ng'weno (2007a), Paschel (2010), Restrepo (2004a, 2013), Velasco (2011). On Brazil, see Sansone (2003), Telles (2004). On Honduras, see Anderson (2007), Mollett (2006). On Bolivia, see Postero (2007). More generally on Latin America, see Hale (2002), Hooker (2005), Sieder (2002), Van Cott (2000, 2005), Wade (1997b), Walsh (2004), Whitten and Torres (1998).

2. Chirimía, jota, and contradanza are typical musical styles in the Chocó region.

3. Such an impressive venture mounted by ACADESAN in the San Juan River stands out for the size of its mobilization and the efforts it required. No similar aquatic voyage of "self-discovery" took place on the Cauca Coast. This can partly be explained by a lack of organization in this region at the time the new Constitution came into effect. This fact hints at important regional differences in the organizing processes of black communities. In general the organizations in the northern Chocó Department have a longer history of mobilization than the rest of the Pacific Coast, where most organizations began to form only once AT-55 was in place. This characteristic is also reflected in the fact that the first community councils to be issued collective land titles are in the Chocó Department. The Peasant Association of the Atrato River, ACIA, is still the strongest of all river organizations in the Pacific today.

4. An earlier version of some of the arguments in this section was presented in Oslender (2002).

5. ASODERGUA (Asociación para el Desarrollo del Río Guajuí) is a grassroots organization that emerged in 1992 in the Guajuí River basin with the aim of improving living conditions locally.

6. Since 1988 the mayors have been popularly elected in Colombia. Before then they were nominated by the governors of their respective departments, frequently along clientelist structures of conventional party politics.

7. Interview with Walberto Banguera, Guapi, February 5, 1999. By using this extensive quote, I also hope to provide, at least in part, an arena for Banguera "to make this public to the world."

8. Alvarez et al. (1998) trace the phenomenon of clientelism as "regular political practice" in Latin America back to the system of social authoritarianism in the nineteenth century, a period dominated by an "out-of-place liberalism" orientated toward European political developments and an oligarchic conception of politics characterized by favoritism that regarded politics as the "business of the elites." Although the twentieth century saw partial political incorporation of the popular masses due to increasing urbanization and industrialization, the political system was still characterized by an elite-based democratization that maintained structures of personalism and clientelism. See also Auyero (1999) for a discussion of clientelism as common political practice throughout Latin America. A detailed analysis of Colombia's bipartisan clientelismo structures and hereditary party identification as constitutive of Colombia's political system can be found in Leal Buitrago and Dávila (1991) and Díaz Uribe (1986). For a regional analysis of clientelismo in the Pacific lowlands and in Guapi in particular, see Agudelo (2005).

9. INCORA (Instituto Colombiano de Reforma Agraria) was the government institution responsible for all aspects of the collective land titling processes in the Pacific Coast region. The first six collective land titles were issued on December 13, 1996, all in the Department of Chocó. By the end of 1998 a total of twenty-three collective land titles had been awarded to black communities, comprising an area of over 1.3 million hectares (IGAC 1999:99). In 2003 INCORA was dissolved and replaced by the Colombian Institute of Rural Development (Instituto Colombiano de Desarrollo Rural [INCODER]), which is now the state agency in charge of executing agricultural policies and overseeing land tenure. By 2013, 159 land titles had been issued over five million hectares, 50 percent of the entire Pacific lowlands.

10. In February 1997 the community council carried out a census (as prescribed in Decree 1745, Chapter 4, Article 20.4) that numbered its population as 1,561. The technical visit by INCORA, carried out April 26–30, 1997 (as prescribed in Decree 1745, Chapter 4, Article 22), determined the official census to be a

population of 1,352. These differences can partly be accounted for by high levels of spatial mobility and migration, both short term and long term, a characteristic of rural black populations on the Colombian Pacific Coast (Arboleda 1998; Whitten 1986).

11. The name *naidí* is said to derive from the indigenous Embera language. The same palm is known in the Chocó as *murrapo* and in parts of Antioquia as *tapafrío* or *palma triste* (sad palm) (Vallejo et al. 2011:193).

12. See also Losonczy (1993) on nutrition patterns in the symbolic system of black populations on the Pacific Coast.

13. Corponariño, Resolution 157 of April 20, 1999.

14. Personal communication from Jorge Yoría, Guapi, February 11, 1999. Yoría also showed me a copy of the proceedings of the First Seminar on the Sustainability of the Naidí Palm, sponsored by ALENPAC (1995).

15. Similar practices have been observed in the exploitation of the bark of mangrove trees to derive tannin for the processing of leather. As in naidí extraction, the mangrove tree has to be cut down to strip it of its bark. The companies Liscano Hermanos e Hijos Ltda. of Cali and Industria de Mangle S.A. of Bogotá extracted mangrove bark between the 1950s and 1980s, first on concessionary lands granted by the Ministry of Agriculture, and from 1968 onward, following the creation of the National Institute of Renewable Natural Resources, INDERENA, with a class A permit on awarded lands (Leal 1998:417–19). However, just as in the naidí case, the companies also processed mangrove bark from other areas. As Colombian geographer Claudia Leal (1998:418) observes, "Although the companies principally worked in the awarded areas, they also exploited mangroves outside the delimited zones along the entire coastline."

16. For a fifteen-minute video clip on palm heart extraction and processing in the Guapi area, see http://www.youtube.com/watch?v=t04EP9ywux8 (clip uploaded in December 2012). The name of the canning plant is not actually mentioned in the video. Interestingly enough, however, the plant owner and manager were still the same as in 1999, when I conducted ethnographic fieldwork in the area and interviews with company officials.

17. Corponariño, Resolutions 357 of June 2, 2006, and 967 of November 23, 2009, respectively.

18. INCORA Resolution 1178, May 12, 1998.

19. For more detail on Guapi-based COADEPAL, see Grueso and Escobar (1996:95–102). For an English-language account of cooperatives in the Pacific, see Escobar (2008:176–80). However, the experience narrated by Escobar in a slightly more positive light, entailing a higher degree of campesino participation, refers in fact to a posterior agricultural cooperative, Coagropacífico, based in Tumaco and established in 1989. Somewhat confusingly, both COADEPAL and Coagropacífico are referred to as Cooperativa Agrícola

del Pacífico in Grueso and Escobar (1996). While both were run by INCORA, the latter was an attempt at correcting the mistakes of the former.

20. Interview with Ricardo Castro (nickname "Don Ricard"), Guapi, April 27, 1999.

21. Interview with Porfirio Becerra (nickname "Don Por"), Tumaco, January 16, 1999. Don Por's clarity of vision and unwavering commitment to the grassroots organizing processes made him a fascinating interview partner, who was frequently sought out by fellow academics as well. See Restrepo (2013:174), for example, for a careful reading of Don Por's vision of "biodiversity" (Restrepo calls him "Don Po," which might or might not be a more adequate transcription of his nickname).

22. COCOCAUCA (Coordinación de Comunidades Negras de la Costa Pacífica del Cauca; Coordination of Black Communities on the Cauca Coast) is the first regional organization with an ethnic-territorial discourse that aims at coordinating the struggles of black communities on the Cauca Coast. It was born in 1993.

23. Interview with Walberto Banguera, Guapi, February 5, 1999. Banguera did not go into detail during our conversation as to what arrangement was finally found to justify the use of these funds from Bogotá. However, after the Community Council Guapi Abajo was established, the contractor was consequently expelled from the colony of guapireños living in Bogotá, as they accused him of having operated in Guapi under the name of the association without their knowledge and consent. In September 2000 I myself got caught up in this messy situation. I had presented some of my fieldwork results at a forum on black communities organized at the Colombian Institute of Anthropology and History (Instituto Colombiano de Antropología e Historia [ICANH]) in Bogotá. Although the contractor was not present at the forum, he subsequently sent a letter to ICANH, in which he accused me—a "researcher of black people most likely reproducing retarded models of the awful colonialism that has so much hurt our communities"—of defamation of his person (letter dated August 15, 2000). He circulated this letter to various organizations of black communities and state institutions (including the Ministry of Culture, Ministry of the Interior, and the Attorney General's Office), leaving me in the awkward situation of having to write to all these institutions, explaining the absurd situation and sending them a copy of my paper in the hope of proving my integrity with the grassroots organizations of black communities. I did this with the necessary seriousness that the case required, although most of my friends and black movement leaders found the situation rather funny. As one of the activists in Guapi told me, "It is good that this has happened to you. So you know what it felt like for us when the local political elite here in Guapi started to attack us and accuse us of all sorts of things" (telephone conversation with Dionisio Rodriguez, COCOCAUCA, Guapi, September 3, 2000).

I should say that I received support from many Afro-Colombian leaders in this case. Thanks in particular to Juan de Dios Mosquera, general secretary of CIMARRÓN, who was present at the conference and who expressed his support for me in an open letter to ICANH, dated September 11, 2000. This case serves to illustrate the multiple ways in which one can get caught up as a "committed researcher" in the messy field of identity politics.

24. Interview with Humberto Villa, Guapi, April 24, 1999.

25. Resolutions 1081, 1082, and 1083 assign collective land titles to the Community Councils of the Rivers San Francisco (26,232 hectares), Napi (47,007 hectares), and Alto Guapi (103,742 hectares). They were signed by INCORA's director on April 29, 1998, but they were published in a regional newspaper, *Costa Caucana*, only on April 20, 1999 (INCORA 1999:3–8).

26. See Paddison (1983) on the notion of the "fragmented state," the idea that the modern state cannot be regarded as a homogeneous unit deploying a unilinear politics but that, on the contrary, different state institutions may in fact articulate different politics toward the same issue. While such an analysis can be applied to all forms of states, be they dictatorships, democracies, or socialist varieties of the two, Paddison argues that it is a particularly common phenomenon in today's Western-style democracies, where at times quite disparate state politics are put into practice by diverse institutions.

5. Ideals, Practices, and Leadership

1. It is telling that Law 70 has much less to say about other regions or the urban black population in Colombia. While some authors see "a misplaced and until recently un-self-aware centering of the Pacific basin in academic works on Afro-Colombians" (Ng'weno 2007b:114 in her ethnographic narrative of two black communities in Colombia's northern Cauca region), and others stress that "not all [blacks] come from the rivers" (Agudelo 2004b)—in fact most Afro-Colombians live in cities today—the focus on the Pacific lowlands in academic work is neither misplaced nor un-self-aware; on the contrary, it is the logical direction, given the intentionality of Law 70 as a mechanism of state governance in that region. Obviously this does not dismiss the need to inquire into issues of race and ethnicity more widely in Colombia.

2. This fact was recognized, for example, with the award of the prestigious Goldman Environmental Prize 2004 to a prominent Afro-Colombian activist. This "Nobel Prize for the Environment" is given every year to grassroots ecological activists from six geographical regions. Libia Grueso from PCN won the prize in April 2004 in the category South/Central America. See Goldman Environmental Prize, http://www.goldmanprize.org/recipient/libia-grueso/.

3. For a fascinating account of Proyecto Biopacífico, in which different models of nature (local and global) were held in tension, and how the search for an

alternative and sustainable production paradigm in the Pacific region has to negotiate these, see Escobar (2008:185–97).

4. For more detail on Matamba y Guasá, see Asher (2009:130–53), where the women's network is at the center of the author's inquiry into gender, ethnicity, and development in the Pacific region.

5. INCORA Resolution 1081, April 19, 1998.

6. Harvey (1996:295) explains the "spatial fix": "There are two facets to this process. Excess capital can be exported from one place (city, region, nation) to build another place within an existing set of space relations. . . . Space relations may also be revolutionized, through technological and organizational shifts. Such revolutions alter relations between places and affect internalized processes of place construction, sustenance, and dissolution (as has happened through the recent history of rapid deindustrialization in many cities of the advanced capitalist world)."

7. An interesting exception to this trend can be observed in places where a significant rethinking of humankind's relationship with nature is under way. For example, in 2008 Ecuador issued a new constitution that has garnered international attention because of its pioneering treatment of what it called "the rights of nature." On par with human rights, nature is endowed, constitutionally, with the right to be protected and to be treated with respect. In this conceptualization nature is no longer seen as an inert object for humans to appropriate, nor is it infused with the kind of management overtone that the term *environment* implies. According to Escobar (n.d.:66), nature's inclusion in the Ecuadorian Constitution is based on an ecological worldview in which all beings exist in relation to others: "To endow Nature with rights means to shift from a conception of nature as object to be exploited to one in which Nature is seen as subject; indeed, in this conception the idea of rights of Nature is intimately linked with the humans' right to exist. This notion implies an expanded ecological notion of the self, which, unlike the liberal notion, sees the self as deeply inter-connected with all other living beings and, ultimately, with the planet as a whole."

8. The first contradiction refers to capitalism's relation to labor, which is exploited in the process of capitalist surplus value accumulation. Initially capitalism's profit increases proportionally to labor's exploitation. However, as labor as necessary production condition deteriorates, surplus value decreases. As Harvey (1982) has argued, this contradiction shows up the "limits to capital," which have temporarily been overcome by capitalist restructuring in the form of benefits given to labor. These benefits include the creation of unions to defend workers' rights and the introduction of legislation on social security, pensions, health services, and so on. Harvey has argued that both capital and labor may benefit from such a restructuring of capital in what he

refs to as a "territorially based alliance": "Production capital which cannot easily move may support the alliance and be tempted to buy local labour peace and skills through compromises over wages and work conditions—thereby gaining the benefits of co-operation from labour and a rising effective demand for wage goods in local markets. Factions of labour that have, through struggle or historical accident, managed to create islands of privilege within a sea of exploitation may also rally to the cause of the alliance. Furthermore, if a local compromise between capital and labour is helpful to local accumulation, then the bourgeoisie as a whole may support it. The basis is laid for the rise of a territorially based alliance between various factions of capital, the local state and even whole classes, in defence of social reproduction processes (both accumulation and the reproduction of labour power) within a particular territory" (420).

9. García Márquez has frequently commented on the way he dresses up Colombian reality in his fictionalized accounts: "All my work corresponds to a geographic or historical reality. It is not magical realism and all these things which are said. When you read Bolívar, you realise that all the others have, in some way, a documented base, an historical base, a geographic basis which is proved with The General" (quoted in Pearce 1990:4).

10. I obtained one of these leaflets later from a Guapi resident.

11. Aerial fumigation is still carried out in 2015 by Colombia's antidrug police spraying suspected coca crops with a mixture of the herbicide Roundup Ultra, a Monsanto product that contains glyphosate and polyethoxylated tallowamine, and Cosmo-Flux 411F. Pesticides containing glyphosate are considered "slightly toxic" in Colombia (registered under toxicological class IV). The U.S. Environment Protection Agency registers glyphosate in Toxicity Category III (with Category I being the most toxic and IV the least; Rincón-Ruiz and Kallis 2013:70).

12. "Colombia Must Stop Coca Fumigations," *Guardian*, August 6, 2010, http://www.guardian.co.uk/world/2010/aug/07/colombia-must-stop-coca-fumigations#history-link-box. The following is the text of the letter sent to the Colombian Embassy in London, dated May 11, 2010:

> Dear Sir/Madam:
> *Sustained poisonous fumigations in the area around Guapi, Costa Caucana—your crime against humanity and biodiversity*
> We, the undersigned academics, lawyers and economists, have confirmed knowledge that since the month of January Colombia's antinarcotics police have established a base in the small town of Guapi on the Cauca Coast, from where they have led operations to fumigate large parts of the rainforest, pretending to eradicate coca cultivation. While aware of

the purpose of these fumigations, we are highly concerned about their detrimental effect on everyday life in the communities affected who live along the river banks in this part of the country.

We demand an IMMEDIATE HALT to your fumigation campaign. You are directly responsible for committing a double crime against humanity and the environment.

As you know, rural black and indigenous communities who live along the river banks in the Pacific Coast region, have established for hundreds of years a peaceful form of living together in harmony with their surrounding environment—*una convivencia pacífica*. These communities have been responsible and successful in the preservation of this unique ecosystem that has a world-renowned reputation for being one of the hotspots of biological diversity in the world. This was recognised by the World Bank–supported research project Proyecto Biopacífico that ran from 1992 to 1998. It is in utter disregard of the recommendations drawn up by this acclaimed study that you have decided to start a massive, indiscriminate fumigation campaign in the region, hoping to eradicate illegal coca cultivation.

It is an act of utterly unacceptable cynicism that you should even consider spraying poisonous liquids—*glifosato*—onto this biodiverse region, thereby killing off the very vegetation, for which the region has become so importantly recognised. The United Nations have declared 2010 as the Year of Biodiversity. And the Colombian government is destroying this biodiversity in front of our eyes. This is a scandal of most utter cynicism. History will not absolve you!

Moreover, the implications of the widespread fumigation campaign for the local communities are devastating. Not only do you target the illegal coca plants, but all vegetation, including cultivations of important everyday crops—the *pan coger*—that local populations depend upon. Rivers are contaminated, elderly and children are particularly affected by skin rashes and asthmatic attacks. The true and long-lasting effects of this poisonous contamination that you have begun will become obvious in the weeks and months ahead.

We cannot sit idly by and let you commit these crimes against humanity and the environment. We most strongly condemn your practice of fumigation.

An added irony is the fact that the anti-narcotics police have taken over the Hotel Río Guapi (a hotel in which some of the undersigned have stayed themselves in the past). This hotel is run by a Spanish NGO—*Levante en Marxa*—that aims at providing support for the poorest of children and young people in the municipality of Guapi. It is one of the Macondoan ironies that your anti-narcotics police, which destroy the life base of these children by fumigation, should operate from the hotel run by this NGO.

Many of us have a long-standing commitment to the communities in and around the region of Guapi. We have been to the area many a times and know what we are talking about. Based on this first-hand experience we repeat our demand for an IMMEDIATE HALT TO FUMIGATION in this area and the whole region of the Pacific Coast.

Yours sincerely.

13. This difference is reflected in Decree 1332 of August 11, 1992, which created the Special Committee for Black Communities. Article 1 stipulates that three representatives of each Departmental Advisory Committee should be present in the Special Committee, and Article 3 names the organizations that form part of each Departmental Advisory Committee. The smallest number of such organizations is given for the Cauca Department, with only five. Ten of the twelve organizations of the Department of Nariño are "campesino associations," whereas six of the eight organizations of the Chocó carry the denomination "campesino."

14. Unless otherwise noted, all quotes from Humberto Villa come from an interview recorded with him in Guapi, April 24, 1999.

15. Unless otherwise noted, all quotes from Walberto Banguera come from an interview recorded with him in Guapi, February 5, 1999.

16. Unless otherwise noted, all quotes from Mirna Rosa Herrera come from an interview recorded with her in Timbiquí, February 17, 1999.

17. JUNPRO (Juventud Unida para el Progreso) was the first community organization to emerge in Guapi, mainly consisting of young professionals and former students. They were also the founding members of COCOCAUCA.

18. For more detail on PCN's organizational strategy, see Escobar (2008:216–28; 2015).

19. Interview with Silvio Sinisterra, director of the regional office of Plan Pacífico in Guapi, February 12, 1999, and documents presented there. Studies conducted in 1998 by UMATA and the national Agrarian Institute (Instituto Colombiano Agropecuario) showed a rice yield of 1,000 kilograms and 1,750 kilograms, respectively, per hectare in the Pacific Coast region, compared to an average of 5,000 kilograms per hectare in the Departments of Huila and Tolima. This discrepancy is still used today by state institutions as an argument to discourage local rice production in the Pacific lowlands.

20. Braun (2002) applies the concept of "technologies of displacement" to the ways forest management experts in British Columbia have discursively situated the temperate rain forest as a domain within wider geographies of "the nation," "the market," and "the global biosphere," separate from the cultural geographies

of Native communities already inhabiting the forest. In this way new actors have been authorized to "speak for the forest," displacing Native community voices and representations (32–33). Much of the development critique can be usefully read through this lens of "technologies of displacement" (see Escobar 1995, 2007; Esteva 1992; Ferguson 1990; Peet and Watts 1996; Ziai 2007).

21. As further conflict in the region, locals identified the impact of *retroexcavadoras*, or backhoes, which since 1995 had been employed in gold mining at a place called El Mero, some ten minutes from the largest settlement San Antonio de Guajuí in the middle section of the river. This activity resulted in the contamination of the river as well as considerable social costs, a situation that reminded locals of the experience of the inhabitants of Santa María de Timbiquí on the neighboring river, where in the 1980s Russians had exploited gold resources and their spending habits had led to a sharp increase in the prostitution of local women and other conflicts with locals. The communities of the Guajuí River also used the report that accompanied their application for a collective land title to denounce the educational system in the region and to voice strong criticism of the teachers themselves as being interested only in the economic benefits of their jobs and without a real commitment to the education of the youth. Apart from the lack of resources, such as libraries and books, the report denounced the "de-contextualization and the uselessness of the education in the region to which the adolescent is subject," which it argued was one of the reasons for emigration out of the region (Consejo Comunitario Río Guajuí 1998).

22. Interview with Guillermo Santamaría, managing director of Fundación La Minga, Cali, December 16, 1998.

23. Comment of Florentino Carvajal, legal representative of the Community Council Unicosta in Nariño, made during my conversation with the board of directors, Madrid, Nariño, May 8, 1999.

24. In general the term *paisa* is used in Colombia to refer to people from the western highlands, in particular from the Department of Antioquia. In the Pacific lowlands, however, it is frequently used to refer to any white outsider to the region, myself included at times.

25. Unless otherwise noted, all quotes from Porfirio Becerra come from an interview recorded with him in Tumaco, January 16, 1999.

26. It is quite common for locals to inquire about the "mission" of strangers on their lands. See the experience narrated by Taussig (2004:2), for example, when he paid a visit to the Russian mining company in the Timbiquí basin: "What is your mission? What is your mission?, people asked as we struggled through the mud to the village that had once housed slaves from Africa brought to mine gold by hand."

27. Interview held in Madrid, Nariño, May 8, 1999.

28. I am not the only one who finds Agnew's framework useful. Both Routledge (1993) and Miller (2000) draw on it in their respective attempts to conceptualize the spatialities of social movements.

Epilogue

1. What may appear to some surprising is actually a quite common collaboration. In May 2001 the Colombian Army and paramilitaries joined forces in "Operation Tsunami" under the same pretext, this time to combat FARC guerrillas in the area around Tumaco and Barbacoas in the Nariño Department, which paved the way for paramilitary control and land seizure. The local district attorney in Barbacoas at the time documents "Operation Tsunami" in her memoir *Revelations of a Prosecutor under Siege* (Márquez 2007:100). See also Taussig (2005) for an account of a village in Colombia's Cauca Valley under siege. There too paramilitaries enjoyed the tacit support of the police in their "cleansing" of the village, rounding up, torturing, and killing their victims and leaving their bodies on display as a warning to others (see also Taussig 2004:18).

2. Interview held in Bogotá, November 28, 2004. Interviewee's name withheld on request.

3. Such a terrorized sense of place permeates the personal narratives of the forcefully displaced. In an interview on December 13, 2004, in Guapi, a woman displaced from the nearby Iscuandé River told me that her village would never be the same again for her: "I won't go back to live there. No, I won't. I'm afraid. I wouldn't be at ease, I have this psychosis now. . . . Before then, we lived well there, because my husband had work, my sons also worked, and we lived well. But now, everything has fallen apart. We are in a limbo." Such a state of forlornness grips many displaced people in their new surroundings, but the sense of terror and fear they experience when thinking about their homeplace is such that they frequently do not consider a return.

4. Remembering the massacre of Bellavista has become an emblematic rallying cry for black activists to denounce what they consider an ethnocide committed against their communities. Every year on May 2 rallies in Bogotá and Quibdó, the regional capital of the Chocó Department, commemorate this single most traumatic event in the collective Afro-Colombian memory of recent times.

5. I have written elsewhere on these changing relations in the region and attempted to conceptualize these in a framework I have called "geographies of terror" (Oslender 2007b, 2008a, 2012). See also Bocarejo (2009) and Grajales (2011) on paramilitary violence as affecting land grabs in Colombia. See Carrigan (1995), Guillén (1997), Gutiérrez Sanín (2001), Pécaut (2000, 2001), Raphael (2010), and Richani (2002) on wider connections between paramilitarism and state terror in Colombia.

6. Website no longer available.

7. AFRODES was created in 1999. It is a grassroots organization consisting of more than fifteen thousand Afro-Colombian families who live in conditions of forced internal displacement. Its mission is to guide, support, and speak in defense of Afro-Colombians' rights and their cultural identity. AFRODES aims to create dignified life choices for their affiliates by sensitizing Colombian society to the displacement of black communities and proposing to the government policies capable of solving problems effectively; see www.afrodes.org.

8. It should be added that in step 4 a landless proletariat from other regions of the country is brought in to work those emptied lands for their new landlords.

9. Cárdenas (2012), for example, examines how in the Mira River basin (Nariño) small oil palm cooperatives function on collectively titled land through co-optation. She calls the appropriation of these lands for oil palm cultivation and biofuel "green land grabs." See also Restrepo (2004b) on the complex situation of oil palm cultivation in the area around Tumaco.

10. Thirty-two Colombian oil palm companies are part of this CDM Umbrella Project backed by FEDEPALMA. It consists in capturing, modifying, and making use of methane gas released from residual water treatment plants. Methane, as a greenhouse gas and a contributor to global climate change, is able to emit about twenty-one times more heat than carbon dioxide. Therein, it is argued, lies the importance of being able to modify it and make use of it to generate electricity or cogenerate and sell the excess. The project is intended to result in reductions of methane (CH_4) and carbon dioxide (CO_2) emissions by burning CH_4 emissions from the waste treatment process instead of passively venting to the atmosphere. These results in reductions of CH_4 and CO_2 emissions are believed to give long-term benefits to the mitigation of climate change. Specifically the project intends to lead to a reduction of 757,067 metric tons CO_2 equivalent per annum. It is to run for seven years initially, from 2010 to 2017, and was certified in 2009 as fulfilling the United Nations Framework Convention on Climate Change criteria for the CDM and as correctly applying ordinance AM0013 to avoid methane emissions from organic wastewater treatment. For a project design report, see United Nations Framework Convention on Climate Change, "Project 1942: FEDEPALMA Sectoral CDM Umbrella Project for Methane Capture, Fossil Fuel Displacement and Cogeneration of Renewable Energy," May 25, 2009, http://cdm.unfccc.int/Projects/DB/DNV-CUK1215586512.61/view.

11. The Kyoto Protocol (1997) committed developed countries to reduce their carbon dioxide emissions by 5.2 percent by 2012 (based on levels registered in 1990) and allowed them the possibility of doing this by receiving Certificates of Emission Reductions generated in developing countries through projects designed to reduce emissions or the planting of woodland.

12. In 2010 a group of sixty academics and intellectuals, concerned about the war scenario in the Pacific Coast, formed the Grupo de Académicos e Intelectuales en Defensa del Pacífico (GAIDEPAC). The group emerged in response to a declaration of social emergence issued on April 15, 2010, by some twenty Afro-Colombian and indigenous ethnic-territorial organizations, mainly of the southern Pacific Coast. This declaration, Declaración de Buenaventura, denounced the social and ecological costs—an ethnocide and ecocide—incurred by, among other factors, the expansion of gold mining in the region, aerial fumigation, constant threats to community leaders, and the increasing militarization of the river basins (by guerrillas, armed forces, and paramilitaries). GAIDEPAC aims to provide public support for these social organizations on the Pacific Coast, inform the international community about their plight, and provide a space for experts and interlocutors on this region. I am a founding member of GAIDEPAC.

13. In the conclusion to their book *Liberation Ecologies*, Peet and Watts (1996:263, 268) describe social movements as articulating "environmental imaginaries" and as contesting normative visions and the "imperialism of the imaginary."

GLOSSARY

agua de panela: commonly found drink on the Pacific Coast; an infusion made from hardened sugarcane pulp

alabao: ritual yearning chant, interpreted mainly by women during the wake for a deceased adult

angelito: "little angel"; soul-spirit of a deceased child

anillo rojo: "red ring"; a beetle pest that attacks coconut palms on the Pacific Coast

arrullo: a spiritual sung during patron saint festivities and during wakes for deceased children

automanumisión: "self-liberation"; process by which the enslaved bought their freedom making use of the judiciary system

azotea: raised platform garden typically kept near the main lodging and planted with medicinal and alimentary herbs

baldíos: "empty lands"; terrains of national domain

batea: wide shallow bowl carved out of wood; used in traditional placer gold mining to wash auriferous sands and gravels; name possibly of Carib Indian origin

bateadoras: girls and women who use a *batea* in alluvial gold panning

bombo: large double-headed membrane bass drum, made from a tree trunk; beaten with a cloth-covered stick

botella curada: "cured bottle"; usually prepared by women traditional healers, the *curanderas*; filled with a mix of forest herbs, leaves, and roots, and cured with *viche*, the rurally distilled unrefined sugarcane spirit (sometimes also spelled *biche*). Botellas *curadas* are often highly sought after and can be quite expensive.

bozal: enslaved person in the Americas who was brought directly from Africa

cabecera: head waters

cantadora: female singer; often referring to women singing spirituals during death wakes and patron saint festivities; also spelled *cantaora*

chigualo: wake for a deceased child, usually under seven years of age

chontaduro: *Bactris gasipaes*; peach palm tree; also refers to the fruit, which is often sold by *revendedoras*, or re-resellers, mostly women who buy large bunches of the fruit on the local market to then resell individual fruits for a profit in the local neighborhood.

cimarrón: maroon, runaway slave

concha: edible mussel, shellfish

conchera: woman who gathers shellfish in the mangrove swamps

cuadrilla: relatively small and mobile slave gang used in gold mining during the colonial era

cununo: hollowed single-head membrane tubular drum; resembling conga drum

curandera: traditional healer (female)

currulao: marimba dance typical of the southern part of the Pacific Coast

décima: the most important poetic structure among Afro-Colombians in the Pacific lowlands, often with a complex rhyme structure; *décimas* deal with disputes, the rules of generational and interpersonal relations, seduction, stories of historical events, tales, social critique, and protest.

decimero: man who recites *décimas*; according to Pedrosa and Vanín (1994:12), *decimeros* are "a kind of collective conscience, critics and historians of local, national and sometimes international events, tale-tellers and praisers of love, loss of love, fortune, and setbacks of fortunes."

estero: tidal estuary in the mangrove swamp

guandal: backswamp of palm thickets of largely inundated lands found mainly in the southern part of the Department of Nariño; a similar ecosystem in the Chocó Department is referred to as *palmar*

guapireño: person from Guapi

guasá: tubular rattle, made of a carved bamboo stem filled with small black seeds, maize, or pebbles; shaken by women in *arrullos* and in the *currulao*

invierno: period of heavy rains

jaguar: black concentrate consisting of a mixture of tiny flakes of heavy magnetic iron oxide, ilmenite, and gold dust, which is washed in the *batea* in placer mining to retain the gold

libre: "free"; self-liberated, formerly enslaved person; occasionally still found as self-denomination of Afro-Colombians on the Pacific Coast

maravelí: maritime "vision"; an apparition-vessel with a crew of satanic spirits that calls on those who have made a pact with the devil

marimba: suspended xylophone, inspired by the Mandingo *balafon*; central instrument in the *currulao*; it consists of twenty-four hard *chonta* palm-wood keys, which are arranged above resonance tubes made of *guadua* bamboo wood; played with rubber-tipped sticks, often by two players at the same time, one playing the lower register, the other the high notes

mazamorreo: stream placering

minga: cooperative labor group that works for the benefit of the community; a Quechua word that originally meant compulsory labor imposed on the common workers by the Inca governors; it retained that meaning in colonial times under Spanish rule, but since independence has been applied to the system of cooperative work groups

molino: sugarcane press

el monte: fluid category used to refer to the uninhabited forest, jungle, and backlands

naidí: *Euterpe oleracea*, also known as *Euterpe cuatrecasana*; açaí palm tree that grows in clusters; harvested for its palm hearts, referred to as *palmito*; locals prefer the dark fruit of the tree, with which they prepare a rich fruit juice known as *pepiao*; the name *naidí* is said to be derived from the indigenous Embera people; the same palm is known in the Chocó as *murrapo*

el ojo: the "evil eye"; an illness from which small children frequently are thought to suffer and which can result in the child's death; treated by the *curandera* with a variety of magic-religious rituals, including the application of specially prepared balsamic oils and prayers

palenque: fortified village of free blacks during slavery times; used today as an organizational category in the social movement of black communities

papa china: *Colocasia esculenta*; tuber popular in the southern Pacific Coast; often deep-fried and served with fried fish

pie de monte: foothill section

politiquería: term used to refer to political corruption, favoritism, and clientelism

potrillo: dugout canoe

puja: spring tide; in the Pacific littoral the weeks of the lunar cycle during which high tides reach their highest level

quiebra: neap tide; the period during which low tides are at their lowest level

quilombo: Brazilian equivalent of *palenque*, a fortified settlement of runaway slaves

real de minas: mining camp and administrative center founded in the eighteenth century

retroexcavadoras: backhoes, or retro power shovel earthmovers, employed in industrial gold mining in the Pacific lowlands; they are used to clear rain forest and chew up river bottoms and banks, causing significant environmental degradation and concern

riviel: dangerous maritime spirit/vision

tagua: *Phytelephas spp.*; palm nut sometimes referred to as "vegetal ivory"; important resource at the end of the nineteenth century in the production of buttons before mass production of plastic set in

tapao: traditional dish consisting of fish and plantain boiled together with herbs added for flavor

trapiche: hand-operated sugar mill

troncos: "consanguineal kinship groups whose members trace their descent to a common ancestor" (Friedemann 1985:207)

tunda: malign female forest spirit said to "possess" children

velorio: death wake for a deceased adult

verano: less rainy period

viche: popular alcoholic drink in the Pacific lowlands, a rurally distilled unrefined sugarcane spirit (sometimes also spelled *biche*). It is drunk on its own as a "shot" or mixed with forest herbs, leaves, and roots in cured bottles known as *botellas curadas*.

REFERENCES

AFRODES. 2010. *Bicentennial: Nothing to Celebrate! Report on the human rights of Afro-Colombian communities in the context of the "celebration" of two hundred years of republican life in Colombia*. July. Bogotá: AFRODES/Global Rights.

Agier, Michel. 2002. "From local legends into globalized identities: The devil, the priest and the musician in Tumaco." *Journal of Latin American Anthropology* 7(2), 140–67.

Agier, Michel, Manuela Álvarez, Odile Hoffmann, and Eduardo Restrepo. 1999. *Tumaco: Haciendo ciudad*. Bogotá: ICAN-IRD.

Agnew, John. 1987. *Place and politics: The geographical mediation of state and society*. Boston: Allen and Unwin.

———. 1994. "The territorial trap: The geographical assumptions of international relations theory." *Review of International Political Economy* 1, 53–80.

———. 2005. "Space: Place." In P. Cloke and R. Johnston, eds., *Spaces of geographical thought*, 81–96. London: Sage.

———. 2009. *Globalization and sovereignty*. New York: Rowman and Littlefield.

Agnew, John, and Ulrich Oslender. 2013. "Overlapping territorialities, sovereignty in dispute: Empirical lessons from Latin America." In W. Nicholls, B. Miller, and J. Beaumont, eds., *Spaces of contention: Spatialities and social movements*, 121–40. Aldershot, UK: Ashgate.

Agudelo, Carlos. 2004a. "La constitución política de 1991 y la inclusión ambigua de las poblaciones negras." In J. Arocha, ed., *Utopía para los excluidos: El multiculturalismo en África y América Latina*, 179–203. Bogotá: CES, Universidad Nacional de Colombia.

————. 2004b. "No todos vienen del río: Construcción de identidades negras urbanas y movilización política en Colombia." In E. Restrepo and A. Rojas, eds., *Conflicto e (in)visibilidad: Retos en los estudios de la gente negra en Colombia*, 173–93. Popayán: Universidad del Cauca.

————. 2005. *Retos del multiculturalismo en Colombia: Política y poblaciones negras*. Medellín: La Carreta Editores.

ALENPAC Ltda-Alimentos Enlatados del Pacífico. 1990. "Inventario forestal: Requisito para prórroga permiso de aprovechamiento persistente de la palma naidí en los municipios de El Charco e Iscuandé, Pasto-Nariño." Unpublished document.

————. 1995. "Memorias del Primer Seminario de sustentabilidad de la palma naidí, Guapi-Cauca." Unpublished document.

Almario, Oscar. 2003. *Los renacientes y su territorio: Ensayos sobre la etnicidad negra en el Pacífico sur colombiano*. Medellín: Universidad Pontificia Bolivariana.

Alvarez, Sonia, Evelina Dagnino, and Arturo Escobar. 1998. "Introduction: The cultural and the political in Latin American social movements." In S. Alvarez, E. Dagnino, and A. Escobar, eds., *Cultures of politics, politics of cultures: Re-visioning Latin American social movements*, 1–29. Oxford: Westview Press.

Anderson, Mark. 2007. "When Afro becomes (like) indigenous: Garifuna and Afro-indigenous politics in Honduras." *Journal of Latin American and Caribbean Anthropology* 12(2), 384–413.

Andrade Bazán, Eusebio. 1999. "Guapi, tierra querida." *Costa Caucana*, Guapi, 21 (May), 8.

Aprile-Gniset, Jacques. 1993. *Poblamiento, hábitats y pueblos del Pacífico*. Cali: Universidad del Valle.

Arboleda, Santiago. 1998. *Le dije que me esperara, Carmela no me esperó: El Pacífico en Cali*. Cali: Univalle.

————. 2007. "Los afrocolombianos: Entre la retórica del multiculturalismo y el fuego cruzado del destierro." *Journal of Latin American and Caribbean Anthropology* 12(1), 213–22.

Arocha, Jaime. 1992. "Los negros y la nueva Constitución colombiana de 1991." *América Negra* 3, 39–54.

————. 1998. "Inclusion of Afro-Colombians: Unreachable national goal?" *Latin American Perspectives* 25(3), 70–89.

————. 1999. *Ombligados de Ananse: Hilos ancestrales y modernos en el Pacífico colombiano*. Bogotá: CES.

Arrázola, Roberto. 1970. *Palenque: Primer pueblo libre de América*. Cartagena: Ediciones Hernández.

Asher, Kiran. 2009. *Black and green: Afro-Colombians, development, and nature in the Pacific lowlands*. Durham, NC: Duke University Press.

Auyero, Javier. 1999. " 'From the client's point(s) of view': How poor people perceive and evaluate political clientelism." *Theory and Society* 28(2), 297–334.

Bachelard, Gaston. (1958) 1994. *The poetics of space*. Boston: Beacon.

Bakhtin, Mikhail. 1986. *Speech genres and other late essays*. Translated by Vern W. McGee. Edited by C. Emerson and M. Holquist. Austin: University of Texas Press.

Bandy, J., and J. Smith, eds. 2004. *Coalitions across borders: Transnational protest and the neoliberal order (people, passions, and power)*. Boulder, CO: Rowman and Littlefield.

Barbary, Olivier, and Fernando Urrea, eds. 2004. *Gente negra en Colombia: Dinámicas sociopolíticas en Cali y el Pacífico*. Cali: CIDSE-IRD-COLCIENCIAS.

Barnet, Miguel. (1968) 2003. *Biography of a runaway slave*. Willimantic, CT: Curbstone.

Bateson, Gregory. 1972. *Steps towards an ecology of mind*. New York: HarperCollins.

Bejarano, Edgar, Bernardo Pérez Salazar, and Cesar Velásquez Monroy. 2003. "Megaproyectos, corporativismo global y violencia en Colombia." Unpublished report. Universidad Externado de Colombia, Bogotá.

Benford, Robert. 1993. "Frame disputes within the Nuclear Disarmament Movement." *Social Forces* 71(3), 677–701.

———. 1997. "An insider's critique of the social movement framing perspective." *Sociological Inquiry* 67(4), 409–30.

Blaser, Mario. 2010. *Storytelling globalization from the Chaco and beyond*. Durham, NC: Duke University Press.

Bocarejo, Diana. 2009. "Deceptive utopias: Violence, environmentalism and the regulation of multiculturalism in Colombia." *Law and Policy* 31(3), 307–29.

Bosco, Fernando. 2008. "The geographies of Latin American social movements." In E. Jackiewicz and F. Bosco, eds., *Placing Latin America: Contemporary themes in human geography*, 177–90. Boulder, CO: Rowman and Littlefield.

Bourdieu, Pierre. 2003. *Firing back: Against the tyranny of the market*. London: Verso.

Braun, Bruce. 2002. *The intemperate rainforest: Nature, culture, and power on Canada's west coast*. Minneapolis: University of Minnesota Press.

Breitbart, Myrna. 2010. "Participatory research methods." In N. Clifford, S. French, and G. Valentine, eds., *Key methods in geography*, 141–56. London: Sage.

Bunge, William. 1977. "The first years of the Detroit Geographical Expedition: A personal report." In R. Peet, ed., *Radical geography: Alternative viewpoints on contemporary social issues*, 31–39. London: Methuen.

Bushnell, David. 1993. *The making of modern Colombia: A nation in spite of itself*. Berkeley: University of California Press.

Buttimer, Anne. 1976. "Grasping the dynamism of lifeworld." *Annals of the Association of American Geographers* 66(2), 277–92.

Caballero, Rodrigo. 1996. *Etnobotánica de las comunidades negras e indígenas del delta del río Patía.* Quito: Abya-Yala/Biopacífico/Universidad Nacional de Colombia.

Calhoun, Craig. 1995. " 'New social movements' of the early nineteenth century." In M. Traugott, ed., *Repertoires and cycles of collective action,* 173–215. Durham, NC: Duke University Press.

Cárdenas, Roosbelinda. 2012. "Green multiculturalism: Articulations of ethnic and environmental politics in a Colombian 'black community.' " *Journal of Peasant Studies* 39(2), 309–33.

Carpentier, Alejo. (1946) 1995. *El reino de este mundo.* Barcelona: Grijalbo Mondadori.

Carrigan, Ana. 1995. "A chronicle of death foretold: State-sponsored violence in Colombia." NACLA *Report on the Americas* 28(5), 6–10.

Casamán, Sabás. 1997. *Historia, política y sociedad: Nuestra historia vista por un negro.* Dialogue with and edited by William Mina Aragón. Cali: Univalle.

Casas, Fernando. 1993. "Conservación, conocimiento y valoración de la biodiversidad: Cuestión de desarrollo." In P. Leyva, ed., *Colombia Pacífico,* vol. 2: 8–11. Bogotá: Fen-Biopacífico.

Casey, Edward. 1997. *The fate of place: A philosophical history.* Berkeley: University of California Press.

Castells, Manuel. 1983. *The city and the grassroots: A cross-cultural theory of urban social movements.* London: Edward Arnold.

———. 1997. *The power of identity.* Oxford: Blackwell.

Castree, Noel, and Bruce Braun, eds. 2001. *Social nature: Theory, practice and politics.* Oxford: Blackwell.

Castree, Noel, David Featherstone, and Andrew Herod. 2008. "Contrapuntal geographies: The politics of organizing across sociospatial difference." In K. Cox, M. Low, and J. Robinson, eds., *The Sage Handbook of Political Geography,* 305–21. London: Sage.

Colburn, F., ed. 1989. *Everyday forms of peasant resistance.* Armonk, NY: M. E. Sharpe.

Colmenares, Germán. 1976. *Histórica económica y social de Colombia, 1537–1719.* Medellín: Editorial Lealón.

———. 1994. "Capítulo I: Formación de la economía colonial." In J. A. Ocampo, ed., *Historia económica de Colombia.* Bogotá: Tercer Mundo Editores.

Consejo Comunitario Guapi Abajo. 1998. "Solicitud de título colectivo del Consejo Comunitario Guapi Abajo." Unpublished document prepared by the community council applying for a collective land title.

Consejo Comunitario Río Guajuí. 1998. "Solicitud de título colectivo del Consejo Comunitario Río Guajuí." Unpublished document prepared by the community council applying for a collective land title.

Córdoba, Eva. 1994. "Por los senderos de los cimarrones." *El Universal (Dominical)*, Cartagena (Colombia), 3–4.

Córdoba, Marino. 2001. "Trágico amanecer." In M. Segura Naranjo, ed., *Éxodo, patrimonio e identidad*, 248–52. Bogotá: Ministerio de Cultura.

Cortés, Hernán. 1999. "Titulación colectiva en comunidades negras del Pacífico nariñense." In J. Camacho and E. Restrepo, eds., *De montes, ríos y ciudades: Territorios e identidades de la gente negra en Colombia*, 131–42. Bogotá: Ecofondo/ICAN/ Fundación Natura.

Cresswell, Tim. 2006. *On the move: Mobility in the modern Western world*. New York: Routledge.

Daniels, Stephen, and Hayden Lorimer. 2012. "Until the end of days: Narrating landscape and environment." *Cultural Geographies* 19(1), 3–9.

Davies, Andrew, and David Featherstone. 2013. "Networking resistances: The contested spatialities of transnational social movement organizing." In W. Nicholls, B. Miller, and J. Beaumont, eds., *Spaces of contention: Spatialities and social movements*, 239–60. Aldershot, UK: Ashgate.

Del Castillo, Nicolás. 1982. *Esclavos negros en Cartagena y sus aportes léxicos*. Bogotá: Instituto Caro y Cuervo.

Deleuze, Gilles, and Félix Guattari. (1983) 2007. *A thousand plateaus: Capitalism and schizophrenia*. Translated by Brian Massumi. Minneapolis: University of Minnesota Press.

Della Porta, Donatella, and Sidney Tarrow, eds. 2005. *Transnational protest and global activism*. Lanham, MD: Rowman and Littlefield.

Diario Oficial. 1993. *Ley 70 de 1993*. Bogotá: Ministerio de Justicia.

Díaz Uribe, Eduardo. 1986. *El clientelismo en Colombia*. Bogotá: El Ancora.

DNP (Departamento Nacional de Planeación). 1998. "Plan de desarrollo 1998–2002: Bases para una política de desarrollo sostenible en la región del Pacífico colombiano." Unpublished working document.

Dowler, Lorraine, and Joanne Sharp. 2001. "A feminist geopolitics?" *Space and Polity* 5(3), 165–76.

Eckstein, Susan, ed. 1989. *Power and popular protest: Latin American social movements*. Berkeley: University of California Press.

Entrikin, J. Nicholas. 1991. *The betweenness of place: Towards a geography of modernity*. Baltimore: Johns Hopkins University Press.

Escalante, Aquiles. 1954. "Notas sobre el Palenque de San Basilio, una comunidad negra de Colombia." *Divulgaciones Etnológicas* 3(5), 207–358.

Escobar, Arturo. 1995. *Encountering development: The making and unmaking of the Third World*. Princeton, NJ: Princeton University Press.

———. 1996. "Constructing nature: Elements for a poststructural political ecology." In R. Peet and M. Watts, eds., *Liberation ecologies: Environment, development and social movements*, 46–68. London: Routledge.

———. 2007. "Post-development as concept and social practice." In Aram Ziai, ed., *Exploring post-development*, 18–32. London: Zed Books.

———. 2008. *Territories of difference: Place, movements, life, redes*. Durham, NC: Duke University Press.

———. 2015. "Activism as history-making: The collective and the personal in collaborative research with the Process of Black Communities in Colombia." In B. Reiter and U. Oslender, eds., *Bridging scholarship and activism*, 105–22. East Lansing: Michigan State University Press.

———. N.d. "Notes on the ontology of design." Unpublished manuscript. University of North Carolina, Chapel Hill.

Escobar, Arturo, and Sonia Alvarez, eds. 1992. *The making of social movements in Latin America: Identity, strategy, and democracy*. Oxford: Westview.

Escobar, Arturo, and Alvaro Pedrosa, eds. 1996. *Pacífico: ¿Desarrollo o diversidad? Estado, capital y movimientos sociales en el Pacífico colombiano*. Bogotá: Cerec.

Esteva, Gustavo. 1987. "Regenerating people's space." *Alternatives* 12, 125–52.

———. 1992. "Development." In W. Sachs, ed., *The development dictionary: A guide to knowledge as power*, 6–25. London: Zed Books.

Fals Borda, Orlando. 1978. *Mompox y Loba: Historia doble de la costa*. Vol. 1. Bogotá: Carlos Valencia Editores.

———. 1979–86. *Historia doble de la costa*. 4 vols. Bogotá: Editores Carlos Valencia.

———. 1987. "The application of participatory action-research in Latin America." *International Sociology* 2(4), 329–47.

———. 1992. "Social movements and political power in Latin America." In A. Escobar and S. Alvarez, eds., *The making of social movements in Latin America: Identity, strategy, and democracy*, 303–316. Oxford: Westview.

———. 1993. "Los constituyentes de 1991 también defendimos a los Afrocolombianos." *América Negra* 6, Bogotá, 221–27.

Featherstone, David. 2008. *Resistance, space and political identities: The making of counter-global networks*. Oxford: Wiley-Blackwell.

FEDEPALMA. 2007. *The faces of the oil palm*. Bogotá: FEDEPALMA. Available at www.fedepalma.org.

Feld, S., and K. Basso, eds. 1996. *Senses of places*. Santa Fe, NM: School of American Research Press.

Ferguson, James. 1990. *The anti-politics machine: "Development," depoliticization, and bureaucratic power in Lesotho*. Cambridge: Cambridge University Press.

Fisher, William, and Thomas Ponniah, eds. 2003. *Another world is possible: Popular alternatives to globalization at the World Social Forum*. London: Zed Books.

FitzSimmons, Margaret. 1989. "The matter of nature." *Antipode* 21, 106–20.

Foucault, Michel. 1972. *The archaeology of knowledge*. London: Tavistock.

———. 1980. *Power-knowledge: Selected interviews and other writings, 1972–1977.* Brighton, UK: Harvester.

Foweraker, Joe. 1995. *Theorizing social movements.* London: Pluto.

Freire, Paulo. 1971. *Pedagogy of the oppressed.* New York: Herder and Herder.

Friedemann, Nina. S. de. 1974. "Minería del oro y descendencia: Güelmambí, Nariño." *Revista Colombiana de Antropología* 16, 9–52.

———. 1979. *MaNgombe: Guerreros y ganaderos en Palenque.* Bogotá: Carlos Valencia Editores.

———. 1984. "Estudios de negros en la antropología colombiana." In J. Arocha and N. S. de Friedemann, *Un siglo de investigación social: Antropología en Colombia,* 507–72. Bogotá: Etno.

———. 1985. "*Troncos* among black miners in Colombia." In T. Greaves and W. Culver, eds., *Miners and mining in the Americas,* 204–25. Manchester, UK: Manchester University Press.

———. 1989. *Criele, criele son: Del Pacífico negro.* Bogotá: Planeta.

———. 1992. "Negros en Colombia: Identidad e invisibilidad." *América Negra* 3, 25–38.

———. 1998. "San Basilio en el universo Kilombo-Africa y Palenque-América." In A. Maya, ed., *Geografía humana de Colombia: Los afrocolombianos,* vol. 6: 81–101. Bogotá: Instituto Colombiano de Cultura Hispánica.

Friedemann, Nina S. de, and Jaime Arocha. 1986. *De sol a sol: Génesis, transformación y presencia de los negros en Colombia.* Bogotá: Planeta.

———. 1995. "Colombia." In Minority Rights Group, *No longer invisible: Afro-Latin Americans today,* 47–75. London: Minority Rights.

Friedemann, Nina S. de, and Mónica Espinosa. 1993. "La familia minera." In P. Leyva, ed., *Colombia Pacífico,* vol. 2: 560–69. Bogotá: Fondo FEN.

Friedemann, Nina S. de, and Carlos Patiño Rosselli. 1983. *Lengua y sociedad en el Palenque de San Basilio.* Bogotá: Instituto Caro y Cuervo.

Friedemann, Nina S. de, and Alfredo Vanín. 1991. *El Chocó: Magia y leyenda.* Bogotá: Litografía Arco.

FUNCOP (Fundación para la Comunicación Popular). 1996. *Identidad, desarrollo sostenible y organización social en la costa Pacífica: Estudio de caso, San Antonio del Guajuí, Guapi.* Popayán: FUNCOP.

Fundación Chiyangua. 1998. *Desde las azoteas.* Newsletter, June, Guapi.

Gal, S. 1995. "Language and the 'arts of resistance.'" *Cultural Anthropology* 10(3), 407–24.

García Márquez, Gabriel. (1967) 2006. *One hundred years of solitude.* New York: HarperCollins.

GEF-PNUD (Global Environment Facility—Programa de las Naciones Unidas para el Desarrollo). 1993. *Proyecto Biopacífico.* Bogotá: DNP/Biopacífico.

Giddens, Anthony. 1979. *Central problems in social theory*. London: Macmillan.

Goffman, Erving. 1972. *Relations in public: Microstudies of the public order*. London: Penguin.

Gould, Peter, and Rodney White. 1974. *Mental maps*. London: Penguin.

Grajales, Jacobo. 2011. "The rifle and the title: Paramilitary violence, land grab and land control in Colombia." *Journal of Peasant Studies* 38(4), 771–92.

Granda, Germán de. 1977. *Estudios sobre un área dialectal hispanoamericana de población negra*. Bogotá: Instituto Caro y Cuervo.

Greenhouse, C. 2005. "Hegemony and hidden transcripts: The discursive arts of neoliberal legitimation." *American Anthropologist* 107(3), 356–68.

Gregory, Derek. 1994. *Geographical imaginations*. Oxford: Blackwell.

Grueso, Jesús Alberto, and Arturo Escobar. 1996. "Las cooperativas agrarias y la modernización de los agricultores." In A. Escobar and A. Pedrosa, eds., *Pacífico: ¿Desarrollo o diversidad? Estado, capital y movimientos sociales en el Pacífico colombiano*, 90–108. Bogotá: Cerec.

Grueso, Libia, Carlos Rosero, and Arturo Escobar. 1998. "The process of black community organizing in the southern Pacific Coast region of Colombia." In S. Alvarez, E. Dagnino, and A. Escobar, eds., *Cultures of politics, politics of cultures: Re-visioning Latin American social movements*, 196–219. Oxford: Westview.

Guillén, Gonzalo. 1997. *Crónicas de la guerra sucia*. Bogotá: Planeta Colombiana.

Gutiérrez Sanín, Francisco. 2001. "The courtroom and the bivouac: Reflections on law and violence in Colombia." *Latin American Perspectives* 28(1), 56–72.

Gutmann, Matthew. 1993. "Rituals of resistance: A critique of the theory of everyday forms of resistance." *Latin American Perspectives* 20(2), 74–92.

Habermas, Jürgen. 1987. *The philosophical discourse of modernity: Twelve lectures*. Cambridge, UK: Polity.

Hale, Charles. 2002. "Does multiculturalism menace? Governance, cultural rights and the politics of identity in Guatemala." *Journal of Latin American Studies* 34, 485–524.

Harvey, David. 1972. "Revolutionary and counterrevolutionary theory in geography and the problem of ghetto formation." *Antipode* 4(2), 1–12.

———. 1973. *Social justice and the city*. London: Edward Arnold.

———. 1982. *The limits to capital*. Oxford: Basil Blackwell.

———. 1985a. *Consciousness and the urban experience*. Oxford: Basil Blackwell.

———. 1985b. "The geopolitics of capitalism." In D. Gregory and J. Urry, eds., *Social relations and spatial structures*, 128–63. London: Macmillan.

———. 1989. *The condition of postmodernity: An enquiry into the origins of cultural change*. Oxford: Basil Blackwell.

———. 1991. Afterword. In H. Lefebvre, *The production of space*, 425–34. Oxford: Blackwell.

———. 1996. *Justice, nature and the geography of difference*. Oxford: Blackwell.

Hazlewood, Julianne. 2012. "CO$_2$lonialism and the 'unintended consequences' of commoditizing climate change: Geographies of hope amid a sea of oil palms in the Northwest Ecuadorian Pacific region." *Journal of Sustainable Forestry* 31(1–2), 120–53.

Hellman, Judith. 1992. "The study of new social movements in Latin America and the question of autonomy." In A. Escobar and S. Alvarez, eds., *The making of social movements in Latin America: Identity, strategy, and democracy*, 52–61. Oxford: Westview.

———. 1995. "The riddle of new social movements: Who they are and what they do." In S. Halebsky and R. L. Harris, eds., *Capital, power, and inequality in Latin America*, 165–83. Oxford: Westview.

Hidalgo, Laura. 1995. *Décimas esmeraldeñas*. Quito: Libresa.

Hobsbawm, Eric. 1990. "La revolución." In R. Porter and M. Teich, eds., *La revolución en la historia*, 16–70. Barcelona: Editorial Crítica.

Hoffmann, Odile. 1999. "Territorialidades y alianzas: Construcción y activación de espacios locales en el Pacífico." In J. Camacho and E. Restrepo, eds., *De montes, ríos y ciudades: Territorios e identidades de la gente negra en Colombia*, 75–93. Bogotá: Ecofondo/ICAN/Fundación Natura.

———. 2004. *Communautés noires dans le Pacifique colombien: Innovations et dynamiques ethniques*. Paris: IRD-Karthala.

Hooker, Juliet. 2005. "Indigenous inclusion / black exclusion: Race, ethnicity and multicultural citizenship in Latin America." *Journal of Latin American Studies* 37, 285–310.

hooks, bell. 1991. *yearning: race, gender, and cultural politics*. London: Turnaround.

Human Rights Everywhere. 2006. *The flow of palm oil Colombia–Belgium/Europe: A study from a human rights perspective*. Madrid: HREV. Available at http://www.cbc .collectifs.net/doc/informe_en_v3-1.pdf.

Hyndman, Jennifer. 2003. "Beyond either/or: A feminist analysis of September 11th." *ACME: An International e-Journal for Critical Geographies* 2(1), 1–13.

IGAC (Instituto Geográfico "Agustín Codazzi"). 1999. *Paisajes vividos, paisajes observados: La percepción territorial en la zonificación ecológica del Pacífico colombiano*. Bogotá: Editorial Gente Nueva.

IIAP (Instituto de Investigaciones Ambientales del Pacífico). 1997. *Plan estratégico*. Quibdó: IIAP.

———. 2000. *Plan de Manejo del Consejo Comunitario del Río Napi*. Quibdó: IIAP.

INCODER (Instituto Colombiano de Desarrollo Rural). 2005. *Los cultivos de palma de aceite en los territorios colectivos de las comunidades negras de los ríos Curvaradó y Jiguamiandó, en el Departamento del Chocó*. Informe técnico, March 14. Bogotá: INCODER.

INCORA (Instituto Colombiano de Reforma Agraria). 1997. *Informe técnico visita Consejo Comunitario Unicosta*, 26–30 April. Unpublished report, Bogotá.

————. 1998a. *Visita técnica al Concejo Comunitario Alto Guapi*, 19–23 January. Unpublished report, Bogotá.

————. 1998b. *Visita técnica al Concejo Comunitario Río Guajuí*, 6–8 May. Unpublished report, Bogotá.

————. 1998c. *Visita técnica al Concejo Comunitario Río San Francisco*, 26–30 January. Unpublished report, Bogotá.

————. 1998d. *Visita técnica del* INCORA *al Concejo Comunitario del Río Napi*. Unpublished report, Bogotá.

————. 1999. "Resoluciones: 'Tierras de las comunidades negras del Pacífico-Caucano.'" *Costa Caucana: Agenda Turística*, 3–8.

Jacobs, Jane. 1988. "Politics and the cultural landscape: The case of Aboriginal land rights." *Australian Geographical Studies* 26(2), 249–63.

Jessop, Bob, Neil Brenner, and Martin Jones. 2008. "Theorizing sociospatial relations." *Environment and Planning* D: *Society and Space* 26, 389–401.

Joseph, G. 1990. "On the trail of Latin American bandits: A reexamination of peasant resistance." *Latin American Research Review* 25(3), 7–53.

Keck, Margaret, and Kathryn Sikkink. 1998. *Activists beyond borders: Advocacy networks in international politics*. Ithaca: Cornell University Press.

Kindon, Sara, Rachel Pain, and Mike Kesby, eds. 2007. *Participatory action research approaches and methods: Connecting people, participation and place*. London: Routledge.

Kropotkin, Peter. (1899) 1995. *Fields, factories and workshops*. London: Freedom.

Laclau, Ernesto, and Chantal Mouffe. 1985. *Hegemony and socialist strategy: Towards a radical democratic politics*. London: Verso.

Leal, Claudia. 1998. "Manglares y economía extractiva." In A. Maya, ed., *Geografía humana de Colombia: Los afrocolombianos*, vol. 6: 397–429. Bogotá: Instituto Colombiano de Cultura Hispánica.

Leal Buitrago, Francisco, and Andrés Dávila. 1991. *Clientelismo: El sistema político y su expresión regional*. Bogotá: Tercer Mundo Editores.

Leal Buitrago, Francisco, and León Zamosc, eds. 1991. *Al filo del caos: Crisis política en la Colombia de los años 80*. Bogotá: Tercer Mundo Editores.

Lefebvre, Henri. 1976. "Reflections on the politics of space." *Antipode* 8(2), 30–37.

————. 1991. *The production of space*. Oxford: Blackwell.

Leitner, Helga, Eric Sheppard, and Kristin Sziarto. 2008. "The spatialities of contentious politics." *Transactions of the Institute of British Geographers* 33, 157–72.

Levi, Jerome. 1999. "Hidden transcripts among the Rarámuri: Culture, resistance, and interethnic relations in northern Mexico." *American Ethnologist* 26(1), 90–113.

Ley, David. 1977. "Social geography and the taken-for-granted world." *Transactions of the Institute of British Geographers* 2(4), 498–512.

Ley, David, and Marwyn Samuels, eds. 1978. *Humanistic geography: Prospects and problems.* London: Croom Helm.

Limón, José. 1994. *Dancing with the devil: Society and cultural poetics in Mexican-American South Texas.* Madison: University of Wisconsin Press.

Losonczy, Anne Marie. 1993. "De lo vegetal a lo humano: Un modelo cognitivo afrocolombiano del Pacífico." *Revista Colombiana de Antropología* 20, 37–58.

———. 1999. "Memorias e identidad: Los negro-colombianos del Chocó." In J. Camacho and E. Restrepo, eds., *De montes, ríos y ciudades: Territorios e identidades de la gente negra en Colombia,* 13–24. Bogotá: Ecofondo/ICAN/Fundación Natura.

Low, S., and D. Lawrence-Zúñiga, eds. 2003. *The anthropology of space and place: Locating culture.* Oxford: Blackwell.

Lyons, B. 2005. "Discipline and the arts of domination: Rituals of respect in Chimborazo, Ecuador." *Cultural Anthropology* 20(1), 97–127.

Maglia, Graciela, and Armin Schwegler, eds. 2012. *Palenque (Colombia): Oralidad, identidad y resistencia.* Bogotá: Pontificia Universidad Javeriana.

Majrouh, Sayd Bahodine, ed. 2003. *Songs of love and war: Afghan women's poetry.* Translated from the French by Marjolijn de Jager. New York: Other Press. Originally published as *Le suicide et le chant: Poesie populaire des femmes pachtounes.*

Márquez, Gaby. 2007. *Revelaciones de una fiscal amenazada: De Telembí a Canadá.* Bogotá: Intermedio.

Mason, Ann. 2005. "Constructing authority alternatives on the periphery: Vignettes from Colombia." *International Political Science Review* 26(1), 37–54.

Massey, Doreen. 1994. *Space, place and gender.* Cambridge, UK: Polity.

———. 2005. *For space.* London: Sage.

Massey, Doreen, and John Allen, eds. 1984. *Geography matters! A reader.* Cambridge: Cambridge University Press.

Maya, Adriana. 1998. "Demografía histórica de la trata por Cartagena, 1533–1810." In A. Maya, ed., *Geografía humana de Colombia: Los afrocolombianos,* vol. 6: 9–52. Bogotá: Instituto Colombiano de Cultura Hispánica.

McAdam, Doug, John McCarthy, and Mayer Zald, eds. 1996. *Comparative perspectives on social movements: Political opportunities, mobilizing structures and cultural framings.* Cambridge: Cambridge University Press.

McAdam, Doug, Sidney Tarrow, and Charles Tilly. 2001. *Dynamics of contention.* New York: Cambridge University Press.

McCarthy, John, and Mayer Zald. 1977. "Resource mobilization and social movements: A partial theory." *American Journal of Sociology* 82, 33–47.

Melucci, Alberto. 1989. *Nomads of the present: Social movements and individual needs in contemporary society.* London: Hutchinson Radius.

Merrifield, Andrew. 1993. "Place and space: A Lefebvrian reconciliation." *Transactions of the Institute of British Geographers* 18(4), 516–31.

Mignolo, Walter. 2005. *The idea of Latin America.* Oxford: Blackwell.

Miller, Byron. 2000. *Geography and social movements: Comparing antinuclear activism in the Boston area*. Minneapolis: University of Minnesota Press.

Mina, Mateo. 1975. *Esclavitud y libertad en el valle del Río Cauca*. Bogotá: Fundación Rosca.

Minority Rights Group. 1995. *No longer invisible: Afro-Latin Americans today*. London: Minority Rights.

Mitchell, Timothy. 1990. "Everyday metaphors of power." *Theory and Society* 19(4), 545–77.

Mollett, Sharlene. 2006. "Race and natural resource conflicts in Honduras: The Miskito and Garifuna struggle for Lasa Pulan." *Latin American Research Review* 41(1), 76–101.

Moore, Donald. 1998. "Subaltern struggles and the politics of place: Remapping resistance in Zimbabwe's Eastern Highlands." *Cultural Anthropology* 13(3), 344–81.

Mosquera, Gilma. 1999. "Hábitats y espacio productivo y residencial en las aldeas parentales del Pacífico." In J. Camacho and E. Restrepo, eds., *De montes, ríos y ciudades: Territorios e identidades de la gente negra en Colombia*, 49–74. Bogotá: Ecofondo/ICAN/Fundación Natura.

Mosquera, Juan de Dios. 1985. *Las comunidades negras de Colombia: Pasado, presente y futuro*. Bogotá: Movimiento Nacional Cimarrón.

———. 1998. *La etnoeducación afrocolombiana: Guía para docentes, líderes y comunidades educativas*. Bogotá: Docentes Editores.

Navarrete, María Cristina. 2008. *San Basilio de Palenque: Memoria y tradición*. Cali: Universidad del Valle.

Ng'weno, Bettina. 2007a. "Can ethnicity replace race? Afro-Colombians, indigeneity and the Colombian multicultural state." *Journal of Latin American and Caribbean Anthropology* 12(2), 414–40.

———. 2007b. *Turf wars: Territory and citizenship in the contemporary state*. Stanford: Stanford University Press.

Nicholls, Walter, Byron Miller, and Justin Beaumont, eds. 2013. *Spaces of contention: Spatialities and social movements*. Aldershot, UK: Ashgate.

Nordstrom, Carolyn, and JoAnn Martin. 1992. "The culture of conflict: Field reality and theory." In C. Nordstrom and J. Martin, eds., *The paths to domination, resistance and terror*, 3–17. Berkeley: University of California Press.

Novak, James. 1993. *Bangladesh: Reflections on the water*. Bloomington: Indiana University Press.

Oberschall, Anthony. 1973. *Social conflict and social movements*. London: Harper and Row.

OCN (Organización de Comunidades Negras). 1996. "Movimiento negro, identidad y territorio: Entrevista con la Organización de Comunidades Negras de Buenaventura." In A. Escobar and A. Pedrosa, eds., *Pacífico: ¿Desarrollo o diversidad? Estado, capital y movimientos sociales en el Pacífico colombiano*, 245–65. Bogotá: Cerec.

O'Connor, James. 1988. "Capitalism, nature, socialism: A theoretical introduction." *Capitalism, Nature, Socialism* 1(1), 11–38.

———. 1989. "Political economy of ecology of socialism and capitalism." *Capitalism, Nature, Socialism* 1(3), 93–108.

O'Connor, Martin. 1993. "On the misadventures of capitalist nature." *Capitalism, Nature, Socialism* 4(3), 7–40.

Offen, Karl. 2003. "The territorial turn: Making black territories in Pacific Colombia." *Journal of Latin American Geography* 2(1), 43–73.

Ogden, Laura. 2011. *Swamplife: People, gators, and mangroves entangled in the Everglades*. Minneapolis: University of Minnesota Press.

Ogden, Laura, Nik Heynen, Ulrich Oslender, Paige West, Karim-Aly Kassam, and Paul Robbins. 2013. "Global assemblages, resilience, and earth stewardship in the Anthropocene." *Frontiers in Ecology and the Environment* 11(7), 341–47.

Olson, Mancur. 1965. *The logic of collective action: Public goods and the theory of groups*. London: Oxford University Press.

Ong, Walter J. 1982. *Orality and literacy: The technologizing of the word*. London: Routledge.

ONU (Organización de Naciones Unidas). 2002. *Informe sobre la Misión de Observación en el Medio Atrato*. Bogotá: Oficina en Colombia del Alto Comisionado de las Naciones Unidas para los Derechos Humanos.

Ortner, S. 1995. "Resistance and the problem of ethnographic refusal." *Comparative Studies in Society and History* 37(1), 173–93.

Oslender, Ulrich. 2002. "The logic of the river: A spatial approach to ethnic-territorial mobilization in the Colombian Pacific region." *Journal of Latin American Anthropology* 7(2), 86–117.

———. 2004. "Fleshing out the geographies of social movements: Black communities on the Colombian Pacific Coast and the aquatic space." *Political Geography* 23(8), 957–85.

———. 2007a. "Re-visiting the hidden transcript: Oral tradition and black cultural politics in the Colombian Pacific Coast region." *Environment and Planning D: Society and Space* 25(6), 1103–29.

———. 2007b. "Spaces of terror and fear on Colombia's Pacific Coast: The armed conflict and forced displacement among black communities." In D. Gregory and A. Pred, eds., *Violent geographies: Fear, terror, and political violence*, 111–32. New York: Routledge.

———. 2007c. "Violence in development: The logic of forced displacement on Colombia's Pacific Coast." *Development in Practice* 17(6), 752–64.

———. 2008a. "Another history of violence: The production of 'geographies of terror' in Colombia's Pacific Coast region." *Latin American Perspectives* 35(5), 77–102.

———. 2008b. "Colombia: Old and new patterns of violence, accumulation and dispossession." In "Violence today: Actually existing barbarisms." Special issue, *Socialist Register* (2009), 181–98.

———. 2010. "Book review: 'Black and Green: Afro-Colombians, Development, and Nature in the Pacific Lowlands' by Kiran Asher (Durham: Duke University Press, 2009)." *Americas: A Quarterly Review of Inter-American Cultural History* 67(1), 143–44.

———. 2012. "The quest for a counter-space in the Colombian Pacific Coast region: Toward alternative black territorialities or co-optation by dominant power?" In J. Rahier, ed., *Black social movements in Latin America: From monocultural mestizaje to multiculturalism*, 95–112. New York: Palgrave Macmillan.

———. 2015. "Leaving the field: How to write about disappointment and frustration in participatory action-research." In B. Reiter and U. Oslender, eds., *Bridging scholarship and activism: Reflections from the frontlines of collaborative research*, 63–74. East Lansing: Michigan State University Press.

———. 2016. "The banality of displacement: Discourse and thoughtlessness in the internal refugee crisis in Colombia." *Political Geography* 50, 10–19.

Ospina Bozzi, Martha Luz, and Doris Ochoa Jaramillo. 2001. *La palma africana en Colombia: Apuntes y memorias.* Vols. 1 and 2. Bogotá: FEDEPALMA.

Paddison, Ronan. 1983. *The fragmented state.* Oxford: Basil Blackwell.

Pain, Rachel. 2003. "Social geography: On action-orientated research." *Progress in Human Geography* 27(5), 649–57.

———. 2004. "Social geography: Participatory research." *Progress in Human Geography* 28(5), 652–63.

———. 2006. "Social geography: Seven deadly myths in policy research." *Progress in Human Geography* 30(2), 250–59.

Pain, Rachel, and Susan Smith, eds. 2008. *Fear: Critical geopolitics and everyday life* Aldershot, UK: Ashgate.

Pararas-Carayannis, George. 1982. *Earthquake and tsunami of 12 December 1979 in Colombia.* Honolulu: ITIC (International Tsunami Information Centre).

Pardo, Mauricio, ed. 2001. *Acción colectiva, Estado y etnicidad en el Pacífico colombiano.* Bogotá: ICANH.

Paschel, Tianna. 2010. "The right to difference: Explaining Colombia's shift from color blindness to the Law of Black Communities." *American Journal of Sociology* 116(3), 729–69.

Pastoral de Etnias. 1999. "Ley de libertad de vientres (28 de mayo 1821)." In Pastoral de Etnias, *Compendio legislativo sobre la población afrocolombiana*, 10–13. Bogotá: Conferencia Episcopal de Colombia.

Paz, Octavio. 1961. *The labyrinth of solitude and other writings*. New York: Grove.

PCN (Proceso de Comunidades Negras). 1999. "El concepto de territorio en las comunidades negras del Pacífico Centro y Sur." Unpublished document.

Pearce, Jenny. 1990. *Colombia: Inside the labyrinth*. London: Latin America Bureau.

Pécaut, Daniel. 2000. "Configurations of space, time, and subjectivity in a context of terror: The Colombian example." *International Journal of Politics, Culture and Society* 14(1), 129–50.

———. 2001. *Guerra contra la sociedad*. Bogotá: Planeta.

Pedrosa, Álvaro, and Alfredo Vanín. 1994. *La vertiente afropacífica de la tradición oral: Géneros y catalogación*. Cali: Univalle.

Peet, Richard, ed. 1977. *Radical geography: Alternative viewpoints on contemporary social issues*. London: Methuen.

Peet, Richard, and Michael Watts, eds. 1996. *Liberation ecologies: Environment, development and social movements*. London: Routledge.

Pile, Steve, and Michael Keith, eds. 1997. *Geographies of resistance*. London: Routledge.

Pizarro, Eduardo. 1993. "Colombia: Hacia una salida democrática a la crisis nacional?" In C. I. Degregori, ed., *Democracia, etnicidad y violencia política en los países andinos*, 137–66. Lima: IEP/IFEA.

———. 2004. *Una democracia asediada: Balance y perspectivas del conflicto armado en Colombia*. Bogotá: Norma.

Portocarrero, Guillermo. 1995. *Sonetos en el puerto*. Cali: Fondo Mixto de Promocion de la Cultura y las Artes del Cauca.

Postero, Nancy. 2007. *Now we are citizens: Indigenous politics in postmulticultural Bolivia*. Stanford: Stanford University Press.

Pratt, Geraldine. 2000. "Participatory action research." In R. Johnston, D. Gregory, G. Pratt, and M. Watts, eds., *The dictionary of human geography*, 4th edition, 574. Oxford: Blackwell.

Pred, Alan. 1984. "Place as historically contingent process: Structuration and the time-geography of becoming places." *Annals of the Association of American Geographers* 74, 279–97.

Price, Richard, ed. 1979. *Maroon societies: Rebel slave communities in the Americas*. Baltimore: Johns Hopkins University Press.

Proyecto Biopacífico. 1998. *Informe final general*. Bogotá: Ministerio del Medio Ambiente.

Rahier, Jean. 1986. *La décima, poesía oral negra del Ecuador*. Quito: Abya-Yala.

———. 1999. "Blackness as a process of creolization: The Afro-Esmeraldian Décimas (Ecuador)." In I. Okpewho, C. Boyce-Davies, and A. Mazrui, eds., *The African diaspora: African origins and New World identities*, 290–314. Bloomington: Indiana University Press.

————. 2013. *Kings for three days: The play of race and gender in an Afro-Ecuadorian festival*. Chicago: University of Illinois Press.

Rahman, Mohammad Anisur. 1991. "El punto de vista teórico de la IAP." In O. Fals Borda and M. A. Rahman, eds., *Acción y conocimiento: Cómo romper el monopolio con investigación-acción participativa*, 21–35. Bogotá: Cinep.

Rahman, Mohammad Anisur, and Orlando Fals Borda. 1991. "Un repaso de la IAP." In O. Fals Borda and M. A. Rahman, eds., *Acción y conocimiento: Cómo romper el monopolio con investigación-acción participativa*, 37–50. Bogotá: Cinep.

Rangel, Alfredo, William Ramírez, and Paola Andrea Betancur. 2009. *Oil palm in Colombia: Conflict, myths and realities*. Bogotá: Fundación Seguridad y Democracia.

Raphael, Sam. 2010. "Paramilitarism and state terror in Colombia." In R. Jackson, E. Murphy, and S. Poynting, eds., *Contemporary state terrorism: Theory and practice*, 163–80. London: Routledge.

Reiter, Bernd, and Ulrich Oslender, eds. 2015. *Bridging scholarship and activism: Reflections from the frontlines of collaborative research*. East Lansing: Michigan State University Press.

Relph, Edward. 1976. *Place and placelessness*. London: Pion.

Restrepo, Eduardo. 1995. "Identidad, poder y cultura entre los 'grupos negros' de los ríos Satinga y Sanquianga, Pacífico Sur colombiano." Report to Proyecto Bosques de Guandal. Medellín: Universidad Nacional.

————. 1996a. "Invenciones antropológicas del negro." *Revista Colombiana de Antropología* 33, 238–69.

————. 1996b. "El naidí entre los 'grupos negros' del Pacífico Sur colombiano." In J. I. Del Valle and E. Restrepo, eds., *Renacientes del guandal: "Grupos negros" de los ríos Satinga y Sanquianga*, 351–83. Bogotá: Biopacífico-Universidad Nacional de Colombia.

————. 1996c. "Los tuqueros negros del Pacífico Sur colombiano." In J. I. Del Valle and E. Restrepo, eds., *Renacientes del guandal: "Grupos negros" de los ríos Satinga y Sanquianga*, 243–348. Bogotá: Biopacífico-Universidad Nacional de Colombia.

————. 1998. "La construcción de la etnicidad: Comunidades negras en Colombia." In M. L. Sotomayor, ed., *Modernidad, identidad y desarrollo*, 341–59. Bogotá: ICAN.

————. 2001. "Imaginando comunidad negra: Etnografía de la etnización de las poblaciones negras en el Pacífico sur colombiano." In M. Pardo, ed., *Acción colectiva, Estado y etnicidad en el Pacífico colombiano*, 41–70. Bogotá: ICANH.

————. 2004a. "Ethnicization of blackness in Colombia: Toward de-racializing theoretical and political imagination." *Cultural Studies* 18(5), 698–715.

————. 2004b. "Un océano verde para extraer aceite: Hacia una etnografía del cultivo de la palma Africana en Tumaco." *Universitas Humanística* 31(58), 73–87.

———. 2013. *Etnización de la negridad: La invención de las "comunidades negras" como grupo étnico en Colombia*. Popayán: Universidad del Cauca.

Richani, Nazih. 2002. *Systems of violence: The political economy of war and peace in Colombia*. Albany: State University of New York Press.

Rincón-Ruiz, Alexander, and Giorgos Kallis. 2013. "Caught in the middle: Colombia's war on drugs and its effects on forest and people." *Geoforum* 46, 60–78.

Rivas, Nelly. 2001. "Ley 70 y medio ambiente: El caso del Consejo Comunitario Acapa, Pacífico nariñense." In M. Pardo, ed., *Acción colectiva, Estado y etnicidad en el Pacífico colombiano*, 149–69. Bogotá: ICANH.

Roa Avendaño, Tatiana. 2007. "Colombia's palm oil diesel push." Research report for IRC Americas Program, February 2. Silver City, NM: International Relations Center.

Romero, Mario Diego. 1993. "Arraigo y desarraigo de la territorialidad del negro en el Pacífico colombiano." In A. Ulloa, ed., *Contribución africana a la cultura de las Américas*, 23–32. Bogotá: ICAN.

———. 1995. *Poblamiento y sociedad en el Pacífico colombiano: Siglos XVI al XVIII*. Cali: Universidad del Valle.

———. 1998. "Familia afrocolombiana y construcción territorial en el Pacífico Sur, siglo XVIII." In A. Maya, ed., *Geografía humana de Colombia: Los afrocolombianos*, vol. 6: 103–40. Bogotá: Instituto Colombiano de Cultura Hispánica.

Routledge, Paul. 1993. *Terrains of resistance: Nonviolent social movements and the contestation of place in India*. London: Praeger.

Routledge, Paul, and Andy Cumbers. 2009. *Global justice networks: Geographies of transnational solidarity*. Manchester, UK: Manchester University Press.

Ruiz Salgero, Magda Teresa, and Yolanda Bodnar. 1995. *El carácter multiétnico de Colombia y sus implicaciones censales*. Bogotá: DANE.

Sábato, Ernesto. 1998. *Antes del fin*. Buenos Aires: Seix Barral.

Safford, Frank, and Marco Palacios. 2002. *Colombia: Fragmented land, divided society*. Oxford: Oxford University Press.

Sansone, Livio. 2003. *Blackness without ethnicity: Constructing race in Brazil*. New York: Palgrave Macmillan.

Schwegler, Armin. 2012. "Sobre el origen africano de la lengua criolla de Palenque (Colombia)." In Graciela Maglia and Armin Schwegler, eds., *Palenque (Colombia): Oralidad, identidad y resistencia*, 107–79. Bogotá: Pontificia Universidad Javeriana.

Scott, James Campbell. 1985. *Weapons of the weak*. New Haven, CT: Yale University Press.

———. 1990. *Domination and the arts of resistance: Hidden transcripts*. New Haven, CT: Yale University Press.

————. 1992. "Domination, acting, and fantasy." In C. Nordstrom and J. Martin, eds., *The paths to domination, resistance and terror*, 55–84. Berkeley: University of California Press.

Sharp, William. 1976. *Slavery on the Spanish frontier: The Colombian Chocó 1680–1810*. Norman: University of Oklahoma Press.

Sieder, Rachel, ed. 2002. *Multiculturalism in Latin America: Indigenous rights, diversity and democracy*. Houndmills, UK: Palgrave Macmillan.

Sivaramakrishnan, K. 2005. "Introduction to 'Moral economies, state, spaces, and categorical violence.'" *American Anthropologist* 107(3), 321–30.

Slater, David, ed. 1985. *New social movements and the state in Latin America*. Amsterdam: CEDLA.

————. 1997. "Spatial politics/social movements: Questions of (b)orders and resistance in global times." In S. Pile and M. Keith, eds., *Geographies of resistance*, 258–76. London: Routledge.

————. 1998. "Rethinking the spatialities of social movements: Questions of (b)orders, culture, and politics in global times." In S. Alvarez, E. Dagnino, and A. Escobar, eds., *Cultures of politics, politics of cultures: Re-visioning Latin American social movements*, 380–401. Oxford: Westview.

Smith, Jackie. 1998. "Global civil society? Transnational social movement organization and social capital." *American Behavioral Scientist* 42(1), 93–107.

Smith, Jackie, Charles Chatfield, and Ron Pagnucco, eds. 1997. *Transnational social movements and global politics: Solidarity beyond the state*. Syracuse: Syracuse University Press.

Smith, Neil. 1990. *Uneven development: Nature, capital and the production of space*. Oxford: Blackwell.

Snow, David, Burke Rochford, Steven Worden, and Robert Benford. 1986. "Frame alignment processes, micromobilization and movement participation." *American Sociological Review* 51, 464–81.

Soja, Edward. 1980. "The socio-spatial dialectic." *Annals of the Association of American Geographers* 70, 207–25.

————. 1985. "The spatiality of social life: Towards a transformative retheorisation." In D. Gregory and J. Urry, eds., *Social relations and spatial structures*, 90–127. London: Macmillan.

————. 1989. *Postmodern geographies: The reassertion of space in critical social theory*. London: Verso.

Sousa Santos, Boaventura de. 2006. *The rise of the global left: The World Social Forum and beyond*. London: Zed Books.

Sparke, Matthew. 1998. "A map that roared and an original atlas: Canada, cartography, and the narration of nation." *Annals of the Association of American Geographers* 88(3), 463–95.

Spicker, Jessica. 1996. "Mujer esclava: Demografía y familia criolla en la Nueva Granada 1750–1810." Master's thesis, Universidad de los Andes, Bogotá.

Spivak, Gayatri Chakravorty. 1996. *The Spivak reader: Selected works of Gayatri Chakravorty Spivak.* Edited by Donna Landry and Gerald MacLean. London: Routledge.

Stemper, David. 1998. "Arqueología y movimientos sociales en el Pacífico colombiano." *Revista Colombiana de Antropología* 34, 166–93.

Tarrow, Sidney. 1994. *Power in movement: Social movements, collective action, and politics.* Cambridge: Cambridge University Press.

———. 2005. *The new transnational activism.* Cambridge: Cambridge University Press.

———. 2012. *Strangers at the gates: Movements and states in contentious politics.* Cambridge: Cambridge University Press.

Tarrow, Sidney, and Doug McAdam. 2005. "Scale shift in transnational contention." In D. Della Porta and S. Tarrow, eds., *Transnational protest and global activism,* 121–47. Lanham, MD: Rowman and Littlefield.

Taussig, Michael. 1979. *Destrucción y resistencia campesina: El caso del litoral Pacífico.* Bogotá: Editorial Punta de Lanza.

———. 2004. *My cocaine museum.* Chicago: University of Chicago Press.

———. 2005. *Law in a lawless land: Diary of a limpieza in Colombia.* Chicago: University of Chicago Press.

Telles, Edward. 2004. *Race in another America: The significance of skin color in Brazil.* Princeton, NJ: Princeton University Press.

Tilley, Christopher. 1995. *A phenomenology of landscape: Places, paths, and monuments.* Oxford: Berg.

Tilly, Charles. 1978. *From mobilization to revolution.* London: Addison-Wesley.

———. 1991. "Domination, resistance, compliance . . . discourse." *Sociological Forum* 6(3), 593–602.

Tilly, Charles, and Sidney Tarrow. 2007. *Contentious politics.* Boulder, CO: Paradigm.

Tilly, Charles, and Lesley Wood. 2009. *Social movements: 1768–2008.* 2nd edition. Boulder, CO: Paradigm.

Touraine, Alain. 1988. *The return of the actor.* Minneapolis: University of Minnesota Press.

Tuan, Yi-Fu. 1975. "Place: An experiential perspective." *Geographical Review* 65(2), 151–65.

———. 1976. "Humanistic geography." *Annals of the Association of American Geographers* 66(2), 266–76.

Udani, Jay, Betsy Singh, Vijay Singh, and Marilyn Barrett. 2011. "Effects of açai (Euterpe oleracea mart.) berry preparation on metabolic parameters in a healthy overweight population: A pilot study." *Nutrition Journal* 10(45), 1–7.

UNCED. 1987. *Our common future.* Basel: UNCED.

Urrea, Fernando, Santiago Arboleda, and Javier Arias. 1999. "Redes familiares entre migrantes de la costa pacífica a Cali." In *Revista Colombiana de Antropología* 35, 180–241. Bogotá: ICANH.

Valencia, Alonso. 1991. *Resistencia indígena a la colonización española.* Cali: Univalle.

Vallejo, Martha Isabel, Natalia Valderrama, Rodrigo Bernal, Gloria Galeano, Gerardo Arteaga, and Claudia Leal. 2011. "Producción de palmito de *euterpe oleracea* mart. (arecaceae) en la Costa Pacífica colombiana: Estado actual y perspectivas." *Colombia Forestal* 14(2), 191–212.

Van Cott, Donna Lee. 2000. *The friendly liquidation of the past: The politics of diversity in Latin America.* Pittsburgh: University of Pittsburgh Press.

———. 2005. *From movements to parties in Latin America: The evolution of ethnic politics.* Cambridge: Cambridge University Press.

Vanín, Alfredo. 1996. "Lenguaje y modernidad." In A. Escobar and A. Pedrosa, eds., *Pacífico: ¿Desarrollo o diversidad? Estado, capital y movimientos sociales en el Pacífico colombiano,* 41–65. Bogotá: Cerec.

———. 1998. "Mitopoética de la orilla florida." In A. Maya, ed., *Geografía humana de Colombia: Los afrocolombianos,* vol. 6: 265–78. Bogotá: Instituto Colombiano de Cultura Hispánica.

Vargas, Patricia. 1999. "Propuesta metodológica para la investigación participativa de la percepción territorial en el Pacífico." In J. Camacho and E. Restrepo, eds., *De montes, ríos y ciudades: Territorios e identidades de la gente negra en Colombia,* 143–76. Bogotá: Ecofondo/ICAN/Fundación Natura.

Velasco, Marcela. 2011. "Confining ethnic territorial autonomy in Colombia: The case of the Naya River basin." *Journal of Environment and Development* 20(4), 405–27.

Velásquez, Rogerio. (1959) 2000. *Cuentos de la raza negra.* In R. Velásquez, *Fragmentos de historia, etnografía y narraciones del Pacífico colombiano negro,* 173–233. Bogotá: ICANH.

Velásquez Runk, Julie. 2009. "Social and river networks for the trees: Wounaan's riverine rhizomic cosmos and arboreal conservation." *American Anthropologist* 111(4), 456–67.

Vélez Torres, Irene. 2010. *International mission to verify the impact of agrofuel production in 5 zones affected by oil palm and sugarcane monocrops in Colombia: Impacts on the territories, rights, food sovereignty and environment (3–10 July 2009).* Bogotá: Censat-PCN.

Villa, William. 1998. "Movimiento social de comunidades negras en el Pacífico colombiano: La construcción de una noción de territorio y región." In A. Maya, ed., *Geografía humana de Colombia: Los afrocolombianos,* vol. 6: 433–49. Bogotá: Instituto Colombiano de Cultura Hispánica.

———. 2000. "El territorio colectivo de comunidades negras más allá de la titulación." In IIAP, *Una aproximación al estado de la titulación colectiva*. Bogotá: IIAP.

———. 2013. "Colonización y conflicto territorial en el bajo Atrato: El poblamiento de las cuencas de la margen oriental." *Revista Estudios del Pacífico Colombiano* (Quibdó, Chocó) 1, 9–56.

Visvanathan, Shiva. 1991. "Mrs. Brundtland's disenchanted cosmos." *Alternatives* 16(3), 377–84.

Von Prahl, Henry, Jaime Cantera, and Rafael Contreras. 1990. *Manglares y hombres del Pacífico colombiano*. Bogotá: Fondo Fen.

Wade, Peter. 1993. *Blackness and race mixture: The dynamics of racial identity in Colombia*. Baltimore: Johns Hopkins University Press.

———. 1995. "The cultural politics of blackness in Colombia." *American Ethnologist* 22(2), 341–57.

———. 1997a. *Gente negra, nación mestiza: Dinámicas de las identidades raciales en Colombia*. Bogotá: Universidad de Antioquia/ICAN/Siglo del Hombre/Uniandes.

———. 1997b. *Race and ethnicity in Latin America*. London: Pluto.

———. 1999a. "The guardians of power: Biodiversity and multiculturality in Colombia." In A. Cheater, ed., *The anthropology of power: Empowerment and disempowerment in changing structures*, 73–87. London: Routledge.

———. 1999b. "Working culture: Making cultural identities in Cali, Colombia." *Current Anthropology* 40(4), 449–71.

———. 2000. *Music, race, and nation: Música tropical in Colombia*. Chicago: University of Chicago Press.

———. 2002. "Introduction: The Colombian Pacific in perspective." *Journal of Latin American Anthropology* 7(2), 2–33.

———. 2005a. "La política cultural de la negritud en Latinoamérica y el Caribe." *Guaraguao: Revista de Cultura Latinoamericana* 9(20), 8–38.

———. 2005b. "Rethinking mestizaje: Ideology and lived experience." *Journal of Latin American Studies* 37, 239–57.

Wainwright, Joel, and Trevor Barnes. 2009. "Nature, economy, and the space-place distinction." *Environment and Planning D: Society and Space* 27(6), 966–86.

Walsh, Catherine. 2004. "Colonialidad, conocimiento y diáspora afro-andina: Construyendo etnoeducación e interculturalidad en la universidad." In E. Restrepo and A. Rojas, eds., *Conflicto e (in)visibilidad: Retos en los estudios de la gente negra en Colombia*, 331–46. Popayán: Universidad del Cauca.

Watts, Michael, and Richard Peet. 1996. "Conclusion: Towards a theory of liberation ecology." In R. Peet and M. Watts, eds., *Liberation ecologies: Environment, development and social movements*, 260–69. London: Routledge.

West, Robert. 1952. *Colonial placer mining in Colombia*. Baton Rouge: Louisiana State University Press.

———. 1956. "Mangrove swamps of the Pacific Coast of Colombia." *Annals of the Association of American Geographers* 46(1), 98–121.

———. 1957. *The Pacific lowlands of Colombia.* Baton Rouge: Louisiana State University Press.

Whitten, Norman. 1986. *Black frontiersmen: Afro-Hispanic culture of Ecuador and Colombia.* Prospect Heights, IL: Waveland.

Whitten, Norman, and Arlene Torres. 1998. "To forge the future in the fires of the past: An interpretive essay on racism, domination, resistance, and liberation." In N. Whitten and A. Torres, eds., *Blackness in Latin America and the Caribbean: Social dynamics and cultural transformations.* Vol. 1: *Central America and northern and western South America,* 3–33. Bloomington: Indiana University Press.

Wilches-Chaux, Gustavo. 1993. "La pesca milagrosa." *Ecológica,* nos. 15–16 (May–October), 79.

Wolford, Wendy. 2010. *This land is ours now: Social mobilization and the meanings of land in Brazil.* Durham, NC: Duke University Press.

Yacup, Sofonías. 1934. *Litoral recóndito.* Bogotá: Editorial Renacimiento.

Zapata Olivella, Manuel. 1964. *En Chimá nace un santo.* Bogotá: Biblioteca Formentor.

———. 1985 [1967]. *Chambacú: Corral de Negros.* Bogotá: Editorial El Bolsillo.

———. 2000. "Omnipresencia africana en la civilización universal." PALARA (Publication of the Afro-Latin American Research Association) 4, 5–15.

———. 2002. *El árbol brujo de la libertad.* Buenaventura, Colombia: Universidad del Pacífico.

———. 2010. *Changó, the biggest badass.* Translated by Jonathan Tittler. Lubbock: Texas Tech University Press.

Ziai, Aram, ed. 2007. *Exploring post-development.* London: Zed Books.

Zuluaga, Francisco, and Amparo Bermúdez. 1997. *La protesta social en el Suroccidente colombiano siglo XVIII.* Cali: Editorial Facultad de Humanidades, Universidad del Valle.

Zuluaga, Francisco, and Mario Diego Romero. 2007. *Sociedad, cultura y resistencia negra en Colombia y Ecuador.* Cali: Universidad del Valle, Programa Editorial.

agro-industrial development, 8, 213. *See also* oil palm cultivation

Agudelo, Carlos, 13, 18, 198, 221n2, 222n4, 233n5, 234n7, 237n1, 238n8, 241n1

alabaos (chants), 49, 251

ALENPAC (Alimentos Enlatados del Pacífico), 126, 144–49, 157, 239n14

alternative future, for Pacific Coast region, 24, 218

alternative life project: in Pacific lowlands, 21, 27, 42; PCN and, 32, 139, 159, 219

Anansi, 48, 110–12, 228n4

Anthropocene, 166

ANUC (Asociación Nacional de Usuarios Campesinos), 191

Aprile-Gniset, Jacques, 96–97, 112–16, 235n15, 235n19

aquatic epistemologies, 14, 18, 51–52; *decimeros* and, 65; mobilization of, 23; sense of place and, 91; *sentipensamiento* and, 48

aquatic sense of place, 35, 46–47, 59, 91, 142, 207

aquatic space, 5, 10–12, 27, 47–48, 198, 202; as assemblage of relations, 11–12, 22, 34, 47, 54, 111–12, 119, 126, 130–33, 217; mobility and, 58; mobilization of, 135–37, 198, 202; oral tradition and, 76–89; in political context, 23, 35, 137; as relational ontology, 137; river travel and, 54–55; sense of place and, 47–48; storytelling and, 84, 88; terror and, 207

Arboleda, Julio: airport in Guapi, 44–45; slave owner, 44, 102, 109

Arboleda, Santiago, 48, 192, 231n26, 237n1, 238n10

Arocha, Jaime, 10, 18, 48–49, 74, 90, 102, 110, 126, 132, 156, 209, 221n2, 222n4, 228n4

arrullo (traditional chant), 49, 51, 85–86, 252

ASODERGUA (Asociación para el Desarrollo del Río Guajuí), 142, 184–85, 191, 238n5

assemblage, 21, 49, 112, 215; aquatic space as, 11–12, 22, 34, 47, 54, 111–12, 119, 130, 133, 217

AT-55 (Artículo Transitorio 55): black mobilization and, 3, 153, 193, 200, 222n4, 237n3; collective land rights and, 1–3, 136; debates over, 221n2; quote from, 162

Atrato River, 93, 112, 122; Bellavista massacre on, 207; black mobilization along, 2, 221n3, 237n3; forced displacement from, 206; mental map of, 123; social cartography of, 122–23, 180

automanumisión (self-liberation), 100, 108–12. *See also* slavery

azoteas, 128–29, 201–2

Balsitas (settlement), 51–52, 56, 59, 110, 127, 228n8

Banguera, Walberto, 174–75, 196–98, 238n7, 240n23

Barbacoas: gold mining around, 112, 235n15; paramilitaries in, 209, 247n1

Becerra, Porfirio (Don Por), 153–55, 188–89, 193, 197, 240n21, 246n25

Bellavista massacre (May 2002), 207, 247n4

Benford, Robert, 15–16, 188

Betancourt, Teófila, 64, 120, 125, 130, 229n16

biche (unrefined sugarcane spirit), 51, 67, 69, 228n5, 252, 254

biodiversity: conservation of, 9, 37, 163–67, 171, 186, 208, 213; discursive fix and, 165–68; Law 70 and, 213–15; in Pacific lowlands, 8–9, 94, 163–67, 210, 215–16, 232n1, 240n21, 243–45n12

biofuels, 212, 248n9

Bioho, Benko, 104–6, 235n10, 235n13. *See also* palenques

Chocó (department), 107, 122, 231n26, 233n4, 235n10, 237n34, 237n2, 239n11; Bellavista massacre in, 247n4; forced displacement in, 205–9; gold mining in, 98, 101, 112; land titles issued in, 238n9; mobilization in, 2, 138, 173–76, 188, 237n3, 245n13; oil palm plantations in, 213–16; Operation Genesis in, 205–9; rainfall data of, 93

chontaduro (Bactris gasipaes), 126, 148, 189, 252

church. See Catholic Church

CIMARRÓN (Movimiento Nacional Cimarrón), 2, 19, 240n23

cimarrón (runaway slave), 97, 100, 112, 134. See also maroon; slavery

clientelism, 143, 154, 157, 198, 238n6, 238n8

climate change, 166, 215, 248n10

COADEPAL (Cooperativa Agrícola del Pacífico), 152–53, 190, 239n19

coca cultivation, 21, 168–70, 212, 217, 243n11, 243–45n12

COCOCAUCA (Coordinación de Comunidades Negras de la Costa Pacífica del Cauca), 154, 197, 229n10, 240nn22–23, 245n17

coconut cultivation: around Guapi, 60, 63, 178, 231n31; promoted by INCORA, 63, 152–53, 177–78, 190

cognitive mapping, 121–22, 180, 236n29. See also social cartography

collaborative research, 38, 41–43. See also Participatory Action-Research

collective action, 13, 26, 41–42, 192

collective identity, social movements and, 12–13, 25, 30, 35, 188, 193

collective intellectual, 218

collective labor, 114, 118, 120–21

collective land rights, 2–4, 14, 65, 136, 149, 159, 162–63, 168, 190, 194–97, 214, 222n4

collective lands (of black communities), 14, 143, 182, 211, 202, 209, 211, 248n9; map of, 161. See also land titling

collective memory, 35–38, 41–42, 45, 70, 90; Afro-Colombian, 60, 65, 110, 138–39, 175–77, 247n4

colonialism, 74–75, 99–101, 108; colonial laws, 99–100, 135; gold mining during, 97, 112, 228n7; palenques and, 104–8, 139, 175; religion and, 89

Community Council Guapi Abajo, 142–43, 150, 154, 157, 174–76, 179, 196, 240n23

community councils: clientelism and, 143; conflict over mangrove areas, 156–57; Decree 1745 and, 171–72; formation of, 23, 140–42, 159–60; INCORA and, 150–56; Law 70 and, 14, 136, 150–52, 162–63, 173; leadership in, 23, 83, 142, 149–55, 159, 187–203; local politics and, 142–43; as representational space, 158–59; river basins and, 137, 140–42; scholarship on, 18–19; as territorial authority, 18, 119

Community Council Unicosta, 143–49, 157, 199, 203, 246n23

conchera (shellfish picker), 126–27, 137, 217

conscientization (conscientização), 40, 176, 186, 194–98, 201

conservation: of biodiversity, 9, 37, 163–67, 171, 186, 208, 213; discursive fix and, 165–68; Law 70 and, 160–63, 172; as state strategy, 8, 23, 161–63

Constitution of 1991, 171, 193, 217; black rights and, 1–3, 65, 135–37, 161–63; mobilization prior to, 2, 173–75, 237n3; as political opportunity structure, 12. See also AT-55; Law 70; National Constituent Assembly

contentious politics, 13, 16, 224n6. See also social movements

contextual space, 84, 88–89

counterlanguage, 75–76

counter-space, 22, 27–28, 30–32, 139, 149, 157, 159–60, 207–9, 219. See also Lefebvre, Henri

Gorgona (island), 84, 86, 181, 231n28
grassroots: ecological activists, 241n2;
  organizations in Pacific lowlands,
  2, 193, 203, 238n5, 240n21, 240n23,
  248n7; PAR and, 41, 45
Gregory, Derek, 224n2, 225n3, 227n2
Guajuí River, 118, 127, 190, 200; community council of, 140–42, 152, 157, 179,
  191; Don Agapito and, 60–61, 64, 217;
  map of, 61, 141; resistance to logging
  in, 183–87; tidal range in, 233n2
Guandal forest, 128, 131, 237n34
Guapi, 9–13, 60–64, 76, 93, 118–21, 125,
  154, 177; aerial fumigation in, 168–70;
  death wakes in, 49–51; gold mining
  around, 112; hospital in, 57–58; house
  construction in, 115; leadership in,
  64, 119–20, 142; map of, 61, 141; naidí
  exploitation in, 144–49; organizations
  in, 43; patron saint festivities in,
  85–87; poem to, 92; rain in, 11–13,
  222nn1–2
Guapi River, 10–11, 60, 85, 148, 180,
  196; attachment to, 58; Doña Celia
  and, 51–59, 110; house construction
  along, 115; map of, 61, 141; poem to,
  46, 92; social cartography workshops
  on, 180–81; tidal rhythms on, 125–27;
  travel on, 55, 96–97
guasá (instrument), 49, 86, 252. See also
  Matamba y Guasá
guerrilla, 45, 136, 160, 170, 183–86, 206–8,
  217, 221n1, 235n10, 247n1, 249n12

Hale, Charles, 137, 237n1
Harvey, David, 28–29, 32; on Lefebvre,
  224n2; on limits to capital, 242n8;
  radical geography and, 226n6; on
  spatial fix, 166, 242n6
Herrera, Mirna, 174, 192–93, 200–201
hidden transcript, 23, 46–47, 70–75,
  230n20
homeplace, 72–73, 206, 247n3;
  palenques as, 104

hooks, bell, 72, 104, 227n9
human rights violations, in Pacific Coast
  region, 19–20, 207–16

identity politics, 30, 35, 240n23;
  Afro-Colombian, 9, 19, 23; in Latin
  America, 73
IGAC (Instituto Geográfico Agustín
  Codazzi), 121, 143, 180, 238n9
IIAP (Instituto de Investigaciones Ambientales del Pacífico), 132, 151–52, 232n1
INCODER (Instituto Colombiano de
  Desarrollo Rural), 213, 238n9
INCORA (Instituto Colombiano de
  Reforma Agraria), 96–97, 110, 143,
  146, 149–56, 165, 181, 213, 238nn9–10,
  239nn18–19, 241n25, 242n5; promoting
  coconut cultivation, 63, 152, 177–78, 190
indigenous population in Colombia, 1,
  135, 170, 233n5; demographic data on,
  97; interethnic relations among, 139,
  182–83, 221n2, 232n1, 243n12, 249n12;
  reserves in Pacific lowlands of (map),
  161; resistance to colonization by,
  100–103
intellectuals, 249n12; Afro-Colombian,
  2, 48, 102, 227n3; collective, 218; de-
  professionalized, 40
interethnic relations, 139, 182–83, 221n2,
  232n1, 243n12, 249n12

JAC (Junta de Acción Comunal), 190, 195
JUNPRO (Juventud Unida para el Progreso), 175, 245n17

kinship ties, 23, 116–18, 123, 236nn23–24
knowledge: local, 14, 38, 42, 137, 152,
  194; PAR and, 41–42, 226n3, 227nn8–9;
  power and, 25, 29; practicing, 23, 51;
  traditional sources of, 36, 57–58, 65,
  70, 164–65
knowledge practices of place-based
  cultures, 4, 24, 218
Kyoto Protocol, 166, 248n11

Pacific Coast region: alternative future of, 24, 217–18; anti-fumigation campaign in, 169–70; AT-55 and, 2, 162; as differential space, 32, 209; displacement in, 208–9, 216; extractive economies in, 8, 184, 228n7; as hidden littoral, 8, 74, 96–97, 233n3; human rights crisis in, 19; Law 70 and, 3, 136, 162–63, 168; leadership in, 191–93, 197; map of, 161; migration in, 192; mobilizing dynamics in, 4, 187; navigating by canoe in, 51–59; palm hearts exploitation in, 126, 144–49, 239n16; Proyecto Biopacífico and, 163–64, 167; timber extraction in, 103, 128–33, 147, 177, 183–87; travels through, 7–10. *See also* Pacific lowlands

Pacific lowlands, 3, 8–9, 38, 94–96, 125; aerial fumigation in, 168–70; aquatic space and, 5, 27, 217; biodiversity and, 8, 94, 215; kinship ties in, 116–19; logic of the river and, 23, 121–25; map of, 95, 161; oil palm cultivation in, 8, 21, 24, 211–17, 224n10, 248nn9–10; oral tradition in, 60–70; paramilitaries in, 207–9; political mobilization in, 4–5, 9, 47, 51, 83, 119, 137–39, 189, 197, 237n3; rainfall in inches, 93; rice cultivation in, 60, 63, 177–78, 188, 245n19; self-liberation (from slavery) in, 100, 108–12; settlement patterns in, 23, 97, 112–19, 122, 127, 139–40, 177, 235n19; slavery in, 45, 97–113, 139, 175; tidal ranges in, 96; West (Robert) on, 92–93, 96. *See also* Pacific Coast region

Palenque de Nariño, 153, 175, 188, 216
Palenque de San Basilio, 105–7, 175, 235n11, 235n13. *See also* slavery
palenques, 104–8, 139, 173–75, 234n9, 235n11, 235n17, 253. *See also* slavery
palm hearts, 126, 144–49, 239n16, 253
PAR. *See* Participatory Action-Research

paramilitaries, 136, 170, 175, 183–84, 206–11, 216–17, 221n1, 247n5, 249n12; in Barbacoas, 209, 247n1
Participatory Action-Research (PAR), 38–45, 51, 225n2, 226n3, 226n6, 227n9
Pashtun women (Afghanistan), 73
patron saints, 88–89, 177, 232n34; festivities in Guapi, 85–87, in Tumaco, 87
Paz, Octavio, 70
PCN. *See* Proceso de Comunidades Negras
people's power, 41–43, 51, 89, 186, 232n34. *See also* empowerment
place, 32–35, 48; narrating place, 18–19; relational place, 33–34, 108, 203; social movement theory and, 13–18, 25–27, 224n6; space and, 16–17, 21, 26–27, 32, 224n1, 227n2, 242n6; theories of, 225nn5–6. *See also* critical place perspective
Plan Colombia, 168, 212
political mobilization, 18–20, 23, 44; aquatic space and, 137; imperfections of, 43, 203; Law 70 and, 3, 36; leadership and, 187–93; in Pacific lowlands, 47, 51, 83, 119, 137–39, 177, 180, 237n3; prior to new constitution, 2, 174–75; religious beliefs and, 51. *See also* black mobilization
political opportunity structure, 1, 12–14, 36, 174, 183. *See also* social movements: theories of
politics of reading, 21, 103
politics of space, 28, 224n2. *See also* Lefebvre, Henri
polizontes, 61–62
Popayán, 44, 86, 101, 108–9, 112, 233n4, 235n15
potrillo. *See* dugout canoe
power, 102, 172–73, 189, 230n20; of Anansi, 111; capital and, 146–49, 166, 242n8; critique of, 74; hidden transcript and, 71–73; of identity (Castells), 13; knowledge and, 25, 29;

San Antonio de Guajuí, 127–28, 133, 246n21; photo of, 128

San Basilio (Palenque de), 105–7, 175, 235n11, 235n13

San Juan River, 111–12, 138–40, 151, 176, 201, 221n3, 233n2, 235n10, 237n3

Santos, Juan Manuel (president), 169–70

sawmill operations, 10, 65, 177; conflict in Guajuí River, 184–87; timber supply to, 128–32, 217

scale, in social movement research, 5, 14–18, 203, 218, 223n4

Scott, James, 23, 47, 71–74; responses to, 230n20

self-liberation, 100, 108–12. *See also* slavery

sense of place, 22, 27, 33–35; on Pacific Coast, 35, 46–48, 51, 59, 65, 83, 91, 140–42, 207; terrorized, 247n3

sentipensamiento, 48–51

settlements: maroon, 174–75, 235n17; rural patterns in Pacific lowlands, 23, 97, 112–19, 122, 127, 139–40, 177, 235n19

Slater, David, 13, 172–73

slavery: abolition of, 44, 99–100, 109, 113, 234n7; collective amnesia regarding, 175; hidden transcript and, 74; in Pacific lowlands, 45, 97–113, 139, 175; resistance against, 100–110; self-liberation from, 100, 108–12; transatlantic slave trade, 98–99

social cartography, 42, 180–81, 231n28. *See also* mental maps

social movement of black communities, 13, 20, 37, 103, 119, 164, 194; alternative life projects and, 21, 27; community councils and, 202–3; emergence of, 12; leadership in, 42–45, 64, 83, 101, 139, 143, 155, 157, 173, 181–203; logic of the river and, 218; made up of, 19–21; narrative approach to, 4–5, 218–19; palenques and, 253

social movements: counter-space and, 22; critical place perspective on, 21, 25, 203, 218–19; difference within, 19–20, 103, 189; ethnographic approach to, 5, 219; geographies of, 4, 7, 12–14, 133, 203, 267; identity and, 13, 25, 197; leaders in, 143, 157; place and, 13, 25, 224n6; theories of, 5, 12–16, 26, 35, 74, 119, 172, 187, 193, 218–19, 223nn3–5, 224n6, 225n7

sociospatial relations, 16–17; dialectic of, 89

Soja, Edward, 88–89, 232nn32–33

space: abstract, 30, 32; autonomous, 104; contestation of, 26; place and, 16–17, 21, 26–27, 32, 224n1, 227n2, 242n6; politics of, 28, 224n2; production of, 22, 28–31; relational, 62; socially produced, 84, 88–89, 232nn32–33; in social movement research, 21–22, 27. *See also* aquatic space; counter-space; differential space; representational space; representations of space

spatial fix, 166, 242n6. *See also* capitalism

spatiality: oral tradition and, 83; in Pacific lowlands, 122; in social movement research, 14–18, 25, 224n6; Soja (Ed) on, 88–89, 232nn32–33

spatial trap, 17

storytelling: aquatic space and, 84, 88; collective memory and, 90; narratology and, 11, 18; in Pacific lowlands, 11, 37, 46–47, 119, 125, 138, 231n29; in PAR, 42; as practicing knowledge, 22–23, 51

subsistence economies, 8, 21, 63, 118, 178

sugarcane plantations, in Valle del Cauca, 190–92

sustainability, 121, 132, 146–49, 163–67, 184, 187–89, 241n3; of naidí, 146, 199, 239n14

sustainable development, 9, 147, 163–67, 208, 214